Rights of Women in Islam

Rights of in Women in Islam

Asghar Ali Engineer

STERLING PUBLISHERS PRIVATE LIMITED

STERLING PUBLISHERS PRIVATE LIMITED
A-59, Okhla Industrial Area, Phase-II,
New Delhi-110020.
Tel: 26387070, 26386209; Fax: 91-11-26383788
E-mail: sterlingpublishers@airtelmail.in
ghai@nde.vsnl.net.in
www.sterlingpublishers.com

Rights of Women in Islam
Copyright © 2004 by Asghar Ali Engineer
First Edition: 1992
Second Revised Edition: 2004
Third Enlarged Edition 2008
ISBN 978-81-207-3933-8

Printed and Published by Sterling Publishers Pvt. Ltd., New Delhi- 110 020.

PREFACE TO THE THIRD EDITION

The issues of women continue to dominate the Islamic world in particular, as there has been very slow change in the status of women in the Islamic world as a whole. With the exception of a few Muslim countries, the age-old laws have not changed. These laws, essentially formulated by the Muslim jurists in the early centuries of Islam, were a human effort to understand divine pronouncements in a feudal era. Claimed to be divine, these laws, were in essence a human effort to provide women secondary status as per the then prevalent social ethos. However, the Ul'ama project these laws not only as divine but also immutable.

It will take years of effort to convince believing Muslims that the Shari'ah laws can and should change without injuring the spirit of the Qur'an. The greatest difficulty in bringing about any change is the centrality of medieval texts. In all traditional societies, text is central, not reason. In modern society, it is reason which is central. In most Muslim circles, reason is considered almost blasphemous and a challenge to the divine. Most of the Muslims, both men as well as women, look up to the traditional Ul'ama as a categorical answer to their problems, particularly in matters of marriage, divorce, inheritance, etc.

This is as far as traditional Muslim societies are concerned; but the plight of Muslim women in Western countries, particularly in U.K., France, Germany, USA and Canada, is not very different. Now that the number of Muslims is increasing in Western societies, there are attempts to build pressure on authorities to implement Shari'ah laws as far as Personal laws are concerned. And they have partially succeeded too.

For example, in the Province of Toronto (Ontorio) authorities had almost succumbed to the pressure and declared their intention to implement Shari'ah laws in personal matters. It was the protest by progressive Muslim women and men which forced authorities to stay its application. Recently in U.K. too, Archbishop of Canterbury expressed his view that certain provisions of Shari'ah law may be selectively applied. Again, there was strong criticism by a section of Muslim women and men that relegated the issue to the backyard.

That is why there is great need for literature on proper understanding; about the beginning and the development of Islamic laws from the early centuries and how various jurists interpreted Qur'anic provisions to suit their own social conditions. Thus, it was thought necessary to bring out a third edition of this book *The Rights of Women in Islam* to disseminate such an understanding.

In this edition we thought it fit to add a chapter: *On a Muslim Woman Leading the Congregational Prayer.* This chapter deals with the important aspect of the Muslim women's problems and also hopes to further enhance the Muslim women's understanding of the Shari'ah issues.

It is hoped the third edition with an additional chapter would become a useful tool in the hands of Muslim women, who are struggling to realise their Islamic rights, of which they have been deprived for centuries. The Qur'an empowered them more than 14 centuries ago but the Muslim men have successfully stalled realisation of this divine empowerment through various ingenious interpretations of the Qur'an and the Hadith.

April 2008   **Asghar Ali Engineer**

PREFACE TO THE FIRST EDITION

Democratic polities and both capitalist and socialist economies have brought about a new consciousness of rights for women. Women can no longer be subjugated as they were in feudal society. Indeed, they now refuse to be treated as the property of men. They even refuse to be considered lower in social status than men. Women insist, and rightly so, on being equal to men in every respect.

However, in the countries of South Asia – and other Asian and African countries as well – religion is predominant and everything, including women's rights, is seen through the prism of religion. Religion, moreover, is a strong cultural force and an important constituent of our social consciousness and a significant determinant of our traditions. Hence, religion still plays a crucial role in determining women's rights in our society.

Islam is one of those religions that has discussed in detail women's rights, both in the Qur'an and in the formulations of Shari'ah (Islamic law). These rights pertain to marriage, divorce, property, inheritance, custody of children, evidence and rewards and punishments. Every right has been discussed in great detail. This book is an attempt to set out women's rights in Islam in the true qur'anic spirit for there has been much deviation from this spirit in practice. Islamic society began to be feudalist within a quarter of century after the death of the Prophet. This feudalisation had a telling impact on the concept of the rights of women in Islam. It is this spirit which still predominates. The new consciousness among women makes it necessary once again to go back to the original qur'anic spirit.

The Qur'an not only awards equal status to both the sexes in the normative sense but it also concedes a degree of superiority to men in its own social context. However, the theologians ignored the context and made men superior in the absolute sense. I have attempted in this book to recapture the original spirit of the qur'anic laws with regard to the male-female relationship and to separate what is contextual from what is normative. I hope that this book will equip Muslim feminists with a powerful weapon in their fight for equal status with men.

It is, therefore, highly necessary to interpret the text properly. This book is an attempt to do precisely that. If the qur'anic text and the *hadith* literature can be suitably re-read and reinterpreted, it will not be difficult to accord women an equal status in society. This book is a modest attempt to arm Muslim women with Islamic arguments for their empowerment. It is the experience of this author that when these arguments have been presented publicly, the orthodox elements have found it very difficult to defend their position on women.

It will not be easy to break the hold of fundamentalists and conservatives. We have no such illusions. But these textual arguments would certainly help the cause of Muslim women in Asian and African countries. The Qur'an has accorded concrete rights to women in respect of marriage, divorce, property, inheritance, custody of children and much else, but over time these rights were overlaid with feudal and patriarchal prejudices. This book is no more than an attempt to shake off this dust. It is hoped the book will help many more women and those men too who are struggling to project the women's cause.

April 1996   **Asghar Ali Engineer**

CONTENTS

CONTENTS

1
INTRODUCTION

The question of women's status has acquired great importance throughout the world and among all communities. The reason is obvious. For thousands of years women kept in total subjugation in all patriarchal societies, and it so happened that most societies were patriarchal. Thus, for centuries it was 'considered a natural law' that women were inferior to men and must submit to the latter's authority for the smooth running of family life.

It should be remembered that even religious scriptures could not altogether escape from adopting such attitudes though some did lay down a few norms which transcended them. However, social attitudes are so pervasive that even progressive scriptural norms become affected and are thus interpreted in a way that reflects the prevailing mental attitudes. Thus, the male-dominated societies often harnessed even just and egalitarian norms laid down for women in divine scriptures to perpetuate their hold. The Qur'an, which is comparatively liberal in its treatment of women, also suffered the same fate.

Today many of the old social structures are fast crumbling and new social orders, rational and liberal, are emerging on the scene. In the new social structures it is becoming increasingly difficult to maintain the old attitudes towards women. The scriptures are, therefore, being re-read and reinterpreted, at least, among the progressive sections of these societies. The women's question is, in a way, comparable to that of slavery. In feudal and pre-feudal societies slavery was considered quite justifiable. The slaves themselves accepted it. However, this attitude towards slavery and serfdom began to change rapidly in the emerging capitalist societies, leading ultimately to their total abolition.

Muslim jurists and theologians quoting from the Holy Qur'an continued to justify slavery throughout the Middle Ages and laid down elaborate rules of behaviour for slaves as well as for their ownership, possession and disposal. To own slaves was considered a 'natural right' in Muslim societies throughout the medieval period, just like owning any immovable property. A slave who ran away from his master was regarded as a sinner'. Of course, the scripture was quoted to justify this.

Now that slavery has been abolished and is regarded as intolerable by all civilised societies, no one invokes the scripture to justify it and no one insists upon that 'divine right' vested in those who owned slaves. Muslim theologians no longer invoke the 'right' to have sexual intercourse with a slave girl, something which they had been doing until recently. Some liberal and modernist interpreters and commentators either do not accept the concept of sexual intercourse with slave girls without *nikah* (marriage) or they explain the verses concerning *milk-i-yamin* (those whom the right hand possesses, i.e. (slave girls) in a way to mean entering into *nikah* with them as an alternative to marriage with free women.[1]

Thus, the theory of Divine Law is no longer applicable to the institution of slavery. Human consciousness in modern society is conditioned by the concept of human rights and human dignity. The laws regarding women drawn up during the medieval period by the jurists, though based on interpretations of the scriptures, are unlikely to be accepted by women today. They no longer accept their subordinate position. They demand equal status with men.

Thus the scriptures will either have to be abandoned and laws enacted on a secular basis or they will have to be re-read and reinterpreted so as to suit modern conditions. Here one important question arises. The theologians allege that the liberals and the modernists often violate the fundamentals of the Qur'an and interpret it to suit their own ends, arguing that Divine Law cannot be trifled with. The argument on the face of it appears to be quite weighty but seems less so when closely scrutinised. One has to take into account sociological influence while interpreting a divine scripture. No interpretation, however honest, can be free from such influences.

The theologians and jurists of the 1st century of Islam – who had acquired great prestige and whose opinions, were taken as final – were themselves subject to sociological influences. Their formulations and interpretations must be seen in the sociological perspective of their time, when women were looked upon as nothing more than instruments of perpetuating one's progeny, bringing up children and providing pleasure for their husbands. This is how the pronouncements of the Qur'an were misinterpreted.

If that was so then, will not our views be influenced by our own situation today? And if so, will it be wrong? If the classical view was formulated in the intellectual environment of the time, will it be wrong to imbibe modern values and ethos? Will it amount to a violation of Islamic principles? Can one see principles and values as merely abstract notions transcending all the influences of one's own intellectual environment? The orthodox jurists, while accepting classical primordial views as being the most authentic, rejected the rational and liberal approach as not only unauthentic but also as deviant. Such a qur'anic commentary is simply referred to as *tafsir bi'al-rai* (i.e. qur'anic exegesis according to one's own opinion).

It is undoubtedly, a very delicate matter. How to draw a line between *tafsir bi' al-rai* and a *tafsir* (exegesis) attempted to suit one's convenience? Does it mean that to avoid the charge of *tafsir bi' al-rai* one should continue to follow the classical medieval commentary on the Qur'an, or should one attempt a qur'anic exegesis according to one's own convictions? Sir Syed Maulana Abul Kalam Azad and others struck their own paths and yet they can be hardly accused of *tafsir bi' al-rai* as their commitment to the cause of Islam was second to none.

Yet any one who strikes a new path and interprets the holy book differently is accused of indulging in *tafsir bi' al-rai*.

Maulana Abul Kalam Azad tries to explain the difference between a new interpretation and an interpretation based on one's own opinion (*tafsir bi'al-rai*). He says that in every epoch there is an intellectual environment, and the qur'anic commentary, like other arts and sciences, is affected by it. Though there is no doubt that the true 'ulama in the history of Islam never surrendered themselves to political influences and never approved of Islamic teachings being influenced by them, the influences of one's time enter not only through the doors of politics. There are also psychological influences at work; once these doors open they cannot be closed. Teachings and beliefs can be preserved from political influences but not from psychological ones.

People have made mistakes in understanding the meaning of *tafsir bi'al-rai*. By putting restrictions on *tafsir bi'al-rai* it was not intended that one should not use reason and insight in understanding the Qur'an. If this was so then, the very purpose of studying the Qur'an would be defeated. The Qur'an itself urges upon us to use reason and the faculty of mind and repeatedly says, "Do they not reflect on the Qur'an? Or, are there locks on the hearts?"[2] In fact, in *tafsir bi' al-rai* the word *rai* (opinion) has not been used in its dictionary meaning. It (i.e. *rai*) is a term of the Shari'ah and means an interpretation of the Qur'an which is not in keeping with what is intended by it but is based on our own fixed opinion. Thus, to conform to our opinion we twist the meaning of the Qur'an.[3]

We have quoted at length from Azad's *Tarjuman al-Qur'an* because it has an important bearing on our subject. Today how we deal with the women's question based on the qur'anic teachings depends very much on how we understand and interpret the qur'anic text. When we try to understand it in the light of our own experiences and changed consciousness, we are often accused of indulging in *tafsir bi' al-rai* and are thus condemned in the eyes of the Muslims who are under the influence of the orthodox 'ulama. It is, therefore, vital to understand the differences between *tafsir bi'al-rai* and understanding the Qur'an in the light of one's own experiences and consciousness. Of course, when we refer to consciousness we do not mean a false consciousness, that is, the one based either on illusion or on unprincipled gains. Opinion also is not to be condemned for what it is but should be condemned only when it is guided by falsehood or the desire for calculated benefit. In that sense no one can be allowed to belittle the contents of the holy book. Allah makes clear the meaning of revelation by saying that it is not based on desire': "Nor does he (i.e. the Prophet) speak of desire. It is naught but revelation that is revealed."[4]

When the Prophet himself does not speak of his own desire, how can anyone else do so and yet expect it to be followed by the Muslims? However, it must be admitted that there is a rather thin line between personal desire, *rai*, and true opinion that is the product of a new consciousness. Only a person of unquestionable integrity and honesty is able to disregard an opinion based on personal desire. This is highly relevant as far as the question of women is concerned. One may reinterpret the qur'anic verses simply because one wants to promote permissiveness out of personal desire or one may reinterpret the relevant verses to accord dignity and freedom to women in keeping with the intellectual and moral environment of one's own times. What the liberals and the modernists are doing (of course, those among them who are true followers of Islam and yet want to keep pace with their own times in all sincerity) is to accord dignity and freedom to women as much as to men. This cannot be done if one rigidly follows the orthodox reading, interpretation and meaning of the qur'anic intent.

Here it is also necessary to understand that morality and ethics are not closed concepts uninfluenced by material developments in society. Morality is as much contextual as normative. The normative may be transcendental, but it can be put into practice in certain contexts. When the context changes it may not be possible to practise morality in its old form, yet its normative content cannot be sacrificed while evolving a new form of morality.

When restrictions were imposed on women in the past the normative concept was to protect their chastity, and slowly chastity became synonymous with *purdah* (veil) itself. Those women who observed strict *purdah* were thought to be very chaste and those who violated it even slightly were dubbed as 'immoral'. Thus a particular form of morality evolved in certain circumstances. We do not intend to go into the question of how *purdah* evolved but it may be mentioned briefly here that it was a product of feudal rulers' concept of *izzat* (honour—here used in the sense of inviolable feminine chastity).

This concept of *izzat* and its protection by men itself implied male superiority. Its essential message was that woman needed to be protected and that man was her protector. In Saudi Arabia even today a woman is not allowed to travel without being accompanied by a man though there is nothing to this effect in the Qur'an. During the medieval ages it was a requirement of the time[5], which later became an essential ingredient of Shari'ah. Also, during medieval times there was a large number of women in a ruler's harem. The very word *harem* meant a prohibited enclave where no one other than the ruler or the prince could enter. The very size of the *harem* showed the prestige of the ruler. In other words, the male ego and sense of superiority were expressed through the concept of the 'weaker sex' which supposedly needed to be protected.

Needless to say, this led to the seclusion of women by means of *purdah* with a view to protecting them. This became a part of female morality. It is interesting to note that even in the Holy Qur'an women are urged to pull their upper garment over their faces so that they are recognised as free women and are not harassed (*wala-udhayna*). The Qur'an says:

> Prophet: Tell thy wives and thy daughters and the women of believers to let down upon them their over-garments. This is more proper, so that they may be known, and not be given trouble. And Allah is ever Forgiving, Merciful.[6]

Thus, in the past women were thought to be weak and this was a direct outcome of a concept of male superiority which was sociological, not theological. The problem was that the sociological often became the theological and was defended as such even when the sociological conditions changed. In our own times women are no longer described as the weaker sex and are treated at par with men. They not only move about alone inviolated but can also earn their own livelihood by working outside the home. They no longer depend on male protection (though on account of India's uneven social development sociological conditions vary and some people still argue that women need protection) and hence *purdah* in the conventional sense is not needed.

However, to argue that *purdah* is no longer needed is not to argue that chastity too can be dispensed with. Chastity is the norm while *purdah* was a contextual means to achieve it. A woman can protect her chastity without observing *purdah*. Thus, if our concept of morality is sufficiently dynamic and creative, we will not resist attempts to give *purdah* a new form, discarding the old one and, circumstances permitting, doing so without sacrificing the essential norm. In other words, the sociological and the empirical should be as important to us as the theological. This balance should never be lost. It is a requirement of the moral dynamics of a society.

II

The Evolution of Shari'ah

Connected with this question is the question of the evolution of Shari'ah (the Canon law of Islam). It is often assumed by those not well versed in the origin and development of Shari'ah that, first, it is *totally* divine and, second it is immutable. Such a view is often aired in common discussions and encouraged by the conservative 'ulama. The facts are to the contrary. First, the Shari'ah did not come into being all of a sudden; it went through a tortuous process of evolution over the centuries; and, second, it never remained static, and hence immutable as commonly assumed. Even after it assumed a recognisable shape the jurists had to admit the principle of *ijtihad* (literally, exertion), i.e. creative interpretation and application of Islamic *fiqh* (jurisprudence) in the face of new circumstances. The principle of *ijtihad*, so long as it was applied, constituted a dynamic element in Islamic law. Unfortunately, the gates of *ijtihad* were closed soon after the decline of the Abbasid empire in AD 12th century. The Shari'ah began to acquire a static character and came to be accepted as immutable. From the time of the Prophet to the waning of Abbasid rule, the evolution of the Shari'ah passed through several stages. A noted jurist of the Al-Azhar seminary, Cairo, divides it into six periods.[7]

In all these six periods, the Shari'ah underwent conceptual changes. It is interesting to note that Cantwell Smith, noted scholar of Islam, through his diligent research comes to the significant conclusion that in the early centuries of Islam the concept of *shara'i-ahkam* (injunctions) was moral rather than legal. These *ahkam* in the early Islamic period:

> are each a divine command morally incumbent and immediately personal, for which men will be answerable on the day of judgement. Only later does this phrase become depersonalised and eventually detranscendentalised to the point where it is equivalent to *ahkamal-Shari'ah*.[8]

In works such as *Al-fiqh al-Akbar* 2nd century *hijrah*, Al-Baqillani's *Kitab al-tamhid* (4th century *hijrah)*, Al-Baghdai's *Kitab usul al-din* (5th century *hijrah*), Al-Ghazzali's *Ihya al-'Ulum al-di'n* (5th century *hijrah*) and *Al-Nasafi* and *Al-Shahrastani* (6th century *hijrah)* one hardly finds mention of the concept of Shari'ah.[9] The term Shari'ah is used frequently specially in the legal sense, only after the eighth or probably the 9th century *hijrah*. For a student of the evolution of Shari'ah this is quite important.

Also, there was never any unanimity among jurists on the number of important legal matters which today are considered as immutable, as divine words in the Qur'an. As our subject here is the status of women in Islam we should like to give an example from this area of the Shari'ah only. One very controversial matter has been the concept of three divorces in one sitting which has been causing a great deal of hardship to a number of women today, especially in the Indian subcontinent, where the British enactment known as the Muslim personal law is applicable and which has the status of immutable Divine Law.

Triple divorce in one sitting (*talaqi thalatha fi majlisin wahidin*) is the most widely practised form of divorce, particularly in India where the Sunni Muslims follow the Hanafite school of jurisprudence. In fact, it is the most contentious form of divorce denounced even by the Hanafites as an innovative and sinful form of divorce. There are cogent arguments for and against it, based both on the Qur'an and the *Sunnah*. The qur'anic verses and the Prophet's traditions have been subjected to interpretations which are in conflict with each other, supporting or rejecting this form of divorce.

Those supporting the triple divorce in one sitting maintain that the Qur'an has not laid down any specific method of divorce and that though the Prophet showed his anger against this form of divorce, he did not indicate that such a divorce would not be valid. Some supporters of this *talaq al-bid'a* even maintain that the tradition of the Prophet's anger against it is a weak one. Imam ibn Hazm (d. 456. AH) has given a detailed argument in favour of the triple divorce relying on the Qur'an and the *Sunnah*. He tries to refute all arguments against the triple divorce in one sitting.[10]

Hafiz ibn Qayyim, on the other hand, has argued, again on the basis of the Qur'an and the *Sunnah*, that even if one pronounces three divorces in one sitting, only one revocable divorce shall take place. Ibn Qayyim, who was a disciple of Ibn Taymiyyah, marshals his arguments on the basis of the Qur'an to prove the invalidity of a triple divorce in one sitting. He maintains that the Prophet's companions numbered more than a lakh (1,00,000) and asks whether anyone can show that even twenty of them ever concurred on the validity of a triple divorce in one sitting.[11] Ibn Qayyim advances many other weighty arguments to disprove the validity of such a divorce.

This clearly shows that there are basic differences among fuqaha of the classical period about the Shari'ah formulations. It is, therefore, very difficult to maintain that the Shari'ah is divine in the same way as the Holy Qur'an. Shari'ah, unlike the Qur'an, is not devoid of human opinion. It is for this reason that there are schools of jurisprudence which differ from each other on many questions. It was precisely for this reason that the principle of *ijtihad,* referred to above, was incorporated in the Shari'ah methodology. *Ijtihad,* it will be seen, should very much depend on personal approach, opinion and proclivity. The objective conditions in the world vary so much that it is almost impossible to develop one uniform view of all problems. Moreover, geographical, racial and cultural traditions also influence our judgements in one way or another. There is a civilisation factor too. The four surviving Sunni schools of jurisprudence were also products of these influences working on the minds of their founders, who lived in Medina, Mecca, Kufa (Iraq) and Misr (Egypt). Imam Abu Hanifah and Imam Sahfi'i were more liberal in their approach as they lived in Iraq and Egypt, respectively, which happened to be the melting pots of different cultures, providing a variety and richness of life.[12]

Imam Abu Hanifah, according to Abu Zayd,[13] was a liberal and modernist (*Imam al-mujaddidin*)[14]. Imam Malik was a conservative (*Imam al-muhafizin*)[15]. Imam Sahfi'i was a moderate (*Imam al-wastwa al- 'i' tidal*)[16] and Imam Ahmad bin Hanbal was rigid and orthodox (*Imam al-mutashaddidin*).[17]

Abu Zayd concludes that various schools of jurisprudence (*Madhahib al-Islami*) are nothing but reflections of the evolution of life in the Islamic world and that these schools changed and evolved and were transformed according to time and circumstance.[18]

It is for this reason that the principle of *ijtihad* was used right from the beginning. When Ma'adh, a companion of the Prophet, said he would use *ijtihad* if he did not find an answer to the problems he is likely to face in the Qur'an and the Prophet's *Sunnah* (practice), the *Holy Prophet* approved of it. Hazrat 'Umar, the second Caliph after the death of the Prophet, when confronted with a number of problems, used *ijtihad*. He temporarily suspended, and even abandoned, some of the directives of the Qur'an in view of the circumstances he faced. For example, he suspended the punishment of amputating hands when faced with famine and abandoned the practice of giving a portion of *zakat* (poll-tax levied on Muslims by the Qur'an) to what is known as *mu'allafat al-quiub* (i.e. those whose hearts are to be won for Islam.). There is a clear directive to this effect in the Qur'an.[19] The Prophet also followed this practice, but Hazrat 'Umar refused to do so. His argument, quite a valid one, was that Islam was no longer weak and there was no need to induce people with money to ally themselves with Islam. One can thus infer that the qur'anic injunctions or the Prophet's *Sunnah* have to be applied to the situation one is faced with.

Thus Ahmad Amin, an Egyptian scholar, remarks:

> In twenty-three years the condition that called forth some judgements changed, then as the conditions changed some of the judgements changed. Indeed a question might require a (positive) command, then the circumstances would change and it would require a prohibition... So if this happened in twenty-three years in the life of the Prophet, what do you think when times have changed and more than a thousand years have passed...? Does the observer not think that if the Prophet were alive and faced these circumstances, many verses of abrogation would descend upon him and God the Generous and Merciful would not leave the Islamic nation without flexible legislation confronting this new life with absolute *ijtihad*.[20]

All this makes it very clear that the Shari'ah laws evolved in response to various challenges and problems and must be viewed as such. They cannot be viewed in the abstract. In other words, Shari'ah is a situational, not a transcendental, law and must be creatively applied in the changed circumstances. Muhammad Mujib a noted Muslim scholar, calls Shari'ah an 'approach to Islam'[21] rather than a law. This approach immensely increases the scope of the Shari'ah formulations. M. Mujib says:

> And if it is a matter of approach, why should Muslims confine themselves to texts embodying traditional methods of approach, and not think afresh in the light of present-day needs and realities?[22]

This approach can prove much more fruitful as far as Shari'ah laws regarding women are concerned. Whether it is polygamy or triple divorce in one sitting, all such laws can be reexamined in the light of the new consciousness which is emerging in our own times. Just as the new consciousness led to the abolition of slavery, so should the emergence of women's movements for equal rights lead to Shari'ah laws regarding women being reconsidered. In fact, this has become inevitable.

What is needed is an Islamic approach to the problem, as rightly pointed out by M. Mujib. It has often been argued by Islamic jurists that women have been assigned a role which is primarily that of wives and mothers. Their responsibilities lie in the home, not outside it. But the jurists based their arguments on a selective approach to the Qur'an. There are verses in the Qur'an which emphasise equal status for both the sexes[23] as well as verses indicating differences and even inequalities.[24] There are also verses which together indicate equality of the sexes as well as the superiority of man over woman to some extent.[25]

One selects verses according to one's biases and then tries to prove one's point of view. Here it is necessary to point out one very obvious psychological fact, namely, that interpretation of empirical facts or the text of a scripture always depends on one's position. Everyone has some kind of *Weltanschauung*. In other words, one lives in one's own intellectual universe and draws inferences accordingly. Thus, our selective approach depends on our intellectual approach. Another question arises: why are there verses in the Qur'an which indicate equal status and, at the same time, superiority of men over women? Is this not a contradiction? Can divine word admit contradiction?

We must understand that there are normative statements as well as contextual statements in the Qur'an. What is desired by Allah is also stated and what is empirical reality in society is also mentioned. A scripture indicates the goal in terms of 'should and aught' but also takes into account the empirical reality in terms of 'is. Then a dialectic of both is worked out so that *the scriptural guidance is accepted by real awkward people in concrete circumstances* and guidance does not remain an abstract idea. However, at the same time, a transcendental norm is also indicated so that in the coming times when the concrete circumstances become more conducive to the acceptance of the norm, it is applied or at least an attempt to get closer and closer to it begins in earnest.

The earlier Islamic thinkers had also recognised the necessity for change in view of the changing circumstances and it is for this reason that Imam ibn Taymiyyah came out with the doctrine that religious edicts change according to the changing times.[26] If we bear in mind that Imam ibn Taymiyyah was not a liberal or progressive of his time the significance of this doctrine increases. Even an orthodox thinker like him thought it necessary that ahkam (edicts) should change in accordance with circumstances. And it was in keeping with the spirit of this doctrine that the 'ulama agreed to the abolition of slavery when the time came for it, though the Qur'an had permitted it and the Prophet had not prohibited it altogether.

If the 'ulama still resist change in certain Shari'ah edicts concerning women such as polygamy, evidence, divorce, etc it is not because they are based on the Qur'an and *Sunnah* (slavery was also based on the Qur'an and *Sunnah* and yet it was abolished when the time came for it) but because societies are still male-dominated and it hurts the pride of men to accept change. But times are changing fast and it will not take very long for these changes to become acceptable as many other changes have become acceptable with the passage of time. Films and television no longer evoke protest as they used to some time ago. They have become part of our life just as much as anything else.

Another 18th century Islamic thinker, Shah Waliyullah, in his *magnum opus, Hujjat Allah al-Balighah*, argues at length that the Shari'ah is devised in keeping with the nature of the people and the needs of the time. He devotes an entire chapter of his book to develop this argument.[27] Shah Waliyullah even gives an example of how *ahkam* change with circumstances.[28] When the Prophet migrated from Mecca to Medina, his blood relations were left behind and so he established what is called muwakhat (mutual brotherhood) and the qur'anic verse about inheritance was revealed. However, when those left behind in Mecca came back and joined their families and Islam flourished, the verse making inheritance a right of close blood relatives was revealed, cancelling the earlier one. Thus with the change of circumstances the *hukum* (religious injunction) changed as well.

"As we have seen above, the Shari'ah has, apart from others, two important sources of formulation: the Qur'an and the *Sunnah*, and both, as pointed out above, have two important ingredients: the normative and the contextual. The Qur'an was undoubtedly revealed for the whole of mankind and for all times to come and yet it contained, in order to be acceptable to the Arabs to whom it was revealed, that which had significance for them. Any scripture which has to be acceptable to the people to whom it has been revealed must have immediate relevance for them. The scripture may draw from their history, culture and traditions. This is what I prefer to call contextual. Apart from this, the Qur'an has much that is transcendental, that which laid down norms for human behaviour and also gave an eschatological direction to life.

The Prophetic *Sunnah* too has both these ingredients: the contextual and the normative. If the Prophet's behaviour had to have any relevance for his people, it had to draw from their history, culture and traditions. Also, he had to set out exemplary behaviour before them. For that he drew from what was normative in the Qur'an and thus he exemplified the qur'anic teachings par excellence. This is why the Qur'an also describes the Prophet's behaviour as the best and most exemplary.[29] Thus, from the Prophet's conduct we have to choose what is transcendental, leaving out what is contextual, if we are to cull values and principles from it. For the Arabs of his time, and especially those who lived in the peninsular area, his whole conduct was of great relevance because it exemplified not only the best in the Qur'an but also the best from their history, traditions (*'adat*) and culture.

It was for this reason that when the *fuqaha* (the jurists) formulated the Shari'ah, they drew immensely from both the Qur'an and the traditions of the Prophet. Sometimes, the normative in the Qur'an, which imbibed principles, did not appeal to them as much as certain traditions which were closer to their *'adat* (practices) and hence they even went to the extent of giving precedence to the *Sunnah* over the Qur'an, though Shah Waliyullah quotes the Prophet's tradition to the contrary, namely that the Qur'an can cancel the *Sunnah* but the *Sunnah* cannot cancel the Qur'an.[30] As the Shari'ah is based on the Qur'an and the *Sunnah*, as pointed out before, there is much in it which is contextual and hence needs to be reassessed in the changed context.

As far as the women's question is concerned, cultural and traditional influences tend to be quite strong. The Qur'an undoubtedly gave a great many rights to women and spelled them out in detail. We will throw light on these rights during the course of the book and show that the Qur'an was the first scripture to have conceded so many rights to women and that too in a period when women were very oppressed in the major civilisations, namely the Byzantine, Sassanid, etc.[31] And yet we see that the later *fuqaha* (Islamic jurists) drew much from the Arab *'adat* (pre-Islamic traditions) and resorted to formulations which curtailed, if not trampled upon, women's rights. Some examples might suffice here. The Qur'an never intended to place undue restrictions on the movements of women, nor did it require them to completely hide their faces while moving out of the house. And yet the leading jurists (though there were differences among them, regarding the interpretation of the relevant verses and traditions of the Prophet) required women not to move out of their houses except in an emergency and even then to have their faces covered.[32]

On venturing out of home alone Imam Sahfi'i's view seems to be more reasonable. Justice Aftab Hussain observes:

> The view of Imam Sahfi'i is clearly based upon the principle that the idea underlying the command [Shari'ah, not qur'anic] to travel with mahram (i.e. a man with whom marriage is prohibited) is to provide security for her person and property. A mahram is the best possible security inter alia for the preservation of her chastity. If her safety is otherwise vouchsafed, there is no harm in her travelling with strangers, men or women.[33]

Though the Qur'an puts no such restriction on women, the jurists did so in the context of their situation, and it is considered equally binding in Muslim countries like Saudi Arabia where women still cannot venture out alone.[34] This clearly shows how the rights given by the Qur'an were taken away by the jurists in view of their situation and yet these Shari'ah rules are enforced even when the context has changed.

The Qur'an demanded of women a reasonable degree of submission to their husbands as they maintain them and spend their wealth on them,[35] but the juristic formulations require them to submit totally to their husbands. A Prophetic tradition (*hadith*) often referred to in this respect says that had *sajda* (prostration) not been prohibited (i.e. Prophet Muhammad) would have ordered women to perform *sajda* to their husbands. Another tradition says that a woman cannot enter paradise if her husband is not pleased with her.[36]

We do not wish to attempt a critique of *hadith* literature, but suffice it to say that many a *hadith* (tradition) came into being later in keeping with the cultural and socio-religious prejudices of the 1st and 2nd centuries of the Islamic calendar. These traditions must be treated with great caution and one should not rush to draw conclusions from them. Unfortunately, many Shari'at formulations are based on such traditions and thus many of the rules reflect the cultural prejudices of the Arabs and the Persians rather than the greatness of the Qur'an and its just and liberal outlook. Drawing upon the qur'anic principles and our own experiential context, it should be possible to reformulate many of these provisions, especially those in regard to women. This would be doing a great service to the cause of Islam, on the one hand, and that of women, on the other.

The Qur'an, as pointed out above, has been very fair to the cause of women. However, cultural prejudices in the Indian subcontinent have played a big role in denying them their rightful status. The kind of *purdah* observed by Muslim women in parts of South Asia is but one example. They cover not only their entire body but also their faces. This is not in keeping with the spirit of the Qur'an. All that the Qur'an requires of women is that they not display their sexual charms, but dress in a dignified manner.[37] These prejudices emanated in the feudal era wherein the ruling

Muslim classes wanted to protect their womenfolk from others and hence kept them under strict seclusion. However, that tradition was given Islamic legitimacy along with such traditions that required women to observe *purdah* even in the presence of a blind person.[38]

The Shari'ah should be seen both in its cultural context as well as in its normative and, transcendental spirit. Unfortunately, at present it is viewed more in its cultural context. A diligent search both in the qur'anic text and in the *hadith* literature and exegetic works is required to reconstruct Islamic law in its true, liberal, humanistic and progressive spirit. Here I would like to say a word about the term progressive. It should not be seen as a political approach. What I mean to say is that I consider as progressive anything which ensures the sustenance and purposeful growth and flowering of humankind. This is the broad approach I adopt towards life.

We should not be constrained by what our ancestors thought and did. To be constrained is not the qur'anic way of approaching the truth. The Qur'an often criticises those who reject Allah's message because their forefathers did not think that way.[39] We should also escape from this rut and begin to think afresh in our own experiential context and in the light of the values and principles laid down by the Qur'an. The jurists (*fuqaha*), including the four Imams, may have been highly learned but it was not humanly possible for them not to think in their own experiential context, nor would it have been of much relevance to their times if they had done so. Laws can be meaningful only if they serve the needs of the society for which they are meant. If they are purely normative and not contextual, they would not be acceptable and therefore useful. If we view the Shari'ah formulations of the four Imams and others from this perspective our whole way of looking at things will change.

When we seek to revise certain Shari'ah formulations of those jurists we are neither challenging their wisdom and intelligence, nor their learning and sincerity in the cause of Islam. All we are saying is that they thought and wrote in the context of their own times and that even if they had thought otherwise and beyond their times their formulations would not have benefitted society. They were expressing their opinions in their own experiential context.[40] They were also aware of the limitations of their thinking and the possibilities of error in their inferences; hence after giving their opinions they always took care to say or write *wa Allahu a'alam bi' al-sawab* (the right thing is known only to Allah). Imam Abu Hanifah, the founder of the Hanifah school, followed by the largest number of Muslims in India, Pakistan and Bangladesh, used to say that if two of his disciples disagreed with him he would listen to them as two persons holding an opinion were more likely to be correct. This has to be borne in mind while dealing with the Shari'ah formulations. However, it is often ignored and the Shari'ah is treated as immutable.

All this becomes quite clear if we keep in mind how Shari'ah opinions came to be formulated. Whenever a problem arose and the 'ulama held the same opinion about its Shari'ah position, it would be immediately recorded as the final answer to the problem. But often opinions differed and the issue was hotly debated amongst the jurists. At times it was debated for a long time. Imam Abu Hanifah would listen to the debate patiently and after having heard each side would come out with a balanced formulation. Very often, however, even after the Imam's formulation, opinions continued to differ and people would stick to their own judgements. This process continued for more than thirty years before it was completed.[41]

This shows that unanimity of opinion was rare and on every issue opinions differed. Often the issues were very complex; it was not possible to get direct answers from the Holy Qur'an or the Prophet's tradition, or there were other difficulties. Also, and not infrequently, the Prophet's traditions were reported in contradictory ways and it was not always possible to decide which version or whose version was correct. For example, there were great differences between Imam Bukhari and Imam Muslim, both eminent compilers of *hadith*, whose collections are known as *Sahihayn* (i.e. two correct compilations). Imam Muslim bitterly criticises Imam Bukhari, going to the extent of calling him a plagiarist (muntahil) and one who insults *hadith*.[42]

Throwing light on these differences about the *hadith*, Maulana Shibli N'umani, a noted *'alim*, says that the traditionalists mutually differ about the correctness or otherwise of traditions. One traditionalist considers one tradition as highly authentic and insists on its acceptance, whereas another rejects it as weak. The traditionalist Ibn Jauzi has dubbed many traditions as forgeries while others have accepted them as good and authentic. Ibn Jauzi goes to the extent of describing some traditions of *Sahihayn* (i.e. compilations of Bukhari and Muslim) as forgiveness.[43]

Apart from this there is one more difficulty to be taken into account. The words of *hadith* as reported are not always the words of the Prophet himself. Often it is implied that it is how the companion of the Prophet, with whom the tradition originated, understood him. This means the tradition reaching us is based on the companion's understanding of what the Prophet said or did. And it is said in the *fiqh* literature that the companion's understanding cannot be used as an argument.[44] This naturally leads to differences among the jurists which are very difficult to resolve.

Thus the Shari'ah formulations depend a great deal on the human factor. First, how a legal issue is extracted from the Qur'an and the *hadith*. Secondly, what was the context of the qur'anic verse of the tradition relied on. Thirdly, what is the authenticity of the tradition, whether it is weak or forged or authentic. Acceptance or rejection of a *hadith* would also depend on the person concerned. Fourth, even if the tradition is authentic, how was it understood by the companion of the Prophet reporting it? In all these the human factor is involved and human beings can err.

Also, human prejudices are quite natural. While trying to understand what the Prophet meant, these prejudices, acquired since childhood, cannot be kept at bay. And when it comes to the question of women, male prejudices are bound to play their role. While the Qur'an treats women with dignity and accords them equal status with men (except in some sociological matters on which we have already thrown some light) the traditions are often found to be highly prejudicial to women, treating them as far more inferior to men. Consider, for example, the tradition "that nation can never prosper which has assigned its reign to a woman."[45] Many more such traditions could be quoted which are derogatory to women. It is not difficult to understand that human prejudices were operational, though not always consciously, in producing such traditions. Thus we have to be doubly cautious while dealing with such traditions, especially when we have to draw conclusions of seminal importance with regard to women's questions. The above tradition, i.e. that "a nation can never prosper which has assigned its rulership to a woman" was freely used recently when Benazir Bhutto came to power in Pakistan to show that a woman cannot become the head of an Islamic state.

First, the *hadith* seems to be weak; second, one does not know in what context this was said (as context makes all the difference, ignoring which wrong inferences could be drawn) and how it was understood by the narrator from the Prophet; and third, it conflicts with the Qur'an, which speaks highly of a woman ruler, the Queen of Sheba.[46] Yet this tradition has been widely used by the 'ulama and the Muslim jurists to deny women any role in the political affairs of the Muslim countries.

We, therefore, cannot always accept arguments about the status of women based on such traditions and especially if they directly or indirectly conflict with the qur'anic position. In the Holy Qur'an also one has to take those verses which make normative pronouncements and not contextual ones and while dealing with contextual ones one will have to understand these verses in the context of the society and the status of women in that society. Unless we follow these methodological guidelines we are not going to draw the right conclusions. This methodology will be followed in this book. All the received Shari'ah positions regarding women cannot be accepted uncritically. Using the methodology suggested above, the reconstruction of these positions in the light of our own experiential context is highly necessary.

Notes and References

1. Maulana Abul Kalam Azad, *Tarjuman al-Qur'an* (Delhi, 1980, p. 436. See also Maulana Umar Ahmad Usmani, vol. II, *Fiqh al-Qur'an* (Karachi, 1981) vol. XI, p. 173.
2. The *Qur'an* 47:24.
3. Maulana Abul Kalam Azad, op. cit., vol. I, p. 44 (tr. from Urdu by the author).
4. The *Qur'an* 53:3-4.
5. Ibid., 33:59.
6. Muhammad al-Khadrami, *Tarikh Fiqh Islami*, Urdu tr. Abdus Salam Nadvi (Azamgarh, AD 1364).
7. Wilfred Cantwell Smith, *On Understanding Islam* (Delhi, 1985), p. 99.
8. Ibid., p. 90.
9. Dr. Tanzil-ur-Rahman (compiled), *Majnu'a-i-Qanun-i-Islami*, vol. II (Islamabad, 1965), pp. 501-503.
10. Ibid., pp. 535-539.
11. For an exposition of this point of view see Faruq Abu Zayd's, *Al-Shari'ah al-Islamia bayna al-Muhafizin wa al-Mujaddidin* (Cairo, n.d.).
12. Ibid.
13. Ibid., p. 17.
14. Ibid., p. 31.
15. Ibid., p. 45.
16. Ibid., p. 59.
17. Ibid., p. 16.
18. The *Qur'an* 9:60.
19. Ahmad Amin, *Duha al-Islam*, vol. III (Cairo, 1961), pp. 325-26; cf. William Shephard, *The Faith of a Modern Muslim Intellectual* (Delhi, 1982).
20. M.Mujib, *An Introductory Note to Changes in Muslim Personal Law* (Delhi, 1982).
21. Ibid., p. 4.
22. The *Qur'an* 33:35, 32:4, 4:1, etc.
23. Ibid., 4:34.
24. Ibid., 2:228.
25. Ibn Taymiyyah's words are *tataghayyaru ahkam bi taghayyuriz zaman.*

26. See Shah Waliyullah's *Hujjat Allah al-Balighah*, vol. I (Deoband, n.d.), pp. 216-22.

27. Ibid., p. 290.

28. The *Qur'an* 33:21.

29. Shah Waliyullah, op. cit., vol. I, p. 290.

30. For further details see Asghar Ali Engineer, *The Origin and Development of Islam* (Bombay, 1980).

31. For a detailed discussion on the question of the veil, see Justice Aftab Hussain's *Status of Women in Islam* (Lahore, 1987).

32. Ibid., p. 198.

33. Even if a foreign woman is unaccompanied, she is not allowed to leave the airport. If she cannot find a *mahram* man (in prohibited degree of marriage) to accompany her she may have to go back to where she came.

34. The *Qur'an* 4:34.

35. See *Mishkat hadith*, no. 3116.

36. The *Qur'an* 24:31.

37. For a discussion on this tradition see Justice Aftab Hussain's *Status of Women in Islam*, op. cit., p. 153.

38. The *Qur'an* 11:62, 11:63, 11:87, 21:54, 13:40, 23:68, etc.

39. Here we are referring only to social matters (*mu'amalat*) and not to spiritual matters (*'ibadat*). *'Ibadat* is not affected by social changes unlike the *mu'amalat* which change with time.

40. Shibli Nu'mani, *Sirah al-Nu'man* (Delhi, 1987), p. 27.

41. See Maulana Tahir al-Mulki's introduction to Maulana Umar Ahmad, Usmani's *Rajm asl had hay T'azir* (Karachi, 1981), p. 40.

42. Shibli Nu'mani, op. cit., p. 208 (trans. from Urdu by the author).

43. Ibid., p. 209.

44. Justice Aftab Hussain, op. cit., p. 214.

45. The *Qur'an* 27:32-35.

2
STATUS OF WOMEN DURING JAHILIYAH

The status of women in Islam can be properly understood only when we know their status during *jahiliyah* (the period of ignorance or the pre-Islamic period). The reason is obvious. No revolution can remove all traces of the past. Continuity is always there and it is this continuity which maintains an organic relationship with the past. The total severing of ties with the past, even if attempted, cannot succeed. As we will see in the subsequent chapters, whatever was reformed, or prohibited by the Islamic revolution that prevailed during the *jahiliyah* in respect of women, it was crept back into Islamic Shari'ah through *adat* (i.e. pre-Islamic Arab practices). In fact, in many cases, the Shari'ah provisions were based on the *adat* in the absence of other provisions.

What was the status of women in pre-Islamic society? Was it better or worse than in the Islamic period? The theologians maintain that women enjoyed no rights whatsoever and were treated no better than a commodity. Not only were they enslaved, but they could also be inherited as a possession. The Holy Qur'an prohibited this practice.[1] Also, after inheriting a woman from her father, a man would marry her. The Qur'an strictly prohibited this, too.[2] According to Maulana Muhammad Ali, "Among the pre-Islamic Arabs, when a man died his elder son or other relations had a right to possess his widow or widows, marrying them themselves if they pleased, without settling a dowry on them, or marrying them to others, or prohibiting them from marriage altogether."[3]

The Qur'an also mentions that the Arabs in *jahiliyah* used to bury their daughters alive.[4] This barbaric custom of burying female infants alive, comments a noted qur'anic commentator, Muhammad Asad,[5]

> seems to have been fairly widespread in pre-Islamic Arabia, although perhaps not to the extent as has been commonly assumed. The motives were twofold: the fear that an increase in female offspring would result in economic burdens, as well as the fear of the humiliation frequently caused by girls being captured by a hostile tribe and subsequently preferring their captors to their parents and brothers.

It was not that there was no opposition to this barbaric custom in those days. One of the staunchest opponent of this custom was Zayd ibn 'Amr ibn Nufayl, a cousin of 'Umar ibn al-Khattab, the second Caliph after the Prophet.[6] Another was Sa'sa'ah ibn Najiyah al-Tamimi, grandfather of the noted Arab poet Farazdaq. He also became famous for opposing female infanticide.[7]

However, the Prophet of Islam said that one to whom a daughter is born and who does not bury her alive, does not humiliate her, nor prefers a son to a daughter, will be sent by Allah to paradise.[8] Another tradition of the Prophet makes hell fire prohibited to one who has to go through trials and tribulation due to a daughter and yet who does not hate her and behaves well toward her.[9]

This was undoubtedly a great improvement in the status of women. Islam used both inducements and the threat of hell fire to dissuade Arabs from burying their female infants alive. This becomes all the more important when we remember that even in communist China people still prefer sons to daughters and even started burying daughters alive when the one-child norm was enforced by the government in the early 1980s.[10]

Then we are also told that in the pre-Islamic period there was no restriction on the number of wives a man could have. The tribal chiefs and leaders had many wives in order to build relationships with other families. This practice of wooing other families and forging political alliances through marriage was practised in other feudal societies too on a very wide scale. Even the Bedouins desired to have a large number of wives. The noted commentator on the Qur'an, Imam al-Tabari, tells us in his exegesis that a person belonging to the tribe of Quraysh on an average married ten women. He says there were people who married four, five, six or even ten women and asks who could stop him from marrying more than the others.[11]

When the Islamic revolution took place there were many men who had wives from Banu Thaqif.[12] Islamic historians even name them. Then came the qur'anic revelation:

> And if you have reason to fear that you might not act equitably towards orphans, then marry from among (other) women such as are lawful to you—two, or three, or four; but if you have a reason to fear that you might not be able to treat them with equal fairness, then (only) one—or (from among) those whom you rightfully possess. This will make it more likely that you will not deviate from the right course.[13]

Thus the permission to marry more than one and up to four wives, must be seen in this context. It was a drastic reduction in the number of wives one could take. However, this is only one possible justification for polygamy in Islam. But it is a contextual justification, not a normative one, and hence its applicability must be seen as dated, not for all times to come. We will throw further light on it at an appropriate place.

When this verse was revealed many who had more than four wives (Al-Harith bin Qays had eight, Naufal bin Muawiyah had five) the Prophet advised them to opt for four and divorce the rest.[14] Thus it would be seen that Islam did not take any initiative in allowing more than one wife; on the contrary, it discouraged it, restricted it and reluctantly permitted up to four wives in the then prevailing situation. So it would be unfair to accuse Islam of needlessly allowing more than one wife.

There were instances in the pre-Islamic period of men marrying five hundred, or seventy-three to ninety women.[15] These figures may be exaggerated but they are indicative of the trend. I do not agree with those who tend to justify polygamy on the basis of biology,[16] yet we cannot see anything out of context. It must be related to the situation in the period immediately preceding Islam.

This also brings us to the question of marriage. What was the form or forms of marriage? It must be admitted that the predominant form of marriage in the pre-Islamic period was contractual. There was never any concept of sacramental marriage in Arabia. Islam retained this form with certain improvements. We will discuss this at an appropriate place. However, in the *jahiliyah* period there were many forms of marriage. We will describe these so that we can have an idea as to what status women enjoyed in those days.

The most popular mode of marriage was one that became prevalent after the Islamic revolution, as pointed out above. Its essential elements were *mahr* (dower money given to the bride) and *ijab-wa-qubul* (i.e. proposing and accepting). It was known as *zawaj al-ba 'ulah*.[17] Thereafter it came to be known as *nikah*. This word clearly indicated marriage in the usual sense and it used to take place after *mahr* was paid by the bridegroom to the bride. This form of marriage was undoubtedly the best and was in keeping with the dignity of a woman.

Generally, in this form of marriage a man wanting to marry a woman would send a proposal to her father, brother, uncle or cousin. The rule implicitly accepted was that a man would send his proposal to a woman of equal status, a man of high status to a woman of equal status and a man of lowly social origin to an equally humble woman.[18] On the day of the wedding people of the tribe would collect, animals would be slaughtered and orations delivered. This is what happened on the day of the wedding of the Prophet with Lady Khadijah.[19]

It would be interesting to quote from the *khutbah* (address) delivered by the Prophet's uncle, Abu Talib, on the day of his (Prophet's) wedding. Abu Talib said:

> Praise be to Allah who created us from the progeny of Ibrahim, and that Ismail cultivated and that he made us in charge of His House (i.e. Ka'ba) and made us leaders of the Arabs. Then my brother's son, this Muhammad bin Abdullah, no one can be weighed with him

but the balance of nobility, excellence and intellect will tilt in his favour. Though he is deficient in wealth, wealth is not permanent and he has asked with enthusiasm the hand of your daughter Khadijah and he is her match and he has given twenty young she-camels as dower and I, people of Quraysh, make you witness to this.[20]

This description of the Prophet's wedding is interesting as it underwent very little change in Islam. It clearly shows that at least one of the prevalent forms of marriage was contractual and that it was retained after the Islamic movement came into being. Of course, there were certain anomalies like the father, grandfather, uncle or elder brother exercising the exclusive right to give the bride away in marriage or the *wali* (i.e. a marriage guardian) taking away the *mahr* amount, etc. These were removed, as we shall see in the subsequent chapter. However, one must add here that there is no proof or anything on record to show that the women were forced or compelled against their will to marry men they did not like.[21]

Another form of marriage was known as *nikah al-dayzan*. This provided that when a women's husband died, his eldest son would be entitled to marry her. If he was willing to marry her he would throw a cloth over her and would inherit her as his woman; if he desired, he could marry her or prevent her from marrying anyone else until she died. On her death, he would inherit her wealth. Or, she could free herself from him by paying him suitable compensation or he could marry her off to one of his brothers on payment of fresh *mahr*.[22] This form of marriage – inheriting one's father's wives – was strictly prohibited by the Qur'an (see verse 4:19).

Yet another form of marriage was *muta'* marriage. This is a kind of temporary marriage in which the period of its validity is specified. After this period is over the marriage is dissolved automatically. According to the Sunni Muslims, the Prophet prohibited this form of marriage after having allowed it during certain battles (*ghazawat*).[23] However, the Twelver Shi'as believe that the *muta'* marriage was never prohibited by the Prophet. They maintain that the qur'anic verse 4:24 permits it.[24] This form was generally resorted to during long journeys such as on trade caravans. The children of such marriages were generally known through their mothers and not their fathers as the latter would go away after the period of marriage expired. However, they did have the right to inherit their father's property.[25]

There was also a form of marriage known as *zawaj al-badal* (i.e. mutual exchange of wives). One man would ask another to forgo his wife in his favour and in turn would forgo his wife in the latter's favour. This exchange took place without offering any *mahr*.[26]

Zawaj al-Shighar was a form of marriage like any other common form except that no *mahr* was offered as the man would marry off his daughter or sister to a man who would marry his daughter or sister to him.[27] The Prophet prohibited this form of marriage; he is reported to have said '*la shighar fir al-Islam*', there is no *shighar* form of marriage in Islam).[28] This form of marriage, as can be seen, is very close to *zawaj al-badal*. There is no *mahr* paid in both cases. Muslim jurists consider it invalid but some of them *Hanafis* for example) allow it provided this name is not used and *mahr mithl* (i.e. analogous *mahr*) is paid.[29]

Another interesting form of marriage was known as *zawaj al-Istibd'a*. In this the husband would ask his wife to have sexual intercourse with another man in order to get pregnant. He would refrain from going near her until she has conceived from that person. Generally, people used to send their wives to men known for their bravery, generosity, etc. The child born was considered a gift from him.[30] It must be said that this form of marriage was extremely rare among the Arabs. Usually only when a man was impotent would he resort to it.

Some people maintain that this form of marriage was practised in respect of slave girls. These slave girls were sent to well-built, strong persons so that they would conceive and give birth to healthy children who they could either employ themselves or sell in the market. Thus it was a kind of business and the motive was to make a profit, nothing more.[31]

When a man captured a woman during war and wanted to marry her it was known as *nikah al-za inah*. She could not refuse to marry him as she was his captive. There was no recitation of *khutba* nor was any *mahr* paid.[32] Similarly, this slave girl, if she bore children he could either free them, or accept them as his children or simply keep them as his slaves.[33]

It would be interesting also to note what categories of relations were excluded from being eligible for marriage. The Arabs had evolved certain norms in this respect. A father could not marry his daughter nor could a grandfather marry his granddaughter. Similarly, it was not permissible for a mother to marry her own son. A grandmother could not marry her grandson either. Nor could a brother marry his sister. Thus the Arabs prohibited marriage with mothers, daughters, sisters, paternal aunts and maternal aunts.[34]

Similarly, marriage with one's brother's daughter or sister's daughter was not permissible but the children of two brothers or two sisters or a brother and sister's could marry among themselves. These prohibited degrees of marriage were enforced strictly. Ibn Abbas (a companion of the Prophet) and others went as far as saying the Arabs in *jahiliyah* prohibited what Allah had prohibited, i.e. marrying one's father's wives and marrying two sisters together at a time.[35]

There is one more interesting thing to note. The Arabs in the pre-Islamic period did not approve of marriage with the wife of one's adopted son or his daughter. But Islam did not find anything wrong with such marriages. The Qur'an maintained that there is no blood relation between the adopted son and the adopter and thus the adopter does not become his natural father. The Qur'an says, "Call them (adopted sons) by (the names of) their fathers; this is more equitable with Allah; but if you know not their fathers, then they are your brethren in faith and your friends..."[36] The Qur'an also says: "So when Zaid dissolved her marriage tie, we gave her to thee as a wife, so that there should be no difficulty for the believers about the wives of their adopted sons, when they have dissolved their marriage tie. And Allah's command is ever performed."[37]

It should be noted that Zaid was the Prophet's slave whom he liberated and then treated him as his own son. He was very much attached to the Prophet. He refused to go back to his own parents and chose to remain with the Prophet. He was married to a woman called Zainab. However, they were later divorced and the Prophet married Zainab. As the Arabs prohibited marriage with one's adopted son's divorced wife, there was a furore among the people. Hence this verse was revealed to say that an adopted son is not a real son and should not be treated as such.[38]

Now we come to the question of divorce during *jahiliyah*. The Arabs were well acquainted with *talaq* as they were acquainted with the concept of marriage. This has been so since time immemorial. *Talaq* meant divesting oneself of all the rights one had over one's spouse and separating her from oneself.[39] When someone wanted to divorce his wife he would say, "Go back to your parents", or "I separate you", or "your rope is on your shoulders" or "liberate you" or some other similar words.[40]

The historians of *jahiliyah* have recorded the reasons for divorce. In those days divorce could be given for any reason, even if the wife spoke highly of her people. Hassan bin Thabit divorced his wife for this reason – or if a man did not find in her the love he was looking for, or if they could not develop friendship and intimacy. A 'asha divorced his wife for this reason.[41] There are also instances of men marrying a woman who they thought was young and beautiful but who turned out to be old and ugly. Hence they found no way out other than to divorce her. This happened with Lajham, who married a woman Bani Faq'as thinking she was young and beautiful.[42]

During *jahiliyah* granting divorce was in the hands of men. In certain circumstances women could persuade their husbands to allow them a divorce. For example, there was the case of Al-Hujjaj al-Sahmi who when he became poor called his two wives and divorced them.[43] It would be interesting to note that in Islam also the divorce, according to the jurists, lies in the hands of the husband, not the wife, though the Qur'an does not categorically give such a privilege to the husband. This is inferred from the qur'anic verse 2:237, in which it has been said that the marriage tie is in the hands of the man (bi yadihi 'uqdatun nikah). It would be seen that it is Arab' adat which has influenced the Muslim jurists' view in such matters. We will discuss this at an appropriate place.

During *jahiliyah*, too, there were women who stipulated the condition at the time of marriage that would have the right to divorce; they would live with their husbands as long as they liked and would initiate divorce when they liked too. This was because of their high status in society.[44] However, ordinary women could hardly think of laying down such conditions. It may be said here that such freedom, even to women of high status, was hardly available to women of other contemporary societies.

There was an interesting method of divorce prevalent among some Bedouins who lived in tents made of wool. The method was to change the direction of the entrance to the tent. This was resorted to by women, generally. If a woman desired to divorce her husband she would change the direction of the entrance to the tent, for instance from the west to the east, or from the direction of Yemen to that of Syria. When the husband saw this he knew that his wife had divorced him and he would not go to her. This was so because among the Bedouins in villages the tent was the property of women.[45]

There were some women who had the exclusive right to divorce and who controlled their own affairs. We read in *Al-Muhbir* that Salam bint 'Umru, mother of 'Abd al-muttalib (the Prophet's grandfather), would never marry unless her husband allowed her full authority; if she disliked anything in her husband, she would divorce him. There was another woman, Fatima bint al-Khaushab, who was known for having more children than any other woman and entering into marriage contracts at the fastest possible pace. Similarly, *Al-Muhbir* tells us of several other women who freely divorced their husbands and remarried.[46]

However, this does not mean that the Arab women did not exercise caution in divorcing their husbands. They would not go for divorce unless they were left with no other option; they would not break the marriage tie foolishly. Their self-respect and dignity lay in their own hands and they would never put them at risk, as borne out by the following incident. A man from the family of Abu Talib told his wife in anger, "Thy matter is in thy hands" (i.e. I divorce you). The wife replied "By God, I was in your hands for twenty years; I guarded these years and gave you the best of company. I did not waste a single moment any day and fulfilled all my duties." He admired what she said and so made up with her.[47]

Islam also retained the woman's right to divorce. She could stipulate it as a marriage condition (*talaq al-tafwid*). She was also given the right to divo rce known as *'Khula'*, i.e. she could free herself from the marriage bond if she so desired. She could ask for *'Khula'* for lack of maintenance or maltreatment by her husband, or if he disappeared for a long period. She was also given the right to annul the marriage, if she was married in childhood, on reaching the age of puberty, or to go ahead with it.[48] We will discuss the question of divorce in Islam in detail at an appropriate place.

Ibn Abbas, an eminent companion of the Prophet, tells us that during *jahiliyah* men had an absolute right over women in matters of divorce. After one or two divorces a man could take back his wife if he so wished but after the third divorce he had no rights over her.[49] The Qur'an does not mention this form of divorce, but unfortunately the Muslim jurists borrowed it from Arab *adat*. This form of three divorces, as we shall see, came to be practised most widely. However, Ibn Zayd tells us that in the pre-Islamic period a man could divorce his wife one hundred times and still take her back.[50] Al-Razi also says that a man could divorce his wife a thousand times and yet could take her back.[51]

During *jahiliyah* a man who had divorced his wife thrice could marry her again only after she had married a stranger. In *talaq al-ba'in* a man could take back his wife after a fresh *nikah* but after Islam this was made conditional on her marrying another man and only then could she acquire legitimacy to marry her former husband. In *jahiliyah* they used to pronounce three divorces in one sitting but as far as Islam is concerned the jurists differed on this. Most of the jurists think that two or three divorces can take place in one sitting itself, whereas some others maintain that only one divorce takes place regardless of how many times it is pronounced.[52] The three divorces in one sitting has re-emerged as the most controversial issue among the conservatives and modernists and we will discuss it further in detail later.

Another form of divorce widely prevalent during the pre-Islamic period was known as *zihar* (literally meaning 'back'). The man would tell his wife she was like his mother's back, like her womb, like her thigh, like her sexual organ or like the back of his sister or aunt.[53] This meant that he treated the wife like his mother, sister or aunt.

The Qur'an prohibited the practice of *zihar*. It says:

> Those of you who put away their wives by calling them their mothers, they are not their mothers. None are their mothers save those who gave them birth, and they utter indeed a hateful word and a lie. And surely, Allah is Pardoning, Forgiving.[54]

And for doing such a hateful thing the Qur'an laid down punishments for those who indulged in it. It said,

> And those who put away their wives calling them their mothers, and then go back on that which they said, must free a captive before they touch one another. To this you are exhorted; and Allah is aware of what you do.[55]

The Qur'an further says:

> But he who has not the means should fast for two months successively before they touch one another, and he who is unable to do so should feed sixty needy ones. That is in order that you may have faith in Allah and His Messenger. And these are Allah's limits.[56]

Naturally, this punishment was prescribed with a view to discouraging this practice, which was an absurd one. There were some practices in *jahiliyah* which were based on superstitions and the Qur'an abolished them and prescribed punishments in order to discourage them as in the case of *zihar*.

It should be remembered that *zihar* was among the worst and most stringent kinds of *talaq*.[57] Even the *muzahir* was forced to marry off his wife to someone else.[58] Islam was categorical in prohibiting *zihar* as a wife could not become a mother simply by making such a declaration, just as an adopted son could not become a real son just by adoption. The Qur'an says:

> Allah has not made for any man two hearts within him, nor has He made your wives whom you desert by *zihar* your mothers, nor has He made those whom you assert (to be your sons) your sons. These are the words of your mouths.[59]

In another form of *talaq* called al-'ila' a man takes a vow to leave his wife for a period of time, may be a few months, a year or two years, during which he does not go near her as a sort of punishment.[60] But Islam limited the period of waiting to four months. There is no question of increasing it. Thereafter either one should divorce his wife or take back the oath.[61] The pronouncement of the Qur'an on Ila is as follows:

> Those who swear that they will not go to their wives should wait for four months; then if they go back, Allah is surely Hearing, Knowing.[62]

In the *'Khula'* form of divorce, already referred to, the woman had the right to ask for liberation (literal meaning of *'Khula'* if she was maltreated, or felt tortured in staying with the husband or if the husband refused to leave her either out of greed or in order to humiliate her or because he had spent too much money to acquire her.[63] Islam retained *'Khula'*. Allah says in the Qur'an:

> And it is not lawful for you to take any part of what you have given them (i.e. women), unless both fear that they cannot keep within the limits of Allah. Then if you fear that they cannot keep within the limits of Allah there is no blame on them for what she gives up to become free thereby.[64]

During *jahiliyah* there was another form of divorce called 'al 'adl which literally meant forcing the woman not to marry. A man who married a free woman and then could not carry on with her could divorce her on the condition that she would not remarry without his permission. When somebody wanted to marry her, he would offer something to her former husband and persuade him to obtain his permission. If he so chose he would give his permission, otherwise he would refuse and not allow her to marry.[65] But Islam categorically banned the practice of 'adl. The Qur'an says:

> And when you divorce women and they end their term, prevent them not from marrying their husbands if they agree among themselves in a lawful manner.[66]

There is a controversy whether there was *iddah* (waiting period) after divorce during *jahiliyah*. Some researchers say there was such a period while others maintain there was none. A woman carrying a child in her womb would marry and go to live with her new husband and give birth to the child in his house. The child so born was known after the man she had later married though it was known that she had conceived it from her former husband. It was Islam which fixed the period of *iddah*.[67]

In *jahiliyah* the period of waiting (*iddah*) after the husband's death was one year. The widow used to be confined to a small room (*hafsh*), was prohibited from touching things, could not apply collyrium to her eyes or even pare her nails or comb her hair until one year had passed. Naturally, her physical condition worsened. She would be given an animal—as ass, goat or bird— to rub her skin with, after which she could return to normalcy.[68]

Islam abolished all this. It also reduced the *iddah* period to four months and ten days. The Qur'an says:

> And (as for) those of you who die and leave wives behind, such women should keep themselves in waiting for four months and ten days; when they reach their term, there is no blame on you for what they do for themselves in a lawful manner.[69]

However, if she were pregnant then her waiting period would last until the delivery of the child.[70] The Qur'an also ended all the other superstitious practices associated with widows, as described above.

During *jahiliyah* a divorcee was given nothing by way of maintenance. She was not entitled to a house or anything else in *talaq al-ba'in* (i.e. irreconcilable divorce)[71] The child was invariably related to the father. It was the Prophet who said that *Al-waladu li'i firash* (the child is of the mother).[72] In the pre-Islamic period the father would claim that the child belonged to him and the child would be ascribed to him just on the basis to this claim alone. Similarly, if the slave girls who were compelled to have sexual relations with their masters gave birth to children, the masters would hardly ever claim them but the children would be ascribed to them if they died without claiming the children. The same principle applied to their heirs. If they wanted they would ascribe the child to the master or else it remained disinherited. The 'ulama differed about the amount of inheritance for such a child.[73]

As for inheritance, according to Muslim historians a woman was treated like a commodity. She had no right to inherit from either her husband's or her father's property or any other relative's property. Instead, she herself was an object of inheritance. In the pre-Islamic period it was generally thought and accepted that inheritance was not meant for women and small children and that it was for those who wield weapons and capture booty,[74] i.e. for the men only.

We are told that during the Prophet's time Aus bin Thabit died leaving behind two daughters and a small son. Aus's cousins came and took away his entire property as neither wife nor daughters or son could inherit it. Aus's wife went to complain to the Prophet, pleading her inability to feed her children since the entire property belonging to her husband had been taken away by his cousins. At that time, the following qur'anic verse was revealed:

For men is a share of what the parents and the near relatives leave, and for women a share of what the parents and the near relatives leave, whether it be little or much—an appointed share.[75]

And also the following verse:

And they ask thee a decision about women. Say: Allah makes known to you His decision concerning them; and that which is recited to you in the Book is concerning widowed women, whom you give not what is appointed for them, nor to the weak among children, and that you should deal justly with orphans.[76]

Then came the verse on inheritance:

Allah enjoins you concerning your children: for the male is the equal of the portions two females; but if there be more than two females, two-thirds of what the deceased leaves is theirs; and if there be one, for her is the half. And as for his parents, for each of them is the sixth of what he leaves, if he has a child; but if he has no child and (only) his two parents inherit him, for his mother is the third, but if he has brothers, for his mother is the sixth, after (payment of) a bequest he may have bequeathed or a debt. Your parents and your children, you know not which of them is the nearer to you in benefit. This is an ordinance from Allah. Allah is surely Ever-Knowing, Wise.[77]

This was a revolutionary step as far as women were concerned. Maybe women were not so totally deprived of inheritance in the pre-Islamic period as Muslim historians have previously thought, but it is undeniable that men had a far greater share than women and that there was no fixed share for women. They depended on the arbitrary decisions of their menfolk. But the Qur'an removed all uncertainties and fixed a share in inheritance for women which, while less than that for men needs to be seen in its totality. We will throw more light on this problem at an appropriate place.

That there was some share for women during *jahiliyah* is indicated by what Ibn Habib and also Ibn Hazm tell us about Amir bin Jashm, who left by way of inheritance for his male children twice as much as that for female children, thereby following the injunction of Islam.[78] There are other indications as well that women did on many occasions inherit possessions.[79] However, what Islam did was to remove all ambiguities and it fixed a compulsory share in inheritance for women. It was undoubtedly a great improvement over the *jahiti* position. Dr. Byumi Mahran maintains that in the pre-Islamic period women did inherit though their share may not have been substantial. The women also had a right to property, as did Egyptian women. They could take part in selling and buying and the women of the towns, as compared to the Bedouin women, had a better status and commanded greater financial resources in their own right.[80] Dr. Byumi Mahran, gives the example of Saiyyidah Khadijah, the first wife of the Prophet, who commanded great resources and owned several trade caravans which used to travel during winter as well as summer. She used to have a partnership in trade with men and it was in this capacity that she entrusted her trade caravan to the Prophet before Allah entrusted him with Prophethood. As the Prophet was a man of great honesty and integrity, she used to give him much more than she gave to others by way of a share in the profits.[81]

Then there is also the example of Asama' bint Makhramah, who used to deal in perfumes (*'itr*). She would buy perfumes in Yemen and sell them in Medina. This lady lived until the time of the second Caliph, Hazrat 'Umar bin al-Khattab (AD 634-644) and perhaps until later.[82] There was also another woman selling *'itr* in Mecca. Her *'itr* became highly popular and men used to apply it before going to war and even consumed it as they went into battle.[83] Many more examples from the pre-Islamic period can be quoted.

Thus we see the status of women during the pre-Islamic period was not as bad as was made out by later Muslim historians. Women of a higher status commanding greater resources were held in great esteem and certain customs and rules did not apply to them as in our own society today. There are instances of women ignoring their father's decision and opting for marriage to men of their own choice. There is the case of Hind bint 'Atbah bin Rabi'ah.[84]

We now come to the question of *mahr*, also known as *sadaq*. Then, as now, a man would ask for the hand of a woman from a man, pay *sadaq* (dower money) and marry her. Most of the Qurashites and other tribes followed similar customs. In fact, we should remember that in the *jahiliyah* period some women lived an independent life and were free to make their own decisions as did the first wife of the Prophet, Khadijah. Their independence derived from their financial status.

As for *mahr* during the pre-Islamic period, it was given to the family of the woman for asking her hand in marriage. In fact, there was some difference between *mahar* and *sadaq*. The former was paid to the marriage guardian (i.e. *wali*) and the latter to the bride herself.[85] *Mahr* in *jahiliyah* was considered a bride price, just as in other tribal societies. At times the marriage guardian would spend it on buying those things which the bride would take along with her to her husband's house. And sometimes he would keep the entire amount for himself without spending any of it. This was because he thought it was his right to do so.[86] However, Islam prohibited the bride's people from taking anything from the mahr. It was designated as the bride's property. The Qur'an says: "And give women dowries as free gifts. But if they of themselves be pleased to give you a portion thereof, consume it with enjoyment and pleasure."[87]

Usually, during the pre-Islamic period the father used to take away the amount of *mahr* and the daughter who brought a lot of wealth by way of *mahr* was known as *Al-Nafijah*. Whenever a daughter was born the people would congratulate the parents saying , "*hanian laka al-nafijah*" (congratulations for a daughter who will bring wealth) or "May Allah grace you with more such wealth bringers". This shows that in *jahiliyah* the father used to add the *mahr* amount to his own wealth.[88] There were contradictory practices in regard to *mahr*. At times *mahr* was also referred to as *Al-Hulwan*, i.e. a kind of fee or brokerage. It was deducted from the *mahr* amount of the daughter, sister or any other woman for that matter though it was not approved of by the Arabs. Many Arab women would say as a matter of pride that their husbands did not take their share while marrying off their daughters.[89]

Thus we see that there was no common practice in regard to *mahr*. Some gave the entire amount to the daughter, some even added to it to honour their daughter and others took away either the entire amount or a part of it.

Also, there was no fixed limit for *mahr* in the pre-Islamic period. Mostly it depended on the financial status of the person concerned and the social status of the bride. At times the *mahr* used to be as high as 100 or 150 camels.[90] 'Abd al-Muttalib, the grandfather of the Prophet, gave 100 she-camels and 100 pounds of gold by way of *mahr* to Fatima bint Umru, and Harith bin Salil gave 150 camels and 1,000 *dirham* by way of *mahr* to Zaba bint Alqama.[91]

In some regions like Kindah, people used to ask for an exaggerated amount by way of *mahr*. They would not marry off their daughters to anyone for less than 100 camels and, in some cases, 1,000 camels. The king of Kindah, when he married Umm Inas, granted her by way of *mahr* that he would fulfil all the desires of her *qaum* (her tribe, her people) whatever they might be.[92] The Prophet, on the other hand, is reported to have given Khadijah, his wife, 20 young camels or 500 *dirhams* or about 12 *awqiyah* (about 100 grams) of gold.[93]

Religious Status of Women during the Pre-Islamic Period

What was the religious status of women in the pre-Islamic period? Of course, there can be no clear answer to this question, but one can say that on the whole it was not too bad. There were a number of *kahinahs* (priestesses) amongst them. From very ancient times women in Arabia, especially in the south (Yemen), have performed the functions of priestesses. During the regime of Qutban,[94] as early as 150 BC, we find mention of a woman priestess called Barat. We also learn about a priestess for the Moon God ('Am') in the south.[95]

We also hear of another priestess, 'Tarifah', in southern Arabia, who predicted the fall of the dam of M'arib. We also know of another priestess, 'Afira, in the same region. She used to interpret dreams successfully.[96] Similarly, in Thamudic inscriptions we find mention of a kahinah (priestess) called Aflakat. From these inscriptions (which were found in the north of Arabia) we learn that Aflakat, played a very important religious role.[97]

In northern Arabia we learn about another *kahinah* called Hudaym. She was one of the children of S'ad and lived in Syria. Her importance can be understood from the fact that to her was referred for arbitration the dispute about the sharing of the waters of the well of Zamzam in Mecca. The case was referred to her by no less a person than 'Abd al-Muttalib, the grandfather of the Prophet. The dispute was decided in his favour.[98]

There is another interesting incident associated with 'Abd al-Muttalib involving a priestess called' 'Arafah. 'Abd al-Muttalib had taken a vow that he would sacrifice one of his sons if ten sons were born to him. When the tenth son was born, he threw a dice to decide who should be sacrificed. Unfortunately, the dice pointed to his son 'Abd Allah, the Prophet's father, whom 'Abd al-Muttalib loved most of all. The people of Mecca tried to dissuade him from sacrificing him in the House of Allah (*K'aba*). But he would not listen. He wanted to fulfil his vow. At last, the matter was referred to 'Arafah. She said that the dice should be thrown again, each time increasing the number of camels to be sacrificed until it fell in favour of the camels, instead of his son. When the lot fell in favour of the camels, the number had increased to 100. Thus, at the instigation of a woman priestess, he sacrificed 100 camels and saved the life of 'Abd Allah.[99]

There was another priestess called Al-Ghitalah who belonged to Bani Marrah bin 'Abd Manat. It is said she predicted the birth of the Prophet of Islam twenty years before his Prophethood.[100] Yet another was Fatma bint Marr al-Khath 'amiyyah, who was both a poetess and a priestess.[101] Similarly, there were several others. It should be remembered that *kahinah* (the oracle) was an institution which had many functions. The *kahinah* not only predicted events but also arbitrated in disputes referred to him or her. The people attached great significance to the *kahinah's* forecasts and decisions, whether right or wrong. Thus the *kahinah* had her place in society and by inference one can say that in the people's eyes women enjoyed much influence as they were consulted in matters of great significance. The opinions and advice given by women were followed.[102] Thus we see that women had a religious status; the priesthood in pre-Islamic days was not the monopoly of men alone.

There were also female deities in those days. During the reign of Qatban Hadrmaut and Saba Sun were worshipped. For the people of Yemen the sun was a female deity though the people of Egypt, Sumer, etc considered it to be a male deity. The Arabs named themselves 'Abd Shams (slave, or worshippers of the Sun).[103] The first to be named 'Abd Shams was a person who worshipped among the followers of Queen Sheba in the period around a thousand years before Christ.[104]

Among the female deities in *K'aba* were Al-Lat, Al-Uzza and
Manat. Al-Lat was a very old and highly respected deity
worshipped by several Arab tribes. In Hijaz Banu-i-Thaqif
worshipped it as the Quraysh worshipped Al-Uzza,[105] Al-Lat also
formed part of several names among the Arabs.[106] Al-Uzza was
the most important deity of the Quraysh and *kinanah*. The idol of
Al-Uzza and her temple were demolished by Khalid bin al-Walid
when Islam triumphed in Mecca. Interestingly enough in charge
of the temple was a black woman along with another man.[107]
However, it should be noted that this black woman remained
hidden inside the temple whereas the man acted as its trustee.
Whatever she spoke from behind the idol was ascribed to Al-Uzza
by the man.[108] The third in this series of female deities was Manat
whose temple was situated about seven miles from Medina or in
Qadid, between Mecca and Medina, or at the nearby town of
Wadan or, according to yet another, source, at Fadak.[109] The
Qur'an refers to these deities in the chapter *Al-Najm*. It raises the
question "Are the males for you and for Him the females.?"[110]

The verse points to a contrast in the values and attitudes
prevalent among the Arabs. While they worshipped the female
deities and desired their intercession they did not like to have
female children. They valued sons and boasted if they had a
number of them. It is this contrast to which the Qur'an points.
Why should they ascribe daughters to Allah while they
themselves liked to have sons? It was a contrast between
sociology and theology. While sociologically, sons were more
desirable as they were much more useful, theologically they
desired reverence for the female as a life-giving force. Islam did
resolve this contradiction on an ideological plane but it soon crept
back into practice as sons continued to be more useful in the
production and earning of wealth.

The position of women, however, cannot be viewed only
ideologically. If this could be done, then, Islam had resolved the
problem by granting a high status (in fact, equal status, according
to modern interpretations of the Qur'an) to women and
recognising their individual rights and dignity. But we know that
the whole social set up is such as to make men more valuable in

the process of production, thus enabling them to usurp the primary place in society, relegating women to a secondary position. Even modern society has not been able to resolve this contradiction in practice. Even in the most advanced Western societies women continue to be treated as inferior in status to men. It is men who control the commanding heights of the economy as well, enjoying socio-political superiority.

My aim in this book is to show how the status accorded to women by the Holy Qur'an was soon compromised at the hands of eminent jurists in view of harsh practical realities. Here in this chapter I have tried to show that the position of women during the pre-Islamic period was not as bad as it has been made out to be by some Muslim historians and commentators. In fact, it was far more complex and not very different from what it is today or has been through the ages. It all depended on what status, economically and politically, women enjoyed in society. There were cases of the total subjugation of women as well as of women achieving respected and powerful positions.

What the Qur'an did was to give a definite normative and legal shape to women's rights and duties. It accepted many practices prevalent in Islamic society but rejected those which were derogatory, iniquitous and unjust from the human point of view. In the pre-Islamic period there was neither a scriptural authority nor a legal one at that. There were only traditions and age-old practices which gave sanction to what people did or did not do. The Qur'an and the Prophet filled this vacuum, as did divine injunctions and the prophetic *Sunnah*. In addition to the divine commands, the Prophet also had legal acumen in abundance to weed out all those practices which might be legally termed iniquitous.

Unfortunately, as we will see, the jurists were more concerned with social rather than with value judgements in determining the position of women in Shari'ah. The time has come for us to exercise value judgements again and sort out social judgements which are becoming obsolete due to social changes that have occurred in the meantime.

Notes and References

1. The *Qur'an* 4:19.
2. Ibid., 4:23.
3. See *Holy Qur'an*, English trans. with Arabic text by Maulana Muhammed Ali (Lahore, 1978), f.n. 554 to verse 4:19, p. 194.
4. The *Qur'an* 81:9
5. *The Message of* the *Qur'an* (Gibralter, 1980), p. 933, f.n. no. 4 to verse 41:9.
6. See Bukhari, *Fada'Ashab al-Nabi*; on the authority of 'Abd Allah ibn 'Umar cf. Muhammad Asad, ibid., p. 993.
7. See Ibn Khallikan, *Wafayat al-A'yan ii*, p. 197; cf. Muhammad Asad, ibid.
8. See Sunan Abi Da'ud, *Kitab al-Adab, bab Fadl man 'ala Yatama.*
9. See Sahih Bukhari, *Kitab al-Adab, bab Rahmat al-Walad* wa *taqbilihi.*
10. There have been reports in the press about the buying of female infants in China. This occurs when a girl is born to parents who are forbidden from having a second child due to the one-child norm enforced in China, thus barring the possibility of begetting a son.
11. Tabari, *Jam'i al-Bavan* (Cairo, 1957-69) vol. VII, pp. 534-5.
12. Saiyyid Qutb, *Fi Zilal al-Qur'an* (Beirut, 1967-74), pp. 240-4.
13. The *Qur'an* 4:3.
14. *Al-Qurtabi, Al-Jami 'al-Ahkam al-Qur'an* (Cairo, 1969-70), vol. V, p. 17 see also *Nayl al-Awtar*, vol. V, p. 160.
15. See *Kitab al-Aghani* (Cairo, 1929).
16. See Muhammad Asad, op. cit., pp. 101-2.
17. Dr. Jawwad Ali, *Al-Mufassal fi Tarikh al–' Arab Qabl al-Islam* (Beirut, 1968-71) vol. V, p. 533.
18. See Dr. Muhammad Byumi Mahran's "Markaz al-mar'ah fi al-Hadarat Al-'arabiyyah al-Qadimah" in *Kulliyah al-'ulum al-jtima 'iyyah,* vol. I, Riyadh 1977.
19. See *Tarikh Tabari* (Cairo, 1967-69), vol. II, p. 281.
20. Itiyan Diniyyah and Sulayman Ibrahim, *Muhammad Rasulullah* (Cairo, 1958, p. 93. See also Ibn al-Jawzi, *al-Wafa 'bi Ahwal al-Mustafa* (Cairo, 1966), p. 145.
21. Dr Jawwad Ali, op. cit., p. 532.

22. Ibn Athir, *Al-Nihayah fi Gharib al-Hadith*, vol. I, p. 104. See also Dr. Jawwad Ali, op. cit., vol. V, p. 534.
23. See *Tafsir Ruh al-Mani* (Cairo, 1924-25), vol. III, pp. 5-7. See also *Tafsir al-Kashshaf* (Cairo, 1966), vol. I, p. 360.
24. The Shi'as maintain that the word *famastamt 'atum* hints at *muta'* (marriage).
25. Dr. Jawwad Ali, op. cit., vol. V, p. 537.
26. Ibid.
27. Sunan Abi Daud, op. cit., vol. II, p. 227.
28. See *Sahih Muslim*, p. 139.
29. *Fath al-Bari* (Cairo, 1301 AH).
30. See Sahih al-Bukhari, vol. III, p. 162, and Dr. Jawwad Ali, vol. V, pp. 538-9.
31. Dr. Jawwad Ali, ibid., p. 539.
32. See Dr. Jawwad Ali, ibid., p. 564.
33. 'Abd al-'Aziz Salim, *Dirasat fi Tarikh al-'Arab*, vol. I (pre-Islamic period), (Alexandria, 1968), p. 116.
34. Ab'ul Fida, *Al-Mukhtasar fi Akhbar al-Bashar* (Cairo, 1325), vol. I, p. 99.
35. *Tafsir Ruh al-Mani*, op. cit., vol. IV, p. 261.
36. The *Qur'an* 33:5.
37. Ibid., 33:37.
38. This story is found in all the standard commentaries on the *Qur'an*.
39. *Taj al-'Urus*, op. cit., vol. I, p. 411.
40. Ibid., vol. I, p. 411.
41. Al-Asbahani, *Al-Aghani* (Cairo, 1929), vol. III, p. 14.
42. Dr. Muhammad Byuni Mahran, op. cit., p. 171.
43. *Al-Aghani*, op cit., vol. IX, p. 5.
44. Dr Jawwad Ali, vol. V, p. 554
45. *Al-Aghani*, op. cit., vol. XVI, p. 102.
46. Ibn Habib, *Kitab al-Muhbir* (Hyderabad, 1942), pp. 398-9.
47. Ibn Tayfur, *Balaghat al-Nisa* (Cairo, 1908), p. 132.
48. Ahmad Muhammad al-Haufi, *Al-Mar'ah fi al-sh'ar al-jahili* (Cairo, 1954), p. 215.
49. Al-Haufi, op. cit., p. 210.
50. *Tafsir al-Tabari*, op. cit., vol. IV, p. 547.
51. Al-Razi, *Tafsir al-Kabir* (Cairo, n.d), vol. II, p. 373.
52. Al-Haufi, op. cit., p. 211 and also *Tafsir al-Tabari*, op. cit., vol. IV, pp. 538-600.

53. Jassas, *Ahkam al*-Qur'an III, p. 417; also Tabari, op. cit., vol. II, pp. 417, 421.
54. *Tafsir al-Tabari*, vol. XXVIII, p. 7.
55. The *Qur'an* 58:2.
56. Ibid., 58:3-4.
57. Ibid., 58:4.
58. Dr. Jawwad Ali, op. cit., vol. VI, p. 551.
59. *Tafsir al-Tabari*, vol. XXVIII, pp. 6-7. See also Al-Haufi, op. cit., p. 212.
60. The *Qur'an* 33:4.
61. *Tafsir ibn Kathir* (Cairo, 1971-73), vol. I, p. 268.
62. Al-Haufi, op. cit., p. 213.
63. The *Qur'an* 2:226-27.
64. Al-Qurtabi, *Al-Jam'i al-ahkam al-Qur'an* (Cairo, !969-70), vol. III, p. 137.
65. The *Qur'an* 2:229.
66. Sunan Abi Daud, op. cit., vol. II, p. 230.
67. The Qur'an 2:232 See also verse 4:19.
68. *Tafsir al-Qurtabi*, vol. III, p. 194.
69. See Sahih Bukhari, vol. IX, p. 432, Sahih Muslim, vol. I, pp. 433-5, *Tafsir al-Tabari*, pp. 80-6.
70. The *Qur'an* 2:234.
71. Ibid., 65:4; See also *Tafsir al-Tabari*, op. cit., vol. V, pp. 81-2.
72. *Sahih Muslim*, vol. IV, p. 195.
73. Ibid.
74. *Tafsir al-Tabari*, op. cit., vol. VII, p. 599; *Tafsir al-Kashsha*, vol. I, p. 376; *Tafsir Ruh al-Mani*, op. cit., vol. IV, p. 210.
75. The *Qur'an* 4:7.
76. Ibid., 4:127; see also *Tafsir al-Tabari*, vol. IX, pp. 253-67.
77. The *Qur'an* 4:11; see also *Tafsir al-Razi*, op. cit., vol. IX, pp. 203-18.
78. Ibn Hazm, *Jamaharah Ansab al-Arab* (Cairo, 1948), p. 290.
79. Dr. Ahmad Muhammad al-Haufi, *Al-Mar'ah fi sh 'ar al-jahili* (Cairo, 1954), p. 266.
80. See Dr. Muhammad Byumi Mahran op. cit., p. 187.
81. See *Tarikh al-Tabari* (Cairo, 1967-69), vol. II, pp. 280-1.
82. *Al-Aghani*, op. cit., vol. I, p. 64.
83. 'Umar Rida' Kahhalah, *A'alam al-Nisa* (Damascus, 1959), vol. V, pp.111-12.

84. Ibid., pp. 239-42.
85. Ahmad al-Haufi, op. cit., p. 151.
86. See Jawwad Ali, op. cit., vol. V, p. 531.
87. The *Qur'an* 4:4.
88. Al-Haufi, op. cit., p. 151.
89. See Jawwad Ali, op. cit., vol. V, 532.
90. *Al-Aghani,* vol. VIII, pp. 78, 185.
91. Ibid., vol. XIX, p. 131.
92. Ibn 'Abd Rabbihi, *Al 'Iqd al-Farid* (Cairo, 1968), vol. III, p. 191.
93. Ibn S'ad, *Al-Tabqat al-Kubra,* vol. VIII, p. 115.
94. There are differing opinions about the exact period of this regime, ranging from 1000 BC to 50 BC and extending even up to the 1st century AD. See Fu'ad Hussain, *Al-Tarikh al-'Arabi al-Qadim,* p. 286.
95. The moon 'Am was known by different names during different regimes in Yemen. It was known as "Al-Maqat" in the reign of Saba', "Seen during the Hadramaut regime, and "Wad" i the regime of Mu'in"; see Hasan Zaza, *Al-Samiyun wa Lughatuhum,* pp. 138-9, "Wad" has also been referred to in the *Qur'an;* see 71:23.
96. *Al-Mar'ah fi sh'ar al-Jahili,* op. cit., p. 323.
97. Khalid al-Dasuqi, *Qaum Thamud Bayan Riwayat al-Mu' arrakhun wa Muhtawiyat al-Nuqush,* p. 228; cf. F.V. Winnet, *Study of the Lihyaite and Thamudic Inscriptions* (Toronto, 1937), p. 17.
98. See Ibn Hisham, *Sirah al-Nabi* (Cairo, 1955), vol. I, pp. 151-8.
99. Ibn Kathir, *Al-Bidayah wa al-Nihayah* (Beirut, 1966) vol. II, pp. 248-9.
100. Ahmad al-Haufi, op. cit., p. 324; see also Musnad al-Imam Ahmad I, p. 332.
101. *A'alam al-Nise,* vol. V, op. cit., pp. 141-3.
102. Al-Haufi, op. cit., p. 326.
103. See *Kitab al-Muhbir li ibn Habib,* op. cit., 364.
104. The *Qur'an* 27:22-24.
105. *Tafsir ibn Kathir.* op. cit., vol. IV, p. 253.
106. Jawwad Ali, op. cit., vol. VI, pp. 233, 235.
107. *Tarikh al-Tabari,* op. cit., vol. III, p. 65.
108. Ibid.
109. Ibn Hisham, op. cit., vol. I, p. 94. See also Dr. Jawwad Ali, op. cit., vol. VI, p. 264.
110. The *Qur'an* 53:19-21.

3
CONCEPT OF SEXUAL EQUALITY

Historically speaking, there has been male domination in all societies throughout the ages except in matriarchal societies, which have been comparatively few. Women have been considered inferior to men. From this emanated the doctrine of the inequality of the sexes. A woman cannot match the power and competence of a man and hence she is considered not equal to him. Man must possess and dominate woman, have mastery over her and determine her future, acting either as a father, brother or a husband. It is in her interest, the argument goes, that she should submit to the superior sex. Confined to home and hearth, she was thought incapable of taking decisions outside her domain. There would be absolute disaster, it was said, if she happened to become the ruler of a country.

Here we are mainly concerned with the status accorded to women in the Qur'an and how Muslim jurists viewed it under different circumstances. Today women, especially Western educated women, are demanding equal status with men and they are, as far as this writer is concerned, absolutely right. The question before us is: what status did the Qur'an give to women? Is it an equal status or an inferior one? The 'ulama and the jurists maintain categorically that women have been given an inferior status; some modernists among Islamic scholars would like to believe that the holy book accords equal status to both the sexes.

In my opinion it is difficult to give a categorical answer to this question. First, the Qur'an refers to it in both the normative and the contextual sense. Normatively speaking, the Qur'an appears to be in favour of equal status for both the sexes, as we will see shortly. Contextually speaking, it does grant a slight edge to men over women. But ignoring the context, Islamic jurists tried to give a superior status to men in the normative sense. We will discuss this in greater detail. Second, the interpretation of the qur'anic verses, as in the case of other scriptures, depends very much on one's own point of view. Ultimately it is one's *a priori* position which determines the meaning of a scripture for the reader or the interpreter. The same verse is understood differently by different people depending on their predilection and proclivities.

Third, and this is equally important to remember, the meaning of qur'anic verses unfolds with time. What the verses meant to an Islamic scholar in the medieval period may be quite different from the meaning conveyed to a scholar living in modern conditions. Religious scriptures often use symbolic language which makes them pregnant with several levels of meaning, all of which may not unfold at any given time. It therefore, becomes necessary to interpret this symbolic language creatively to fit in with our own experiential context. Time and experiences are always in flux and so is our understanding.

Now the question is: what is concretely implied by equality of status of the sexes? First, in its generalised sense this means acceptance of the dignity of the sexes in equal measure. Second, one has to see both men and women enjoying equal rights: social, economic and political. Both should have equal rights to contract a marriage or to dissolve it; both should have the right to own or dispose of property without interference from the other; both should be free to choose their own profession or way of life; both should be equal in responsibility as much as in freedom.

First, let us take what the Holy Qur'an has to say about equality of the sexes in the generalised sense of enjoying equal dignity. The Qur'an considers both the sexes as having originated from one living being and hence they enjoy the same status. It says: "O! mankind, be conscious of your Sustainer, who has created you out of one living entity, and out of it created its mate, and out of the two spread abroad a multitude of men and women."[1] Here the verse clearly says that all men and women have been created out of one nafs[2] (living entity) and hence one has no superiority over the other. Again, as Muhammad Asad, a noted contemporary commentator on the Qur'an points out in the footnote to the above verse, the words'. "He created out of it (*minha*) its mate", "He created its mate (i.e. its sexual counterpart) out of its own kind (*minjinshiha*)...."[3]

Maulana Azad, another noted commentator, also interprets this verse more or less in the same manner. He says that divine wisdom creates all others from one person. But he interprets *nafsin vahidatin* (one living being, one person) as father. Whether it is one person, one living being or father[4], the implication is the same: namely, that all have originated from one living being, men and women, and hence enjoy equal status. The Qur'an does not subscribe to the view that Eve was born from the crooked rib of Adam and thus has an inferior status.[5]

It is in this general sense that Maulana Qari Muhammad Tyeb, who was chief of the Dar al-'Ulum, Deoband, accepts equality of rights of men and women. He says the fact is that women enjoy the same rights as men, and, in certain respects, they enjoy even more rights... He goes on to say that Hazrat 'A'isha is the wife of the Prophet (peace be on him). The Prophet says about her that half the knowledge of my revelation should be acquired from all my companions and the other half from 'A'isha (may Allah be pleased with her)[6]. After all 'A'isha Siddiqa is a woman and Allah has given such a status to women that thousands of the Prophet's companions are put on one side and a woman on the other side.[7]

Also the Qur'an says: "We have honoured the children of Adam... "[8] Maulana Usmani maintains that *bani Adam* (children of Adam) include men as well as women and hence, according to this verse of the Qur'an, both are equally honourable without any distinction of sex.[9] The Qur'an also uses the metaphor of *libas* (apparel) for men and women. It says: "They are apparel for you and apparel for them". This clearly implies that, like apparel both need each other and one cannot be complete without the other. There cannot be inequality where there is complementarity.[10]

Maulana Azad has much more eloquently advocated equal rights for women. For this purpose he cites the qur'anic verse, "The rights of wives (with regard to their husbands) are equal to the (husbands') rights with regard to them" in support of his contention. He says very eloquently that the Qur'an not only creates a belief about the rights of women but *it also* clearly declares that they are equal to men in matters of rights. As men have rights over women, women have rights over men.[11] In other words, women have to take in return for what they give. It is not right that men should demand rights from women and forget the latter's rights. As women have obligations towards men, men also have obligations towards women.

Further, he says that by pronouncing these four words (*lahunnamithlul ladhi 'alayhinna*, i.e. the rights of wives are equal to those of husbands)[12], the Qur'an has brought about a great revolution in the life of human beings. These four words gave women all that was their right but was always denied to them. With these words she was lifted out of deprivation and dishonour and was seated on the throne of equality.

Thus there is no doubt that there is a general thrust towards equality of the sexes in the Qur'an. There are various reasons for this. First, as pointed out earlier, the Qur'an gives a place of great honour to the whole of humanity, which includes both the sexes. Second, as a matter of norm it advocates the principle of equality of the sexes. Biological otherness, according to the Qur'an, does not mean unequal status for either sex. Biological functions must be distinguished from social functions.[13]

According to the Qur'an, women's religious status, like their social status, is as high as that of men, It categorically states:

Lo! men who surrender unto Allah and women who surrender, and men who believe and women who believe, and men who obey, and women who obey, and men who speak the truth, and women who speak the truth, and men who preserve, and patient men and patient women and the humble men and the humble women, and the charitable men and the charitable women, and the fasting men and the fasting women, and men who guard their chastity and women who guard it and men who remember Allah and women who remember Allah has prepared for them forgiveness and a mighty reward.[14]

Commenting on this verse, Maulana Muhammad Ali says: "This verse repeats ten times that women can attain every good quality to which men can have access and settles it conclusively that according to the Qur'an women stand on the same spiritual level as men."[15] Thus we see that, unlike in other religions, in Islam there is absolutely no distinction between men and women in religious matters either. In some religions a menstruating woman is considered unclean and kept away from all her normal functions, such as cooking. The Qur'an takes a purely biological view of menstruation. The Qur'an says: "And they ask thee about menstruation, say it is harmful; so keep aloof from women during menstrual discharge and go not near them until they are clean. But when they have cleansed themselves, go into them as Allah has commanded you."[16]

The word used for menstruation is *adhan* which means a *slight evil* or anything that causes a slight harm. Maulana Muhammad Ali maintains that it is not menstrual discharge that is harmful but having sexual relations while the woman is in that condition. Judaic law prescribes complete separation between husband and wife. In Islam it is, however, limited to cessation of sexual intercourse only.[17]

However, the Qur'an does speak of man having a slight edge and social superiority over woman. This, as pointed out above, must be seen in its proper social context. The social structure in the Prophet's time was not such as to admit of complete sexual equality. One cannot take a purely theological view in such matters. One has to adopt a socio-theological view. Even a revealed scripture comprises both the contextual and the normative. No scripture, in order to be effective, can totally ignore the context.

Thus when the Qur'an gives man a slight edge over woman, it clarifies that it is not due to any inherent weakness of the female sex, but due to the social context. The Qur'an says, "Men are maintainers of women as Allah has made some to excel others and as they spend out of their wealth (on women)."[18] Thus from this verse it becomes clear that the *fadilat* (excellence, superiority) which Allah has given one over the other, or to men over women, is not sexual superiority or excellence. It is due to the social functions that were then performed by the two sexes. Since man earns and spends his wealth on women, he by virtue of this fact, acquires functional superiority over women. Of course, today the feminists argue that women's domestic work should also be counted as economically productive and cannot be taken for granted merely as their domestic duty. If men earn, women do domestic work and both are complementary to each other. This position is quite justified and must be vigorously defended. What one does (by way of service or productive work) must be given full recognition. This interpretation of women's domestic work is not against the qur'anic spirit though it may not have been explicitly recognised as such. The Qur'an repeatedly says: *laysalil insane illa ma s'a* (a person gets what he/she strives for).[19]

Thus the Qur'an explicitly recognises that one must be justly rewarded for what one does. None can be deprived of his or her reward for the work done, much less a woman who is equally entitled to the fruits of her labour. Again, to quote the Qur'an: "...and that every soul may be rewarded for what it has earned, and they will not be wronged."[20] There are many more verses in this respect.[21] In view of such categorical statements one cannot deny a woman the reward for her domestic work.

However, the question is why, then, the Qur'an concedes a slight superiority to men over women for what they earn. The real question here is of social consciousness and proper interpretation. The feminine consciousness in those days was no doubt at a low ebb and domestic work was considered a woman's duty. Moreover, men considered themselves superior by virtue of their earning power and spending of their wealth on women. The Qur'an reflects the social situations. It simply says that men are *qawwam* (maintainers or managers of family affairs) and does not say that they *should be qawwam*. It can be seen that *qawwam* is a contextual statement, not a normative one. Had the Qur'an said that men "should be *qawwam*" it would have been a normative statement and would have been binding on women for all ages and in all circumstances to come. But Allah did not will it in that way.

This also shows that with changing circumstances and greater consciousness among women, the concept of their rights will change. In this case the above verse in which man has been declared *qawwam* will have to be read in conjunction with other verses of the Qur'an which speak of reward for any work done.[22] At the time when the Qur'an was revealed there was no such consciousness about work at all. Even the word *qawwam*, was until recently understood quite differently. The commentators of the past rendered it to mean *hakim* (ruler) or *darogha* (an overseer, a prefect of a town) and used this verse to prove the definite superiority of man over woman. Women all through the feudal ages were so suppressed and confined that no other meaning of *qawwam* occurred to these commentators. For them it was the 'obvious' meaning as it was quite 'obvious' to them that women should serve men as part of their duties.

This verse is most important as regards the question of equality or inequality of the sexes. Hence it requires a little more attention. First, we would like this verse to be quoted in full before we discuss it in all its aspects. The verse in full runs as follows:

> Men are the maintainers of women, with what Allah has made some of them excel others and with what they spend out of their wealth. So the good women are obedient, guarding the unseen as Allah has guarded. And (as to) those on whose part you fear desertion, admonish them, and leave them alone in bed and chastise them. So if they obey you, seek not a way against them. Surely, Allah is ever Exalted, Great.[23]

The verse seems to be weighted in favour of men and, as pointed out, has often been used to prove his supremacy by the orthodox 'ulama. First, it is important to know the context in which the verse was revealed. The context must be known to understand the real importance of the verse. The noted commentator, Zamakhshari, throwing light on the context of the revelation of the verse, says that an Ansar leader, S'ad bin Rabi', slapped his wife, Habibah bint Zaid, because she disobeyed him. Aggrieved, she complained to her father, who took her to the Prophet. He complained to the Prophet that his daughter had been slapped by her husband because of her disobedience. The Prophet asked her to retaliate.[24]

However, this was opposed by the men in Medina who protested to the Prophet. Maybe the Prophet realised that his advice would have created an uproar in a society where man was completely dominant. The verse was revealed as soothing advice to control the violence of man towards woman and advising them to adjust themselves in a man dominated society.[25] From today's standards the verse in question (4:35) appears to be quite iniquitous to women. It seems to permit wife-beating. But, as pointed out by Prof. Lokhandwala, the Medinese context could not be ignored, and seen in that context the verse has a moderating effect. First, it says that disobedient women should be admonished and that if they persist in their *nushuz* (rebellion), they should be left alone in bed and if even that has no effect on them then they should be chastised. But again Allah asks the faithful not to seek a way against them and to have reconciliation with them if they obey.

As the story of Habibah bint Zaid shows, the Prophet was himself inclined to give the right to retaliate to the wife, but Allah's revelation willed otherwise. The Prophet, according to Zamakhshari, said that we wanted it one way but Allah wanted it the other way.[26] According to the Qur'an, Allah is just. (*'Adil*),[27] so how can He order the beating of a wife? We see from the available evidence that the idea was not to encourage the beating of wives but rather was meant to discourage it and gradually abolish it. Wife-beating was very common during the Prophet's time. According to Zamakhshari, Asma' bint Abi Bakr was the fourth wife of Zuber bin al-Awwam, who used to beat his wives severely.[28]

The Prophet also exhorted his followers not to be harsh to their wives and not to beat them. He said no one should beat his wife like a slave as at night he will be with her again.[29] In Mishkat there are a number of traditions of the Prophet asking his followers to treat their wives better.[30] One anecdote throws light on this problem. On one occasion the Prophet said, "Beat not your wives". Then Umar came to the Prophet and said: "Our wives will get the upper hand over their husbands from hearing this." He also claimed that Quraysh (the tribe of the Prophet) always ruled their women and that the Ansars (the people of Medina) were always ruled by their women. So the Prophet agreed to keep the Arab social custom unruffled. Then a large number of women collected around the Prophet's family, and complained of their husbands beating them. So the Prophet said: "Verily a great number of women are gathered here in my house complaining against their husbands. Those men who beat their wives do not behave well. He is not of my way who teaches a woman to go astray."[31]

While talking of social structure it is important to note that in Mecca, it was patriarchy which prevailed while Medina in all probability, had experienced matriarchy in the distant past. Scholars like Montgomery Watt have raised along these lines. However Maxime Rodinson, the French Islamicist, rejects this suggestion. He says:

Some accounts of pre-Islamic Arabia suggest the existence of matrilineal characteristics, especially in certain towns, such as Medina. There may be a connection between these characteristics and the traces in certain places of the existence of polyandry, that is, the marriage of one woman to several men at one time. Montgomery Watt has suggested that these disparate signs could be interpreted as an indication that Arab society, which had formerly been matrilinear, was in the Prophet's time in the course of changing to the patrilinear system, and was therefore in a transitional stage associated with the general development towards individualism. This view seems to me, as it does to J.Henninger, somewhat dubious. There is evidence that the patrilinear system

predominated in Arabia from time immemorial, in particular from
the so-called Thamudic inscriptions.[32]

It is difficult to say categorically whether the matrilinear
system ever predominated in Medina though one can certainly
find some traces of it. It is significant that 'Umar, the Prophet's
companion who later became the second Caliph, say in the
tradition referred to above[33] that the Quraysh always ruled their
women and the Ansars *were always ruled by their women*. This
tradition, if true, is certainly indicative of a certain trend in the
treatment of women in Medina. But it also clearly indicated that
in the Prophet's time it was patriarchy which prevailed all over
Arabia. The qur'anic revelations, at least in their immediate
context, could not ignore this. It is also quite a significant
indicator that though the Prophet was in favour of *qisas*
(retaliation) by the wife, the Qur'an did not permit it.

One modern translator of the Qur'an does not agree with this
view and maintains that the Qur'an has never permitted wife-
beating.[34] He translates verse 4:34 as follows:

> Men are the guardians of women as God had favoured some with
> more than others, and because they spend of their wealth (to provide
> for them). So women who are virtuous are *obedient to God* and
> guard the hidden as God has guarded it. As for women your fear are
> averse, talk to them persuasively; then leave them alone in bed
> (without molesting them) and *go to bed with them* (when they are
> willing). If they open out to you, do not seek an excuse for blaming
> them. Surely, God is sublime and majestic.[35]

The italicised words in the translation indicate where it differs
from other translations, and it is to these that we shall now turn.

Ahmed Ali translates the word *qanitat* as 'obedient to God'
and explains in a footnote[36] that "the Arabic word *qanitat* means
devoted, or obedient to God, and does not lend itself to any other
meaning." However, both Zamakhshari and Al-Razi, the two
eminent classical commentators, say that *qanitat* means
"obedience to husband".[37] Al-Razi, however, implies both

meanings: i.e. 'obedience to God' and 'obedience to husband', whereas Zamakhshari insists on the latter meaning. The second key word in this verse is *wadribuhunna*, which Ahmed Ali renders as "and go to bed with them" as against all other translators who render it as "and beat them". For his unusual meaning, Ahmed Ali refers to the *Mufridat* of Al-Raghib. Al-Raghib points out that *daraba* metaphorically means to have intercourse.[38]

This is, however, a modernist interpretation and one of considerable interest to those who champion women's rights and who are persuaded to uphold the equality of the sexes. I doubt whether classical interpreters and commentators would have accepted any such interpretation. Even Maulana Azad, who was a great champion of women's rights, translates *wadribuhunna* as "beat them" and adds in parenthesis "without harming them and only by way of admonition."[39] Zamakhshari also says that beating should be such as not to cause injury. He quotes a tradition from the Prophet to the effect that you do not beat your subordinates as Allah's power over you is much greater than your power over the subordinates.[40]

Mr. Parvez, a noted commentator on the Qur'an from Pakistan, has given an altogether different interpretation of this verse. He says that, first of all, we should bear in mind that the verse does not talk about relations between husband and wife but between man and woman in general. This, according to him, makes all the difference. He maintains that *qawwam*, in Arabic and in this context, means nothing more than provider for the family.[41] Parvez, however, believes in the division of functions between man and woman. Man has to earn while the woman has to perform household duties. In fact, he sees the whole verse in this context. He believes that the verse does not by the word *qanitat* imply that a woman has to be obedient to her husband. According to him, the relation between husband and wife is not one of superior or subordinate position but one of camaraderie (*rafaqat*).[42] What is required of both of them is to submit to the will of God. Therefore, there is no question of the Qur'an permitting a husband to beat his wife, whatever her offence. He maintains that since in this verse the talk is not about husband and wife but between man and woman in general, the word *nushuz* (rebellion) does not refer to the rebellion of the wife against the husband but of women against their assigned functions, which, according to him, leads to *fawdiyat* (anarchy) and hence needs to be checked, if necessary, with the help of physical punishment. According to Parvez, the latter part of the verse refers to a situation in which a woman is bent upon discarding her feminine biological function. So first she should be persuaded not to do so. If she disagrees she may be confined to bed. If even then she persists in her behaviour, she may be physically punished by an appropriate legal authority.[43] Thus, according to Parvez, the word *wadribuhunna* (and beat them) does not refer to the beating of the wife by the husband but rather to the infliction of physical punishment by a suitable authority on those women who rebel from their assigned function.

Even this interpretation may not be acceptable to the feminists of today who do not want to confine themselves to domestic chores and want the right to work outside the home. The rearing of children, according to them must be shared equally between husband and wife. They do not seem to be in the wrong if we consider the modern economic conditions. Thus Parvez's interpretation, though a step ahead of those who find permission for wife-beating in the Qur'an, is still not wholly satisfactory from the modern feminist viewpoint.

Maulana 'Umar Ahmad 'Usmani's interpretation, on the other hand, is more satisfactory. To begin with, he unequivocally opposes the idea of the superiority of husband over wife. He tends to adopt Maulana Azad's interpretation of the verse in its spirit.[44] He does not depart much from his translation of the verse. He also agrees with the interpretation that *qawwamun* means maintainers of women and he rightly concludes that the Qur'an has put on men the responsibility of maintaining women. He also agrees that it is a compensation for looking after children and bringing them up. In a way he suggests that domestic work should be compensated for by men.[45]

More significantly, Maulana Usmani argues that the Qur'an does not give men an edge over women. The words *bima faddal Allahu b'aduhum 'ala b'din* (Allah has made some of them to excel others) do not at all indicate superiority of men over women. Had it been so, Allah could have said *bima faddalahum 'alayhinna*. He made them (men) superior to them (women). But in this verse the masculine and feminine gender, that would indicate superiority of men over women are not used but rather the common pronoun *hum* which includes both men and women.[46] He also maintains that if Allah wanted to bestow superiority to men over women he could have made categorical use of the words *bima faddalar rijala 'alan nisa'* (excelled men over women).

All this goes to show that it is a general statement: Allah has given excellence to some over others and this statement includes both the genders. Maulana 'Usmani, therefore, interprets this verse to mean that men have certain qualities which women do not have, without one gender enjoying superiority over the others.[47] 'Usmani also does not oppose women working outside their homes to earn a living. Thus he says there are many women in our society who serve and earn money through hard work. Even within the home they do sewing and weaving and the rural women (who are at least eighty per cent of the population) plough, water the fields and look after the animals. He has seen, he says, women wielding 20 lb hammers in a smith's shop. Thus men who perform women's duties and women who also perform men's duties are far superior to others and this is what is implied by this verse of the Qur'an.[48] Maulana Usmani also discusses in detail the meaning of the word *nushuz* (rebellion). *Nushuz* has different shades of meaning. *Nashaza* in Arabic means to rise from a place.[49] By implication it means to be above others and it is in this sense that Abu Bakr Jassas says that the real meaning of *nushuz* is for a woman to consider herself superior to her husband and to rise above him.[50] It thus implies opposition, disobedience, quarrel, misbehaviour, resistance, etc. It also includes sexually deviant conduct.

Maulana Usmani says here in this verse that *nushuz* does not refer to ordinary household quarrels but rather to a woman's breach of sexual conduct, her arrogant misdemeanour or the others taking advantage of her husband. It is this conduct which calls for corporal punishment.[51] It is this punishment which the verse prescribes and is intended not to injure her bodily but only to humiliate her for her arrogance.

In his last address to the congregated Muslims on the occasion of the final pilgrimage the Prophet advised the Muslims to remember his (Prophet's) advice. Women, he said, squander their youth on you and soon age (the word used is '*awan* which means middle-aged). You have no right (to maltreat them) except when they indulge in open defiance of sexual conduct; and in that case, too, you have no right over them except to isolate them in bed. The corporal punishment should not result in bodily injury; and then if they submit to it do not seek anything more against them. Your wives have rights over you and you have rights over them. Your right over them is that they should not permit any other man on your bed and they should not allow such men who you dislike to enter your house. And their right over you is that you should behave well with them in matters of food, clothing, etc.[52]

The Qur'an has spoken of *nushuz* even in respect of men. It says: "And if a woman fears ill-treatment (*nushuz*) from her husband or desertion, no blame lies on her if she effects a reconciliation with him. And reconciliation is better."[53] Here in the case of *nushuz* on the part of the husband, a different course is prescribed by Allah, namely reconciliation. The woman is not empowered to beat her husband. One may argue that this is sheer inequality, that when the wife is guilty of *nushuz* the husband can isolate her in bed or even inflict physical punishment on her but when the husband is guilty of *nushuz* both are advised to have a reconciliation. Is this not inequality? One may reasonably argue it is. But the whole thing has to be seen in its proper context. The woman in those days was not an earning member of the family and her rights and her security in the form of marriage had to be protected at any cost. The Qur'an, even in the case of sexual deviancy, tries to protect her marriage by opting for a slight physical punishment (without bodily injury). When a man is guilty of *nushuz* (ill-treatment) it again tries to salvage the marriage by advising both of them to have a reconciliation.

Also, as pointed out before, this verse will be, and should be, interpreted differently in today's context. The light physical punishment prescribed in the verse, after all, is not normative but contextual. The verse, it must be noted, was revealed in a certain sociological context and must be seen as such and not as a normative prescription for all times to come. If we understand this limitation of the verse, much of the problem would be resolved. The difficulty arises when Muslim jurists see this verse as a normative prescription. Then they tend to prove the superiority of men over women. This verse, seen in its proper social context, does not advocate male superiority.

The Qur'an, as we have pointed out before, does not intend to make any difference between men and women in normative terms. Quite a few verses can be quoted from it in support of this position. The Qur'an, for example, says: "And whoever does good deeds, whether male or female, and he (or she) is a believer' these will enter the Garden, and they will not be dealt with a whit unjustly."[54] At yet another place it says: "I will not tolerate work of any worker to be lost, whether male or female, the one of you being from the other."[55]

What the traditional 'ulama do is to ignore the context select certain verses from the Qur'an to prove their point of view. The best example of this is a section of a verse[56] which says *lirrijale 'alayhinna darajatun*, that is, men are a degree above them (women). This verse too is a weapon in the hands of those who are hellbent upon proving the inferiority of women. They do so by tearing the verse out of its context. First, they ignore that the very preceding section of the verse talks of equality of rights and the obligation of a woman ("and women have rights similar to those against them in a just manner"). Second, the slight edge men have over women is not in social but in biological terms. It would be interesting to quote the whole verse here to put it in proper perspective. It says:

And the divorced women should keep themselves in waiting for three course. And it is not lawful for them to conceal that which Allah has created in the wombs, if they believe in Allah and the Last Day. And their husbands have a better right to take them back in the meanwhile if they wish for reconciliation. And women have rights similar to those against them in a just manner *and men are a degree above them*[57] in a just manner. (emphasis added)

The italicised words thus should be read in the total context of the qur'anic verse. Otherwise "men are a degree above them (women)" would not have been added just after. "And women have rights similar to those against them in a just manner". This would be an obvious contradiction. It becomes clear then that "men are a degree above them" is not meant to prove their superiority over women. This statement relates to the other things referred to in the verse, namely that women, on being divorced, have to wait for a period of three courses so as to be sure whether Allah has created life in their womb or not. This does not apply to men, who are free to marry without any biological restriction. Also, even if the husband has divorced his wife by way of revokable divorce (*talaq-e-raj'i*), the wife more often than not, would like to go back to her former husband if reconciliation is possible (and Allah desires reconciliation) but generally husbands have no such consideration. It is in this biological sense that men have a slight edge over women. This verse certainly does not militate against the concept of social equality of the sexes.[58]

There is yet another verse in the Qur'an which explains how women were in charge of men and how they used to control them and their properties. The verse is as follows: And they ask thee a decision about women. Say: Allah makes known to you His decision concerning them; and that which is recited to you in the Book is concerning orphan women in your charge, to whom you do not give that which has been ordained for them because you yourselves may be desirous of marrying them, and about helpless children; and about your duty to treat orphans with equity. And whatever good you may do, behold, God has indeed full knowledge thereof.[59]

The women were thus at the mercy of men, especially orphans and widows were at an even greater disadvantage. Their properties were often misappropriated. The Qur'an repeatedly exhorts men not to do so and to treat orphans with justice and kindness.[60] Similarly, in matters of marriage also men were at an advantage, both biologically and socially, as we have seen in verse 2:228 above. It is to this that the Qur'an refers when it says "men have an edge over women or they are a degree above them." It is a statement of a social situation rather than of a normative principle, as made out by many theologians. Men did stand at an advantage in that society (they do even today in the most advanced capitalist and even socialist societies). The Qur'an at no point says that men should be a degree above women. All it says is that they *are* a degree above in the given social situation. This distinction between 'are' and 'should' has to be borne in mind.

Another sure indication of the equality of the sexes mentioned in the Qur'an is that women have been given the right to hold property in their own right; neither the father nor the husband of a woman has any right to tamper with her property. The Qur'an states: "Men shall benefit from what they earn and women shall benefit from what they earn."[61] It is a very clear statement of the fact that the women would benefit from their own earnings and would be the masters of their own earnings. The Shari'ah law also allows them to be absolute masters of their own property. This property they might have inherited or acquired from their own efforts.

The woman's right to own property is so absolute that even if she is rich and her husband poor, he has to maintain her and she would not be obliged to spend anything from her property or income to maintain herself and her children. Thus the qur'anic injunction is: "Let him who has abundance spend (on his wife) out of his abundance, and let him whose means of subsistence are scanty spend in accordance with what God has given him."[62] Thus what is implied here is that a man must spend on his wife according to his own capacity. He cannot neglect her just because she has an income or property of her own. In the preceding verse it is stated:

> (Hence) let the women (who are undergoing a waiting period) live in the same manner as you live yourselves, in accordance with your means; and do not harass them with a view to making their lives a misery. And if they happen to be with child, spend freely on them until they deliver their burden; and if they nurse your offspring (after the divorce has become final), give them their (due) recompense; and take counsel with one another (about the child's future).[63]

Thus we clearly see here that, according to the Qur'an, a man is obliged to maintain his wife according to his means; second, in the event of divorce, he should keep her (during the waiting period of three courses) as he himself lives and, if she becomes pregnant, he must spend freely on her upkeep and after the delivery of the child she should be paid for nursing it, the future of the child being decided through mutual consultation.

Does this not ensure equal status for the woman? She is allowed to hold her own property and the husband is made to pay for her sustenance. The future of the children, in the event of separation, is to be decided by mutual consultation rather than by the father alone. Also, the husband cannot get away by making provision for bare subsistence. The qur'anic injunction is that she should share fully her husband's standard of living.[64]

Similarly, the dower (*mahr*) amount paid to her is her own. Neither her father nor her husband can claim it. She alone owns it in her own right. The Qur'an also encourages the man to give her dower liberally and with pleasure, not with a sense of compulsion. Also, if the wife wishes, she may allow her husband to enjoy part or all of it. But it will depend wholly on her discretion. Her husband cannot compel her to do so. Thus the Qur'an enjoins on men to "give unto women their dower in the spirit of a gift;[65] but if they, of their own accord, give up to you aught thereof, then enjoy it with pleasure and good cheer."[66]

Also, the husband cannot claim back the *mahr* amount, even if he has given a heap of gold to the wife except in the case of the *'Khula'* that is when the wife herself asks for separation from her husband. "And if you wish", the Qur'an tells husbands, "to have (one) wife in place of another and you have given one of them a heap of gold, take nothing from it. Would you take it by slandering (her) and (doing her) manifest wrong?"[67] The implication of this verse is clear. A wife cannot be deprived of her right to her dower and the husband cannot claim it is the event of divorce either, if it is he who gives it.

From this verse it can be argued that there is no limit to giving *mahr* to a wife. The words 'heap of gold' indicate this. Ibn Kathir, referring to *Musnad Ahmad*, narrates the story of 'Umar, the second Caliph, who sought to put a ceiling of 400 *dirhams* on *mahr*. This was challenged by a woman belonging to the tribe of Quraysh. She referred to the above verse and said when Allah had permitted the payment of a heap of gold who was he to put a ceiling of 400 *dirhams* on it? Umar had to rescind his ordinance and admit that even a woman knew more than him.[68]

It is important to note that the Qur'an does not use the word *mahr* for dower. It often uses two terms' namely *saduqat* or *ujur*, plural of *air* (lit. wage). The word *saduqat* has its root in *sadaqa* which means truthfulness, sincerity and friendship. This word is most appropriate since relations between husband and wife are based on truthfulness and sincerity. The amount paid to a wife is out of sincerity and love and hence it has been called *saduqat*.

However, the other word, *ujur*, is rather disturbing. Does the Qur'an state that the husband pays a wage to the wife by way of *mahr*? Though the Qur'an took some of its words from pre-Islamic usage, it did invest these with a new meaning. *Ujur* was commonly used for *mahr* in pre-Islamic times, too. The Qur'an adopted the usage but tried to give it a new meaning. The word *saduqat* is quite suggestive of that. There are other instances of the use of pre-Islamic words as far as the marital relationship is concerned. We have the use of the word *ba'l*. This word in pre-Islamic usage meant god and by implication was used for husband, as if he were god. The Qur'an also uses word *ba'l* for husband.[69] However, it does not use the word *bu'ul* in that sense. It gives it a new content, as in Islam the relationship between wife and husband is one of equal partners, marriage itself being a civil contract.[70]

It is well-known that revolutionary movements have given new meanings to earlier usages of words. Islam, from both the political and the sociological angles, was a revolutionary movement which discarded not only old categories of thinking but also old usages of language. Wherever it retained an old usage it gave it a new meaning. For example, the word *salat* for prayer existed in pre-Islamic times but Islam gave it not only a new meaning but also a new content. It is very unfortunate that during medieval times Islam lost much of its revolutionary elan and that, what is worse, by the second and third centuries of the Islamic era, many of the pre-Islamic concepts and categories had intruded back into Islamic Shari'ah.

It is certainly not easy to make sexual equality acceptable to all, even in our own times. Various inequalities, some subtle and others obvious, exist even in advanced capitalist and socialist societies. It was much more difficult for the Islamic ideals of human equality in general and sexual equality in particular to be made acceptable at a time when women were treated like chattels and slaves. It is surprising that such an ideal was, at least partially, practised for a few decades. Later the position of women in Islamic society degenerated very fast. By the time the Shari'ah began to be codified, all sorts of pre-Islamic and non-Islamic influences, e.g., non-Arab societies like the Hellenic and Sassanid civilisations, had affected the thinking of Muslim jurists. We do not want to go into those details here, but suffice it to say that it was under these alien and non-Islamic influences that the great thinkers of Islam came to codify their thoughts on women.

To give an idea of how women came to lose the social status given to them by Islam in latter-day Islamic society, we quote here from a Muslim writer, showing what an ideal woman was thought to be. An ideal woman, according to him, speaks and laughs rarely and never without a reason. She never leaves the house, even to see neighbours or her acquaintances. She has no women friends, confides in nobody, and relies only on her husband. She accepts nothing from anyone, except from her husband and her parents. If she sees relatives, she does not meddle in their affairs. She is not treacherous, and has no faults to hide, nor wrong reasons to proffer. She does not try to entice people. If her husband shows the intention of performing conjugal rites, she is agreeable to satisfy his desires and occasionally arouses them. She always assists him in his affairs. She does not complain much and sheds few tears. She does not laugh or rejoice when she sees her husband moody or sorrowful, but shares his troubles, and cheers him up, till he is quite content again. She does not surrender herself to anybody but her husband, even if abstinence would kill her... Such a woman is cherished by everyone.[71]

One can see here that an idea and desirable woman is one who is passive, surrenders herself to her husband without a murmur, allows him to satisfy his carnal desires without protest, does not care for her own sexual desires, does not go out of his house, tries to please her husband and keeps him in good humour all the time. In other words she has no existence of her own at all. She exists for her husband or her father. This was the image of woman during medieval times when she was considered nothing more than an adjunct to her husband or her father. The Qur'an, however, does not approve this. It gave her an independent existence of her own and an active role in life in her own right. Though there were certain constraints in the contextual sense, the intention of the Qur'an was quite clear. A woman has an active, independent role to play and has well-defined rights. She does not exist at the pleasure of her male adjuncts.

It is most unfortunate that in the so-called Islamic states women are seen only in their medieval image, not in the revolutionary Islamic image portrayed in the Qur'an. They are placed in *purdah* and are relegated to a secondary role within the four walls of the house. Islamic jurists in these countries give more importance to certain doubtful traditions than to the clear statements of the Qur'an to see woman in their own image. It is against this tendency that we have to fight.

Notes and References

1. The *Qur'an* 4:1.
2. Here the word *nafs* is important. It means soul, spirit, mind, animate being, living entity, human being, humankind, etc. Many classical commentators choose "human being" and assume that it refers to Adam. Muhammad 'Abduh, however, prefers "humankind" in as much as this term stresses the common origin and brotherhood of the human race (see *The Message of the Qur'an*, Muhammad Asad, Gibralter, 1980), p. 100.
3. Muhammad Asad, Ibid.
4. Abdul Kalam Azad, *Tarjuman al-Qur'an* (Delhi, 1980), vol. II, pp. 422-3.
5. Of course, there is the Prophet's tradition to this effect but it seems to have originated later under Jewish and Christian influences.
6. See *Fadilat al-Nisa* by Qari Muhammad Tyeb in *Fiqh al-Qur'an* (Karachi, 1985), vol. VIII, p. 61.
7. Ibid., pp. 62-3.
8. The *Qur'an* 17:70.
9. *Fiqh al-Qur'an*, op. cit., vol. III, pp. 45-6.
10. The *Qur'an* 2:187.
11. Ibid., 2:228.
12. *Tarjuman al-Qur'an*, op. cit., vol. II, p. 88.
13. Ibid., pp. 188-9.
14. The *Qur'an* 33:35.
15. *Holy Qur'an*, trans. and commentary by Maulana Muhammad Ali (Lahore, 1973), p. 809.
16. The *Qur'an* 2:222.
17. *Holy Qur'an*, op. cit., p. 95, f.n. 287.
18. The *Qur'an* 4:34.
19. Ibid., 53:39. I have rendered *insan* as person not, as is usual, as man. *Insan* has no gender orientation and includes both sexes.
20. The *Qur'an* 45:22.
21. See verses 2:281, 2:286, 2:25, 3:161, 16:51, etc.
22. See verses quoted above, i.e. 2:281, etc.
23. The *Qur'an* 4:35.
24. Zamakhshari, *Al-Kashshaf* (Beirut, 1977), vol. 1, p. 254.

25. S.T. Lokhandwala, "The Position of Women Under Islam", in Asghar Ali Engineer, ed., *Status of Women in Islam* (Delhi, 1987), p. 22.

26. Zamakhshari, Ibid., p. 524.

27. The *Qur'an* 5:8, 6:152, 4:58, etc.

28. Zamakhshari, op. cit., p. 525.

29. *Mishkat* (Delhi, n.d.), p. 701.

30. Ibid., pp. 701-7.

31. *Mishkat,* Babun nikah, cf. Lokhandwala, op. cit., pp. 17-18.

32. See Maxime Rodinson, Muhammad, (London, 1971), p. 230.

33. See ref. 31 above.

34. See Ahmed Ali, *Al-Qur'an: A Contemporary Translation* (Delhi, 1987).

35. Ibid., p. 78.

36. See the f.n. on Ibid., p. 78.

37. Zamakhshari, op. cit., p. 524; Al-Razi, *Tafsir* (Beirut, 1981), vol. V, p. 91.

38. See Raghib, *Al-Mufradat fi Gharib al-Qur'an.* (Beirut, n.d.); see under *daraba,* pp. 294-5.

39. *Tarjunan al-Qur'an,* op. cit., p. 457.

40. Zamakhshari, *Kashshaf,* op. cit., p. 525.

41. Parvez, *Matalib al-Furqan* (Lahore, 1979), vol. III, p. 364.

42. Ibid., p. 365.

43. Ibid., pp. 365-6.

44. *Fiqh al-Qur'an,* op. cit., vol. III, p. 65.

45. Ibid., p. 68.

46. Ibid., p .69.

47. Ibid.

48. Ibid., pp. 70-1.

49. *Al-Munjid Fi Lughat wa al-Adab wa al-'ulum* (Beirut, 1927), p. 809.

50. Abu. Bakr Jassas, *Ahkam al-Qur'an* (Egypt, n.d.), vol. II, p. 230; cf. *Fiqh al-Qur'an,* vol. III, op. cit., p.78.

51. 'Umar Ahmad Usmani, op. cit., vol. III, p. 80.

52. Jam'a al-Fawa'id, *Kitab al-Iman, ahkam al-Li'an,* (Meerut, n.d.), vol. I, p. 14.

53. The *Qur'an* 4:128.

54. Ibid., 4:124.

55. Ibid., 3:195.

56. Ibid., 2:228.
57. Ibid.
58. See also *Fiqh al-Qur'an*, op. cit., vol. III, pp. 72-4.
59. The *Qur'an* 4:127.
60. Ibid., 4:10, 6:152, 17:34, 89:17, 93:9, 107:2, 2:220, etc.
61. Ibid., 4:32.
62. Ibid., 65:7.
63. Ibid., 65:6.
64. See Zamakhshari, op. cit., vol. IV, pp. 121-2.
65. Here the word used is *nihlah*, i.e. something given willingly, of one's own accord, without expecting anything in return for it (see Zamakhshari, op. cit.).
66. The *Qur'an* 4:20.
67. Ibid.
68. *Tafsir ibn Kathir*, Urdu trans. by Maulana Abu Muhammad Junagadhi (Deoband, n.d.), section 4, *Lantanul birrah*, vol. I, p. 83.
69. See verses 2:228, 24:31, 11:72, 4:128, etc.
70. *Matalib al-Furqan*, op. cit., pp. 353-5.
71. Shaykh Nefzawi, The Perfumed Garden, trans. Sir Richard Burton (New York, 1964), p. 97; cf. Vernal L. Bullough, *The Subordinate Sex: History of Attitudes Towards Women* (Chicago, 1974).

4

OTHER ASPECTS OF EQUALITY
OF WOMEN

In the previous chapter we discussed some aspects of equality of men and women. There are several other aspects of this question which will be taken up in this and subsequent chapters. It is not easy to argue for equality of women in a traditional society. Besides other factors, one has to take into account the problem of male prejudices prevalent in such a society. In the past, as we know, women had been assigned household tasks and lived their lives within the four walls of their house. This received 'wisdom' is considered a sacred tradition enjoying theological sanction as well. Theology, it must be remembered, is not born of divine revelation alone; it is as much conditioned by the social circumstances and traditions prevalent in a society. What we receive as theology is a mix of all this, but for us, it assumes the form of 'pure divine knowledge'. Our attitudes are then determined by this received theology.

We have to face tremendous odds if we are to get rid of traditional received knowledge and explore further creative potentialities of the divine revelation as embodied in our scripture, the Qur'an. It should not be forgotten that our understanding of the holy scripture is also conditioned by our prevalent social, political and economic attitudes and our attitudes are determined by the prevalent social structure too. So the understanding of the Qur'an by our ancestors should not deter us from exploring its further possibilities in the context of the changed social structure and economic realities.

How our circumstances and social structure determine our understanding of the qur'anic verses has been discussed to some extent in respect of verse 4:34 in the previous chapter. Here is one more example of the interpretation of the same verse. Riffat Hassan, a feminist theologian from Pakistan, says:

> Another very important term in the Qur'an which occurs in Chapter 4 (called the Women chapter) in verse 34 is the word *qawwamun*. This is the plural form of a word which is translated as lord, master, ruler, governor, manager. Once you make the man the ruler, obviously you make the women the ruled. You have established a hierarchical relationship. In fact, this word does not mean ruler at all. There are many authorities on the basis of which I can say that it means 'breadwinner' and it is an economic term. If we translate that word as breadwinner the interpretation of the entire verse changes. Its talking about, the division of functions, that while women have the primary responsibility of being child-bearers, during that time when they are undergoing the process of childbearing, they should not have the obligation of being breadwinners, and therefore men should be breadwinners *during this period.*[1] (emphasis added).

The italicised words add a new meaning to the verse. It implies that the Qur'an wants women to desist from breadwinning only during the period of childbearing and it is in this period that men will be the sole breadwinners. During normal times women may also earn money. Since Riffat Hassan looks at this verse from the feminist perspective she could add this meaning to it. Thus it would be seen that every interpretation has a human dimension and should not be treated as divine. No one, however great an exegetist, should be an exception to this.

I

The Worth of Women in the Law of Evidence

This has been a very hotly debated issue in Islamic theology. Regarding evidence of women in matters of written financial contracts, the Qur'an says:

> O you who have attained to faith, wherever you give or take credit for a stated term, set it down in writing. And let a scribe write it

down equitably between you; and no scribe shall refuse to write as God has taught him; thus shall he write. And let him who contracts the debt dictate; and let him be conscious of God, his Sustainer, and let him not weaken anything of his undertaking. And if he who contracts the debt is weak of mind or body, or is not able to dictate himself, then let him who watches over his interests dictate equitably. And call upon two of your men to act as witnesses, and if two men are not available, then a man and two women from among such as are acceptable to you as witnesses, so that if one of them should make a mistake, the other could remind her. And the witnesses must not refuse (to give evidence) whenever they are called upon.[2]

We have quoted the relevant verse in full so that it may be properly understood and the context in which two women as witnesses have been recommended may be known. It is from this verse that Muslim jurists have deducted a general rule, namely that one male witness is equal to two women witnesses and hence man is superior to woman. Also, the verse mentions two female witnesses and one male witness in reference to *financial contracts* only. There is no mention of contracts of other kinds and yet the jurists have concluded from this that in any matter, financial or otherwise, a woman would be treated as a half witness. The Zia regime enforced this "Islamic" evidence act in an attempt to Islamise the law in Pakistan. However, just because the Muslim jurists held this view it does not mean that it is a 'true' Islamic view. At best, it should be treated as their interpretation and reading of the verse. A careful reading of it with an open mind would indicate that these jurists sought to read too much into it. Here we will attempt a critique of this traditional approach.

To begin with, it must be understood that the verse is concerned only with financial matters. Many modern commentators, sympathetic to women's rights, imply that it does not indicate inferiority of women. Women in those days were not sufficiently experienced in financial matters, and hence two female witnesses were recommended by the Qur'an so that, in case of forgetfulness, one (due to inexperience) could correct the

other. Since men were sufficiently experienced, no such reminder
was necessary for them.

Thus Muhammad Asad says:

> The stipulation that two women may be substituted for one male
> witness does not imply any reflection on woman's moral or
> intellectual capabilities. This is obviously due to the fact that, as a
> rule, women are less familiar with business procedures than men
> and, therefore, more liable to commit mistakes in this respect.[3]

Muhammad' Abduh, a noted Egyptian theologian, also held a
similar view.[4] It should be noted that the clause is a
recommendatory and not an obligatory one. The Qur'an wants to
be fair to creditor as well as debtor and see that the contract is
written properly and is affirmed by duly qualified witnesses. If the
contracting parties have mutual faith, they may even dispense
with witnesses. What is to be ensured is that the contract is a just
one. It is for this reason that the Qur'an says that it should be
written down *justly (b 'll 'adli),* and that let him who contracts be
conscious of God.[5] These words make it clear that what is
required is justness and equity, and that witnesses should ensure
that they strive for this. It is only by way of caution that the Qur'an
recommends two female witnesses.

The later part of this verse also makes this abundantly clear. It
says:

> And be not loath to write down every contractual provision, be it
> small or great, together with the time at which it falls due; this is more
> equitable in the sight of God, more reliable as evidence, and more
> likely to prevent you from having doubts (later). If however it (the
> transaction) concerns ready merchandise which you transfer directly
> unto one another, you will incur no sin if you do not write it down.[6]

Thus this verse makes it sufficiently clear that everything said
is meant to ensure that the contract is clean without leaving any
dispute or doubt. Witnesses and writing down are required for this
purpose only. In any ready transaction or short-term transaction it
will be no sin if the conditions of the contract are not written
down. It is surprising that despite such clarity of statement, the

jurists have read so much into it and used it to prove the inferiority of women. This reveals more about male prejudice than divine intention.

Another important thing to note about the verse is that though two female witnesses in place of one male witness have been recommended, only one would bear witness, the other's function being nothing more than reminding her in case she falters (on account of her inexperience in financial matters). The words of the Qur'an are: *an tadilla ihdahuma fatudhakkira ihdahumal ukhra* (if one of them should make a mistake, the other could remind her). In those days there was always some possibility of female witnesses making mistakes in financial matter due to their inexperience and not due to any inferior intellectual ability. This verse should be categorised as a contextual and not a normative one. The Qur'an is certainly not laying down any norm that in matters of witnessing two women would be treated as being equal to one man. Had it been so intended the Qur'an, wherever the question of witnessing arises, would have treated the women in this way. However, this is not so. There are seven other verses about recording evidence in the Qur'an[7] but none of them lays down the requirement of two female witnesses in place of one man. One such verse is:

> O you believe, let there be witnesses to what you do when death approaches you and you are about to make bequests: two persons of probity from among your own people, or—if pangs of death come upon you while you are travelling far from home—two other persons from (among people) other than your own. Take hold of the two after having prayed; and if you have any doubt in your mind, let each of them swear by God, "We shall not sell this (our word) for any price even though it were (for the sake of) a near kinsman; and shall we conceal aught of what we have witnessed before God or else, may we indeed be counted among the sinful.[8]

From the above verse it is clear that when a person is about to die, he can choose from among his own people, and if he is in a foreign land, from among others, two witnesses to what he has to say by way of bequest. Here the words used for two witnesses are *ithnani dhwa 'adlin* (two just persons). No gender has been mentioned. Both the witnesses could be men or both could be women or they could be one man and one woman. All that is required is justness and reliability. To witness for the bequest is an important obligation. Had the women been inferior in the eyes of Allah it could have been stipulated that either they could not discharge such an obligation or that two of them, as in the other verse,[9] could have been equated with one man. Thus it is clear that in verse 2:282, two women were recommended in view of a specific situation and context, and not on account of intellectual or moral inferiority.

Justice Hussain, referring to verses 5:106 and 5:107, argues: In the above verse, it is stated that the witnesses may be asked to take oath that they shall be truthful. The verse which follows[10] provides that if it is afterwards ascertained that both of them merit the suspicion of sin, that is, of falsehood, two others from among the near relatives of the deceased take oath that their testimony is truer than that of those witnesses who were with the testator. If women are excluded they will not be able to take oath and their rights will not be guarded, in case there are no male heirs. Verse 106 of Chapter 5 and the verse that follows it apply to members of both sexes and women are competent witnesses according to them.[11]

Similarly, in verse 65:2 and 4:15, for witnesses from "amongst you" the word *minkum* has been used, one which according to Arabic grammar, includes both the sexes. So nothing about the gender of the witnesses has been specified in these two verses either. In verse 24:4, it is no different. This verse deals with accusations of unchastity against honourable women, according to which four witnesses are required to be produced to prove the charge of unchastity. However, again, there is no mention of the sex of the witnesses. It is interesting to note that the jurists (*fuqaha*) generally hold that the testimony of women cannot be accepted for *hudud* punishments (those which have been prescribed by the Qur'an and Shari'ah. This verse deals with the punishment of 80 lashes for bringing a false charge against an *honourable woman,* yet it, does not specify the gender of the witnesses required.

Similarly, verses 6 to 9 of Chapter 24 are important in this respect. These verses deal with *li'an.* (i.e. cursing oneself for speaking falsehood). The verses are as follows:

> And as for those who accuse their own wives (of adultery), but have no witnesses except themselves, let each of these (accusers) call God four times to witness that he is indeed telling the truth, and the fifth time, that God's curse be upon them if he is telling a lie. But (as for the wife) all chastisements shall be averted from her by her calling God four times to witness that he is indeed telling the truth.[12]

It is obvious from the text of these verses that in fact a woman has the right to falsify the testimony of a man (her husband in this case) and by taking an oath herself can prove her husband to be a liar. Thus a woman not only has the right to bear witness but has also the right to falsify the testimony of a man. And it should be remembered that here taking an oath is a substitute for witnesses and that too in the matter of *hudud* punishment, something from which the Muslim jurists have barred her.

In another verse from Chapter 4, which speaks of lewdness on the part of women, the sex of witnesses is not specified. The verse is as follows:

> And for those of your women who become guilty of immoral conduct, call upon four from among you who have witnessed their guilt; and if these bear witnesses thereto, confine the guilty women to their houses until death takes them away or God opens for them a way (through repentance).[13]

All these verses prove, if abundant proof is required, that in matters of bearing witness women are not second to men as commonly assumed by the male Muslim jurists relying solely on verse 2:282, while totally ignoring the overwhelming evidence of the other qur'anic verses which make no such discrimination.

Maulana Umar Ahmad Usmani makes another interesting point. He says that the fact that two women are required to give evidence does not detract from their status of equality. Even for making financial transactions the Qur'an requires the evidence of two men. Does it mean that one man is not reliable or does it detract from his social status? Similarly, in proving *zina* (adultery) four witnesses are required. Does it mean then that one man could not be considered reliable? If two women are required to make evidence reliable why should it be thought that women are inferior?[14]

Also, in matters connected with women such as childbirth, only women can bear witness; no man is required to bear testimony along with them. Imam Sahfi'i, one of the founders of the four Sunni schools of jurisprudence, concurs with this. He enunciates this in his book.[15] Imam Zahri also upholds this doctrine.[16] Imam ibn Taymiyyah, a great theologian of the 14th century, also agrees that if in a place of bathing only women are present and something punishable by *hadd* (rape, adultery, etc.) takes place then the case will be decided on grounds of women's testimony alone, or if a man makes a bequest and frees his slave and only women are present only they will bear testimony. Imam Taymiyyah says this referring to the opinion of Imam Ahmad bin Hanbal.[17]

Ibn Qayyim, a disciple of Ibn Taymiyyah, maintains that a single woman, if she be reliable, can be acceptable as a witness. He says in his book:

> When the woman be perfect in retaining in memory what she observes, is wise and also religious-minded the object is served by her evidence alone... On many occasions the evidence of one woman alone is considered sufficient. The better proposition, therefore, would be that a matter be decided on the evidence of two women and the oath of the right holder plaintiff (which means that is should not be necessary to produce a male witness along with them). This is what is stated by Imam Malik and it is one of the views attributed to Imam Ahmad. Our, revered teacher (Imam Iban Taymiyyah)', however, says that it would also be correct if a decision is given on the basis of the sole evidence of a woman and the oath of the plaintiff, because two women have been made

representatives of one man only at the time of procuring of witnesses so that one may not be forgetful. There is no such thing in the Qur'an and the Sunnah that unless there be two female witnesses their evidence should not be admitted, and the order about (procuration of) two female witnesses does not mean that if the number be less no judgement can be rendered on the basis of that evidence...[18]

Also, the opinion of some Muslim jurists that a woman's testimony in matters of *hudud* (punishments prescribed by the Qur'an) and *qisas* (retaliation) is not admissible cannot be sustained. The Prophet himself is reported to have decided such cases with the help of a single woman's testimony. Here we should mention the case of a woman who, while going for the morning prayer, was raped by a person whose identity was not known. The rapist ran away after committing the crime. The woman raised an alarm and someone ran after the offender. Other men joined in the pursuit. However, they caught a man who was pursuing the culprit and the woman who was raped said that he was the culprit. The man protested that he was the one who was running after the culprit, but ignoring his protestations, they presented him before the Prophet. The woman accused him of committing the rape and the Prophet, accepting her testimony, sentenced him. As he was being taken away for the execution of the sentence, the real culprit appeared before the Prophet and confessed his crime.[19]

Here it is quite clear that the Prophet passed sentence on the strength of a woman's testimony in a case of *hadd*. We may also refer to the case of a girl who was robbed of her ornaments by a Jew, who also caused her grievous injuries to which she later succumbed. When she was taken to the Prophet in her injured condition, he asked her who had done this to her. He (the Prophet) named several persons but she shook her head in denial until he named the Jew, whereupon she nodded by way of approval. The Jew was caught and killed by being beaten about the head, just as he had attacked the girl.[20] Here we see that the Prophet himself accepted the testimony of a woman when there was no one else at the site of the crime to bear witness. Another version of the incident has the Jew confessing his crime. It is difficult to say which of the two versions is correct but the fact is that there exists a version indicating that the Prophet had accepted the testimony of a single woman in a case of *hadd* punishment.

There is also the story of the murder of the Hazrat Uthman, the third Caliph, to which his wife Na'ila alone was witness. Most of the companions of the Prophet demanded *qisas* (revenge) on the killers of the Caliph on the basis of Na'ila's testimony. It is also known that Hazrat Ali, successor to Hazrat Uthman, avoided *qisas* not on the grounds of lack of witnesses (he never objected to the acceptance of a single woman's testimony in a murder case) but on grounds of political expediency, for the killers of Uthman were in a powerful position and it would have caused more complications if an attempt had been made to punish them. Hazrat Ali, therefore, asked for more time rather than reject the case for punishment for lack of evidence.[21]

Imam Zahri says that in all matters in which there is no other source of information, a woman's evidence is acceptable.[22] In fact, the real basis of the widely prevalent assumption that women would not bear witness by themselves is that they were considered intellectually and morally inferior to men. This assumption, to which Muslim jurists also fell victim, has no scientific basis. It was male dominance which created the prejudiced view. It resembles the racist attitude of whites towards the black peoples, who are considered inferior by virtue of the former's dominant position. The qur'anic verse 2:282 was interpreted in the light of prejudiced opinion and a whole range of distortions were attempted to bolster it. In today's changed conditions we can read into the real intent of the Qur'an.

Justice Aftab Hussain, a former Chief Justice of the Federal Shari'at Court of Pakistan, says:

> There is no bar in the Qur'an or the hadith against the admissibility of the evidence of a woman or against her being a competent witness without a male witness. This question came up for

consideration before me as a judge of the Lahore High Court in Fida
Husain V. Naseem Akhtar. It was held that a suit of dissolution of
marriage could be decreed in favour of the plaintiff on her evidence
alone. It was also held that Islam does not fix any particular number
of witnesses to prove a case (of a civil nature). I observed that the
traditions of the Holy Prophet (p.b.h.) also do not lay down any
fixed or rigid rule. The Holy Prophet (p.b.h.) decided a case on:
(1) the testimony of a woman plaintiff; (2) the testimony of a female
witness; (3) the evidence produced by both the parties;
(4) the evidence of the witness and the oath (yamin) of the plaintiff;
(5) the oath of the defendant; and (6) the evidence of two or more
witnesses and on the oath of the defendant.

The jurists have differed widely on the scope of admissibility
of evidence of women. Many such instances have already been
cited.[23] It is interesting to note that in *Musannaf Abd al-Razzaq* we
find all sorts of traditions in respect of evidence of women. Many
of these traditions are contradictory to each other. For example,
according to Ta'us, a woman is a competent witness except in the
matter of *zina* (fornication or adultery) as it does not behoove a
woman to witness such an act.[24] But 'Ata held the view that a
woman can give evidence in matters of *zina* too. But in that case
there should be three other male witnesses.[25] In cases of *zina* all
four witnesses are required as a rule. Thus female witnesses are
allowed in cases of fornication and adultery and according to 'Ata
one female witness is equal to one male witness. Similarly, Ibn
Shahab held that a woman is competent to give evidence in a
murder case as well.[26] Ibn Qayyim held that many jurists also
allow women to be witnesses, in *hudud* (Shari'ah punishments
matters).[27]

Thus it can be seen that the jurists differ widely in the matter
of woman's competence to give evidence and on the question of
whether one man is equal to two women. It would be wrong,
therefore, to adopt one particular jurist's view to enable modern
enactments in such cases, as was done by Zia-ul-Haq of Pakistan.
It betrayed either ignorance of the controversy among the
medieval jurists or was a deliberate attempt to pass a conservative

law for a particular reason. The latter possibility seems to be nearer the truth.

II

Inheritance: Another Instance of Inequality?

It is generally argued that daughters have been given half the share in inheritance compared to their brothers and hence they are considered inferior to men in worth. Many Muslims use this kind of argument. It is an erroneous one on many counts. First, sexual equality is altogether a different category from inheritance. The former is a moral category while the latter is an economic one. If for some reason the share given in inheritance to one or the other sex is less or more, it does not imply that the recipient of the lesser share is considered inferior. Inheritance depends very much on a social and economic structure and the function of a particular sex within it. Women had a role different from that men of in the Arabian society when the Holy Qur'an was revealed. Without keeping this in mind we cannot draw proper conclusions from the concerned verses about inheritance in the Qur'an.

Let us consider first the verse on inheritance which fixes various shares in the property of a deceased person. It says:

Allah enjoins concerning your children for the male is the equal of the portion of two females; but if there be more than two females, two-thirds of what the deceased leaves is theirs; and if there be one, for her is the half. And as for his parents, for each of them is the sixth of what he leaves, if he has a child; but if he has no child and (only) his two parents inherit him, for his mother is the third, but if he has brothers, for his mother is the sixth, after (payment of) a bequest he may have bequeathed or a debt. Your parents and your children, you know not which of them is the nearer to you in benefit. This is an ordinance from Allah.[28]

A careful reading of this verse shows that the Qur'an has taken care to give women a share in the property of the deceased not only as daughters but also as mothers. Similarly, they also inherit as wives according to the Qur'an.[29] ("... and theirs, i.e. the wives' is the fourth of what you leave if you have no child, but if you have a child, their share is the eighth of what you leave"). In the pre-Islamic period there was no regular law in this respect. Sometimes women inherited property, sometimes they did not. According to Al-Razi, a great commentator, during *jahiliyah* (the pre-Islamic period) there were two criteria for inheritance: 1. relationship, and 2. oath. According to the former criterion, male relatives who took part in raids and captured loot were generally entitled to inherit property, while female relatives were excluded. In the latter category, two persons would say: "Your blood is my blood and your garment is my garment, you inherit me and I inherit you", and thus a mutual relationship on oath would be established. Also, an adopted child would inherit similarly.[30]

Al-Razi also tells us about the context of the revelation of this verse, i.e. verse 4:11. According to him, when S'ad bin Rabi' was martyrd he left behind his wife, two daughters and a brother. The brother took away the entire wealth of his deceased brother, leaving the wife and daughters high and dry. The wife went to the Prophet and complained about her husband's brother appropriating all his wealth. The Prophet sent her away saying Allah would decide the matter. After some time she again went to complain about it. It was then that this verse (4:11) was revealed. The Prophet ordered S'ad's brother to pay two-thirds of the property to the daughters and one-eighth to the mother. He could keep the rest.[31]

Thus, seen in this context, too, it becomes clear that whereas women were not regularly, as a rule, given any share in inheritance, the Qur'an ensured that they got it in their capacity as a daughter, a wife and a mother. The fact that they were given half of the share of male heirs is to be seen in its sociological and economic context. It is a well-known principle of Islamic Shari'ah derived from the Qur'an[32] that a wife is to be looked after by her husband even if she possesses a great deal of wealth. She is not obliged to spend any of her wealth and it is her right to claim maintenance from her husband. Not only that, at the time of marriage she gets *mahr* which is hers and hers alone, whatever the amount, and she can demand whatever she wants, which her husband is obliged to pay with good grace.[33] Thus as a wife she adds to whatever she got by way of inheritance as a daughter, and that too without any obligation either to maintain herself or her children.

It would be interesting to quote here from *Ikhwanus Safa*[34] 'an encyclopaedic compilation of the 10th and 11th centuries AD by the leading intellectuals of their time from the Islamic world. It shows that in this age, too, there were progressive thinkers who tried to uphold the real intent of the Law-giver. The text of the discussion on the question of female inheritance runs as follows:

> Brother, many of the intellectuals who engage themselves in the study of philosophy and metaphysics when they reflect with their rationality upon the Divine laws and compare them with their own thoughts, directions and understanding, their judicious acumen *ijtihad* and comparative reasoning (*ciyas*) lead them to feel that most of the divine prescriptions appear to be against justice, truth and rectitude. All this is because of their deficiency in understanding, paucity of discretion and lack of knowledge about the essence of the secrets of the divine law. For example, when they reflect upon the rule of inheritance that a male will have twice the share of a female, they feel that the correct position should have been the female getting twice the portion of a male. For women are feeble and have no avenues for earning money. They (the intellectuals) do not know and understand that the rule laid down in the divine law actually leads to what they hint at and desire for. For example, if you were to inherit from your father one thousand *dirhams*[35] and your sister 500 *dirhams*, at her marriage she will take another 500 *dirhams* as dower, making her share one thousand; whereas when you marry you will give 500 *dirhams* as dower that shall leave with you half of what your sister has received. In this manner, the Divine Law would produce the result they have desired and hinted at. This is the manner you should look at the Divine Law so that the exact rectitude and substance of truth could become apparent. One should be aware that the insight of the Law-giver in

the requirements of his laws in not a partial and fragmentary insight, for the benefit of some and to the exclusion of others, or for the ready present (transitoriness) to the exclusion of the future (eternity), but it is an absolute insight aiming at the good and rectitude of all, for the present as well as the future.[36]

Thus, as very aptly pointed out by the compilers of *Ikhwanus Safal'* the whole thing has to be seen in the proper perspective, taking both the present and the future into account. In the immediate present the daughter might get half of the sons' share but taking the future into account, it is the daughter who ultimately gets more and that to without any obligation to maintain herself. For this purpose one should bear in mind that the *mahr* amount in most of the Muslim communities is usually quite high and puts a substantial amount into her hands. This *mahr* also acts as an insurance against divorce, which is relatively easy in Islam.

However, here one may ask, what about the daughter who does not marry for certain reasons, maybe social, or others? She would have only what she inherits (Half of her brothers' share). Moreover, she may also have to look after herself, i.e. fall back upon her own resources to maintain herself. Such cases may be exceptional but nevertheless they are there and must be taken into account. First, laws are made for normal cases and, second special provisions could be made for women who cannot marry for a number of reasons.

There is a gross misconception about the law of inheritance as enunciated by the Holy Qur'an. It is generally thought that whatever shares have been fixed in verse 4:11 of the Qur'an for inheritors, the testator must strictly adhere to them and has no right to make any will whatsoever. This is simply not true. A noted modern commentator on the Qur'an from Pakistan[37] points out that people in the life of the person, whose inheritors they happen to be, start thinking that they are already entitled to their portion of inheritance and that the person concerned cannot make a will. This is totally wrong. The inheritors can inherit what the deceased has left behind (the Qur'an uses the word *ma taraka*, i.e. what one leaves behind).[38]

Second the Qur'an gives a person the right to make his own will. Whatever is left after the will is executed will be inherited by the inheritors in the proportions fixed by the Qur'an. In other words, the Qur'an does not take away the right of a person to make his own will. If his will gives away his entire property to someone and nothing is left after executing the will, there will be nothing for the inheritors to inherit.[39] Parvez also says that it is definitely wrong to maintain, and it is in opposition to the definite view of the Qur'an (*nass-i-sarih*), that a person cannot make a will. This is the view of the jurists, not of the Qur'an, and it is in conflict with the spirit of the Qur'an.[40]

This becomes all the more obvious if we carefully read the two verse on inheritance.[41] In both of them it is made clear that the inheritors will get what is left after the execution of the will made by the deceased (the words used are *min b'adi wasiyyatin yusi biha*, i.e. after the bequest he may have bequeathed). Maulana Usmani maintains that it is not correct to say that verse 2:180, in which bequest has been permitted, has been abrogated and that after its abrogation one can bequest only one-third and no more. Both the verses make it clear that the relatives shall inherit whatever is left after the bequest by the deceased, as pointed out above.[42]

There is one more weighty reason for this. We find in *Akham al-Qur'an* that the fifth chapter of the Qur'an *Al-Ma'idah* was the last one to be revealed and that nothing in it has been abrogated. Imam Abu Bakr Jassas informs us in this book that there are 18 obligations (*fara'id*) in this chapter and none has been abrogated. As the verses on bequest (5-106-108) also figure in this chapter, it is not correct to say that these have been abrogated. Imam Hasan al-Basari has also supported this view.[43]

We have discussed this at length for the simple reason that it is possible for a person to make a will in favour of someone who he thinks needs additional support. In fact, it is quite in keeping with the spirit of the Qur'an that a bequest may be made in favour of the weak. Thus the Qur'an says: And when relatives and the orphans and the needy are present at the division (of inheritance), give them out of it and speak to them kind words.[44] So if a daughter cannot marry for some reason and she is not well provided for, the parents can make a special bequest in her favour, compensating her for her deprivation. This is an important additional provision of the holy book.

Thus one can say with certainty that the Qur'an takes care of women, who are considered weaker in society, in a fairly reasonable way. If woman marries she receives *mahr* (and she has the right to stipulate whatever amount she desires) and is also maintained by her husband.[45] But in case she cannot marry and the parents are aware of this, they can always make a special provision for her in their bequest, as the Qur'an requires the testator to make some provision for the weak among the relatives.

However, it must be pointed out that Muslim society consistently violated the qur'anic injunction to give women their due share in inheritance. The Qur'an was kind to women and the weaker sections but Muslim society was not so generous. Women were generally deprived of their share, especially in agricultural societies where dividing the land caused problems. It should be remembered that in Arabia, which was by and large a non-agricultural society, there was no danger of division of land if the women also inherited it. Thus its law of inheritance is quite liberal and favours women. In agricultural societies if a woman marries and goes to her marital home, there is a clear possibility of division of land. This possibility was very real as generally women enjoyed no property rights and whatever belonged to them was vested either with their fathers or husbands after marriage. Because of this, landed property could not be transferred to women.

However, there was no such consideration in the Arabian society which was chiefly a non-agricultural one. Second and this is quite important to note, Islam recognises the women's right to property and whatever belongs to her is hers alone and no one, neither her father nor her husband, could claim it. This being so, there was no immediate danger of landed property being distributed as a woman could retain her share without dividing the land as long as she pleased. So the Qur'an fixed her share in all the properties by way of inheritance, movable and immovable.

However, we should always remember that life is governed more by sociological than theological realities, and the law of inheritance, as far as the women are concerned, was observed more in the breach than the observance. This was so because Islam had spread in chiefly agricultural societies where the women enjoyed no rights of inheritance and were in quite a subordinate position. In India, too, most of those converted were directly or indirectly dependant on land and had their own age-old traditions which proved more stubborn than the laws of the new religion which they happened to adopt for social, political and economic reasons.

Not only that but in India landlords and Nawabs succeeded in persuading the British rulers to enact a law in their favour for application of the principle of primogeniture as far as landed properties were concerned. Though Muslim personal law is defended as Divine Law no one campaigns against this un-Islamic provision. During the Shah Bano agitation this question was raised by some people but unfortunately no one from amongst those defending the 'Islamic law' answered it. So much for their defence of Islam. In fact, in the name of Islam what is being defended are the male privileges which became part of Islamic Shari'ah not because of but despite the qur'anic provisions. However, those defending the Shari'ah provisions would never admit it. In fact, if the qur'anic provisions in respect of inheritance are implemented faithfully, the women would benefit greatly. The only condition for successful implementation of the qur'anic provision is that the Shari'ah as formulated by the early jurists should not be treated as final and, wherever necessary, should be reinterpreted or even reformulated in the true qur'anic spirit in view of the changed conditions and new consciousness of women.

III

Can a Woman Become a Head of State?

Another crucial question as regards equality is whether a woman can become a head of state, or an Islamic state, for that matter. This question came to the fore in Pakistan when Benazir Bhutto became prime minister. The mullahs, especially those who were in the opposite camp, had raised a hue and cry even before her appointment. They issued *fatwas* that a woman could not become head of an Islamic state.

What is the real position? Is there any qur'anic provision or provision in the Prophetic *Sunnah,* against a woman becoming a head of state? There is absolutely nothing to this effect in the Qur'an. The qur'anic revelations, more often than not, came in response to one or the other situation. In the Prophet's time no such situation arose, nor did anyone ever raise such a question. However, there was a time when a daughter of a Persian ruler came to the throne. The Prophet is then reported to have disapproved of it. We will discuss this question a little later.

One finds in the Qur'an no disapproval of the rule of the Queen of Sheba who had South Yemen as her domain. She would overrule her male counsellors and act according to her own will. When her kingdom was about to be attacked by Solomon's forces, she consulted them. The Qur'an says:

> She (the Queen of Sheba) said, O chiefs, advise me respecting my affair; I never decide an affair until you are in my presence. They said, We are possessors of strength and possessors of mighty prowess. And the command is thine, so consider what thou wilt command. She said, surely, the kings, when they enter a town, ruin it and make the noblest of its people to be low; and thus they do. And surely I am going to send them a present, and to see what (answer) the messengers bring back.[46]

Thus, it is quite clear from the above qur'anic verses that the Queen of Sheba was a legitimate ruler; she is also shown to be very wise. She overrules her male counsellors and takes her own politically wise decisions. Had Allah disapproved of a woman as head of the state, or had a woman's rule been disastrous, the

Qur'an would have painted the Queen of Sheba in an adverse light and would have shown her to be inferior to her male counsellors. But it is otherwise.

Now we come to the Prophet's *hadith* on the basis of which the theologians argue that a woman cannot become head of a state. The *hadith* is as under: Abu Bakra said that Allah caused me considerable benefit from one sentence. When news reached the Prophet (p.b.h.) that the Iranians had made the daughter of Cusroe their ruler, he observed: That nation can never prosper which has assigned its reign to a woman."[47]

It should be noted that the above *hadith* is from *ahad*, that is, an isolated one and is not *mutawatir*, i.e. one repeated by more than one companion of the Prophet. It is a well-known principle that the *ahad* (i.e. isolated one) is not binding and that it is not necessary to act upon it. Thus how can one make this tradition of the Prophet binding on us and that too for all ages to come? It is strange that the 'ulama of Pakistan made this tradition, which is an isolated one, the basis of their charter of demands saying that a woman cannot become a head of state in that country.[48]

Second, apart from being isolated, there is every possibility that this tradition is a bogus one. Maulana 'Umar Ahmad Usmani shows that this *hadith* did exist before the Battle of Camel in which 'A'isha, the wife of the Prophet, participated. Abu Bakra, the narrator of this *hadith* remembered it only after the battle had started and 'A'isha had assumed command of the army against Ali, who was elected as the fourth Caliph. Abu Bakra did not remember it earlier, which is proof enough of the fact that it was forged in the context of this battle.[49]

In the context of the Battle of Camel we would like to point out that the Prophet's wife, 'A'isha, was in command of the army which had many illustrious companions of the Prophet in it. None of them objected to her being in command, nor did they desert her for the reason. Even Abu Bakra, the narrator of the above *hadith*, did not desert her. Had he been convinced that the Prophet had prohibited women from being *imam* (leader or head) he should have deserted 'A'isha as soon as he recalled this tradition. How then could it be said that a woman cannot become leader of a government when her leadership was accepted by such eminent companions of the Prophet?

Even if the above *hadith* is taken seriously, the question would arise whether a *hadith* which is in conflict with the qur'anic teachings can be accepted? Obviously it cannot. Dr. Abdul Hamid Mutawalli maintains that a *hadith* is not acceptable if: (1) it describes what is impossible to believe, (2) the *hadith* is in conflict with the Qur'an, and (3) it contradicts the facts of history.[50] The above tradition does contradict the teachings of the Qur'an as we have shown with respect to the verses about the Queen of Sheba.[51] More of these verses can be quoted. Thus the Qur'an says: "And the believers, both men and women—they are friends of one another. They enjoin good and forbid evil and keep up prayer and pay the purifying due and obey. Allah and His Messenger. As for these, Allah will have mercy on them. Surely, Allah is Mighty, Wise."[52]

Now the determination of what is right and what is wrong is one of the basic duties of a state and here men as well as women, who are protectors of each other, have been enjoined to perform this task. How can then women be excluded from being leaders of the state? Thus, according to this verse too, a woman can be made head of an Islamic state, and much more so if it has a parliamentary government. Here it would be interesting to quote a *fatwa* (religious opinion) expressed by an eminent theologian from India, Maulana Ashraf Ali Thanavi. He was asked a question quoting Abu Bakra's *hadith*[53] (that nation which makes a woman its head can never prosper) whether a woman can be appointed a head of state and whether the states of which women are heads are also covered by the *hadith*. Maulana Thanavi gave the following reply:

> Governments are of three types. The first type is one which is both personalised (*tam*) and based on popular sanction ('*am*). The *tam* type of government is one in which the ruler rules personally and is not dependant on any other superior's sanction. The second type is

one which is absolute and has no popular sanction. The third type of government is one which has popular sanction but is not absolutist. As an example, the first type of government may have a woman as head of state who has personal authority. The second category can be exemplified by a woman who heads a small group and wields absolute authority without sharing it with anyone else. The example of the third category is one in which the head of state has no authority by herself but is part of a consultative body. If we contemplate on the *hadith* it becomes obvious that what is implied by it is the first category (i.e. personalised rule of a woman). The reason for the pronouncement of this tradition is that the people of Iran had made the daughter of Cusroe their ruler.[54]

Maulana Thanavi refers to the story of the Queen of Sheba in the Holy Qur'an and about whose rule it raised no objection. From the words of the Qur'an, "I never decide an affair until you are in my presence", the Maulana concludes that her rule belonged to the third category of government (democratic) and what was objected to by the Prophet was the rule of the first category. The Maulana argues that since non-welfare (which results from a woman's rule is due to her paucity of reason and that this paucity in a consultative rule is made good by consultation with men, the reason for non-welfare is done away with and hence in this sense a woman's becoming head of state can be allowed.[55]

Today women would not agree with this line of argument as it implies that women's power of reasoning is imperfect. Such a faulty argument must be rejected outright. However, the Maulana at least legitimises democratic rule by a woman, despite that *hadith*. The rival 'ulama in Pakistan, during Fatima Jinnah's candidacy in 1962 and Benazir Bhutto's election campaign in December 1988, freely used this Prophetic tradition to declare even democratic rule by a woman as illegitimate and un-Islamic. In this regard Maulana Ashraf Ali's position seems to be more progressive.

We have already shown that this *hadith* itself is at best an isolated one and isolated traditions cannot be used for enacting laws. Imam Abu Hanifah, the founder of the Hanafi school of Islamic law, himself never accepted *ahad* (isolated traditions) for establishing a rule. There is yet another angle to this issue. Prof. Abdul Hamid says that the 'ulama, while discussing which of the Prophet's *ahkam* (rulings) are part of general law (*tashr'am*) and which are not, admit that those *ahkam* which relate to the *imamah* of the community of Muslims and their general governance cannot be applied for framing general law as these *ahkam* were meant for particular times and were issued in accordance with the prevailing situation. All the constitutional matters are included in this category.[56]

However, our 'ulama thoughtlessly and uncritically want to apply whatever has been reported from the Prophet to our situation without caring to establish the context in which the Prophet had said it. Not only that, they impute other meanings to those traditions which are not implied by them. For example, using the above *hadith* the 'ulama maintain that a woman cannot hold any position of responsibility in administration, let alone the position of head of the administration. Some theologians have even said on the basis of this tradition that the woman cannot even vote as she is imperfect in reasoning (*naqis al-aql*).

Prof. Abdul Hamid rejects the tradition which declares women as *maqis al-'aql wa al-din* (imperfect in reasoning and religion). He says it is one of the thousands of traditions which were forged and ascribed to the Prophet. The *hadith* is neither acceptable to reason nor is it in conformity with the Qur'an. This tradition has all the three elements of forgery and if accepted, would not only deprive women of their political rights but would also result in serious implications. It would conflict with other laws which are there in the Qur'an itself and also with some other traditions. It will also conflict with some of the happenings in the Prophet's time and that of the rightly guided Caliphs.[57]

Abdul Hamid further argues that if women are imperfect in reasoning and religion then it is necessary to impose restrictions on their managing properties or at least make it obligatory for them not to dispose them of without the permission of their husbands or wards. But Islam has accepted that women are able to manage their properties. It has given them the full right to manage properties of their own without referring the matter to their husbands and wards.

If it is true that women are imperfect in reasoning and religion then those historians who say the Caliphs used to consult women and attached importance to their opinion are wrong. And if it is true that women are imperfect in reasoning and religion, Imam Abu Hanifah would not have permitted women in certain circumstances to accept the office of *qadi* (judge) and 'Allamah Tabari would not have permitted this in general. Again, if woman are imperfect then no women could have been counted among those companions of the Prophet who enjoyed a reputation for giving fatwa (religious opinions) and one would not have found any women in the history of Islam who achieved great fame in the qur'anic exegesis, science of *hadith*, jurisprudence and literature.

And if so, how can one accept the fact that the first one to believe in the Prophet was a woman, i.e. his own wife Hazrat Khadija, and that when the Qur'an was first compiled, it was given in the custody of a woman, Hazrat Hafsah bint 'Umar bin al-Khattab. She kept the compilation in her custody from the time of the first to that of the third Caliph Hazrat 'Uaaman. All later compilations of the Qur'an were based on this first compilation and copies of it were distributed throughout the Islamic world.[58]

This tradition also conflicts with another tradition of the Prophet which says that one who honours women is himself honoured and one who insults them is himself lowly.[59] This tradition is much more reliable than the earlier one as was narrated by Hazrat 'Ali and reported by Ibn 'Asakir. How can one maintain that both traditions are true? The tradition which says that women are imperfect in reasoning and religion directly conflicts with the Qur'an too, which says that men and women are one another's friends and men as well as women determine what is good and what is evil.[60] Thus if women were imperfect in reasoning and religion how could they be required to enjoin others to do what is good and not what is evil, which is considered to be the highest kind of duty.

It is true that both Imam Malik and the eminent exegetist and historian Tabari hold that women can become a *qadi* (judge).[61] Many Maliki jurists have given *fatwa* that a woman can become a judge.[62] Also, a section of theologians have always supported the view that a woman can become a head of state, although the majority of them have always opposed it.[63] Not only this, but many women held prominent positions in the administration of an Islamic state. Even the second Caliph, Hazrat 'Umar, appointed a woman as chief of market inspectors.[64]

During the Abbasid period many women wielded great influence in state affairs, Zubeda, wife of Caliph Harun al-Rashid, a very intelligent woman, used to advise her husband on political and administrative matters. Philip Hitti tells us:

> Not only do we read of women in the high circles of that early period achieving distinction and exercising influence in state affairs—such as Al-Khayzuran, Al-Mahdi's wife and Al-Rashid's mother, 'Ulayyah, daughter of Al-Mahdi. Zubaydah, Al-Rashid's wife and Al-Amin's mother, and Buran, Al-Ma'mun's wife—but of Arab maidens going to war and commanding troops, composing poetry and competing with men in literary pursuits or enlivening society with their wit, musical talent and vocal accomplishments.[65]

There is always the instance of a woman becoming head of state in Yemen. During the late 5th and early 6th century AH, Malikah Arwa' bint Ahmad headed the administration of the province of Yemen on behalf of the Fatimid Caliphs of Egypt. Three of the Fatimid Caliphs, Mustansir, Must' ali and Amir, reposed faith in her and gave her a free hand to govern Yemen. She was held in high esteem by all the three. The last of the three Caliphs, Amir, even appointed her *hujjah* (the highest religious office under the Fatimid hierarchy). It speaks volumes for the ability of Hurrah Malikah (*malikah* literally means ruler or empress) that she won the distinction of being a governor of a province as well as rising to the office of *hujjah*. After the assassination of Amir it was she who successfully took charge of the *Fatimid D'awah* (mission) and became ruler of Yemen.[66]

Many such instances can be given from India, too. I need not narrate in detail the stories of Raziyah Sultana, Chand Bibi, Nurjahan and others which are well-known to Indians. The ability of these outstanding women to govern and administer has been recognised by all historians. One cannot but be proud of them. Those who maintain that it would be disastrous and would invite the wrath of God if women were to rule a country should think coolly of these women who came to the fore despite severe restrictions and strong prejudices in society and whose extraordinary talents won them many plaudits.[67]

The view that women should be confined to the four walls of the home and should have no role to play outside it is not a qur'anic one. There is no direct or indirect mention of this in the Qur'an. As far as the Qur'an is concerned, a woman can play any role in life without violating *hudud* Allah (the limits set by Allah). Her right to earn and be master of her properties has been recognised by the Qur'an. Thus, it is said in the Qur'an, "For men is the benefit of what they earn. And for women is the benefit of what they earn."[68] This is a very clear statement, leaving no room for differing interpretations. No wonder that the jurists are unanimously of the opinion that women can earn and deal with their property as they like. Maulana Azad too agrees with this interpretation and quotes the above verse in his defence."[69] Thus he says:

> As far as economic and financial independence is concerned, the Qur'an has categorically refused to accept that only men have this exclusive preserve. It has categorically declared that men's earnings will be for men and women's earnings will be for women. A woman can earn independently of her father as daughter, of her husband as wife and of her brother as sister and can be sole owner of what she earns.[70]

However, Islamic society came under the influence of the highly feudalised societies of Byzantine and Persia – to the disadvantage of women. The 'ulama began to air opinions which were quite contrary to the spirit of the Holy Qur'an. As pointed out earlier, hundreds of *ahadith* (Prophetic traditions) were forged and were uncritically accepted by theologians. The social influences were so strong that these traditions were given greater importance than the pronouncements of the Qur'an in the name of the Prophetic *Sunnah* (practices). The qur'anic pronouncements were subjected to interpretations favouring the forged ones.

From the accounts of women companions of the Prophet we come to know that they were never confined to their homes. They used to take part in activities ranging from politics to religion.[71] Hazrat 'A'isha was a great exegetist; *Sahih Muslim* includes a large part of her exegesis. In *hadith* almost all the Prophet's wives had expertise and, a part from 'A'isha', Umm Salma, Umm 'Atiyyah, Asma 'bint Abu Bakr, Umm Hani and Fatma bint Qays also narrated a number of *ahadith*. Some of the Prophet's women companions had expertise in *tib* (medicine) and surgery (*jarrahi*). Rafidah Aslamiyah,' Umm *muta'*, Umm Kabsha and several others were experts in medicine and surgery and Rafidah had her nursing home next to the mosque of the Prophet.[72]

Women were certainly not behind the men in the sphere of poetry; Khansa, Safiyah, Atikah, Hind bint Harith, Kabshah bint Rafi and several others were known for their excellence in this field. Khansa was a great name. She had published a collection of poetry. Many of the Prophet's women companions were engaged in industry, commerce, agriculture, calligraphy and other fields. We also find that many of them used to weave cloth for their families.[73]

Thus we will hardly find any profession in the Arabia of those days in which women of the Prophet's time did not participate. It was much later that women came to be confined to the home and people generally began to believe that their main role in life was to bear and rear children and cook food. In the famous book of songs, *Aghani*, however, we read about several women who were accomplished in several others fields of activity and were most sought after. Many of them led totally independent lives and even married and obtained divorce whenever they willed.

In other accounts we read about men and women showing their prowess in conversation, poetry and other arts.[74] Thus it would be wrong to assume that women were kept in strict *purdah* in early Islamic society. Had it been so, one would not find so many instances of men and women intermixing in public. One may argue that though Islam prescribes *purdah*, those belonging to high society consistently broke the qur'anic injunctions and violated Islamic *hudud*. It is therefore necessary to discuss the concept of *hijab* (veil) as prescribed by the Qur'an which has often been quoted in its support.

There are three verses in the Qur'an which particularly refer to what is called *hijab* (veil). One such verse is as follows:

O Wives of the Prophet, you are not like any of the (other) women, provided that you remain pious. Hence, be not over-soft in your speech, lest any one whose heart is diseased should be moved to desire (you); but, withal, speak in a kindly way. And abide quietly in your homes, and do not flaunt your charms as they used to flaunt them in the old days of pagan ignorance; and be constant in prayer, and render the purifying dues, and pay heed unto God and His Apostle for God only wants to remove from you all that might be uncleanliness, O you members of the (Prophet's) household, and to purify you to utmost purity.[75]

The jurists have generally used this verse to make *hijab* compulsory for all Muslim women. However, it is not so. Maulana Usmani feels that this verse is particularly addressed to the wives of the Prophet and this shows that whatever has been said in this verse does not apply to other Muslim women. He argues that it is not proper to apply these special instructions meant for the Prophet's wives to ordinary Muslim women.[76] In fact, the Prophet's wives had a special status and had to observe certain stricter rules to distinguish themselves from others. There was a reason why such restrictions were imposed on them. Lots of people, of all sorts, from Medina and elsewhere, used to come to the Prophet with their problems, including those of an intimate nature. If the Prophet were not there or if he was busy with others, these visitors would try to talk with his wives and behave with them in a manner which was not always desirable. We should also remember that among those who came to meet the Prophet were a large number of uncouth Bedouins unfamiliar with the culture of city-dwellers.

We have to keep this background in mind to understand the restrictions proposed on the wives of the Prophet, who were *ummahat al-m 'uminin* (like mothers to the believers). They could not be trifled with. One could not talk of private intimacies and joke with them or even try to court them. So the wives of the Prophet were advised to keep their distance from such visitors in order to preserve their dignity and not to encourage them by their talk. This is why the verse clearly says "O wives of the Prophet, you are not like any of the (other) women, provided that you remain pious." And also, "Hence be not over-soft in your speech, lest anyone whose heart is diseased should be moved to desire (you)."

But this does not mean that the wives of the Prophet were to be arrogant towards visitors or display harshness towards them. Not at all. It would not be in keeping with the behaviour of 'mothers of believers'. Therefore, the Qur'an advises them to "speak in a kindly way". They are also advised to "abide quietly in your homes, and do not flaunt your charms as they used to flaunt them in the old day of pagan ignorance..." As pointed out before, the wives of the Prophet were no ordinary women and they had to avoid displaying their charms so that they could set an example to others of feminine solemnity and dignity. They had leading roles to perform.

As we will see from other verses, during pre-Islamic days women used to display their sexual charms publicly, reducing themselves to sexual objects. They even used to solicit publicly. Tabari has recorded such an instance. He tells us of an event in the life of the Prophet's father. "After sacrificial offerings he ('Abd al-Muttalib, the Prophet's grandfather) was returning from the K'aba holding the hand of his son 'Abdallah. He happened to pass by a women of Bani Asad, Umm-e-Qital bint Naufal, who was present in the K'aba. She, looking at Abdallah's face, said, 'Where are you going?' 'Abdallah said, 'I am with my father, 'Take from me,' she said 'all the camels slaughtered in redemption (of vow) if you (agree to) sleep with me right now.' Abdallah said, 'My father is with me. I do not want to act against his will nor do I want to separate from him'.[77]

This clearly shows that during the *jahiliyah* women not only displayed their sexual charms but they also solicited publicly. A new sexual norm had to be introduced and propagated, which is what the Qur'an did. The Prophet's wives had to be active in propagating the new sexual conduct which would restore to women their dignity and which would not make them mere sexual objects. Moreover, the Prophet's wives, in their role as mothers of all the believers, had to follow the new conduct more rigorously by remaining at home and dealing with the visitors to the Prophet in a prescribed manner. That the Prophet's wives have a special status is hinted at by Al-Razi.[78] Thus it is clear that this verse is not meant for all Muslim women as most of the commentators think and apply these restrictions (to remain confined to one's house, etc) to all Muslim women.

In another verse the Qur'an asks men to talk to the Prophet's wives from behind the curtain (*hijab*). The verse is:

O you who believe, enter not the house of the Prophet unless permission is given to you for a meal, not waiting for its cooking being finished—but when you are invited, enter, and when you have taken food, disperse—not seeking to listen or talk. Surely, this gives the Prophet trouble, but he forbears from you and Allah forbears not from the truth. And when you ask of them any goods, ask of them from behind a curtain. This is purer for your hearts and their hearts. And it behooves you not to give trouble to the Messenger of Allah, nor to marry his wives after him ever. Surely this is grievous in the sight of Allah.[79]

In this verse the believers have been instructed about entry into the Prophet's house; they have been told not to spend more time with him or his wives than is absolutely necessary, and not to wait there after eating food. If they need to talk to the Prophet's wives, should do so from behind the curtain. The other instruction – that the believers should not entertain any desire to marry the

Prophet's wives after his death – is a significant one. This clearly shows that at least some people did entertain such ideas, and this was a repulsive desire (that anyone should intend to marry one whom the Prophet had married – the Qur'an itself calls it "grievous in the sight of Allah").[80] It was necessary to control this by preventing direct contact between the believers and the Prophet's wives. Naturally, all these instructions do not relate to other believing women who have nothing to do with all this. The instruction that the men should talk to the Prophet's wives from behind the curtain cannot apply to other Muslim women. It has a specific reference and deals with a specific situation. In other words, talking from behind the curtain (*min wara'i hijabin*) with the Prophet's wives is not a general but a specific category. It would, therefore, be going beyond the scope of this verse to insist that one should talk to all women from behind the curtain.

For Muslim women in general the restrictions imposed by the Qur'an are as follows:

> And say to the believing women that they lower their gaze and restrain their sexual passions and do not display their adornment except what appears thereof. And let them wear their head-coverings over their bosoms. And they would not display their adornments except to their husbands or their father, or fathers of their husbands, or their sons, or the sons of their husbands, or their brothers, or their brothers' sons, of their sisters' sons, or their women, or those whom their right hands possess, or guileless male servants, children who know not women's nakedness. And let them not strike their feet so that the adornment that they hide may be known.[81]

Here in this verse some restrictions have been imposed on women but they are not such as to confine them to the four walls of their homes or to compel them to wear a traditional kind of veil as insisted upon by many, or most of the theologians. The main restriction imposed here is that the woman, except before certain categories of men, should not display their adornments and sexual charms. Interpreted in a broad way, this is to save women from becoming mere objects of lust, thus losing their individual dignity and merit. This is precisely what is being demanded by the feminists today. Women are much more than mere sexual objects. And if women begin to display their adornments (*zinatahunna*) before everyone they would be reducing themselves to objects of lust, more than anything else. Of course, women have (men too are no exception though this tendency may not be as pronounced in them) an urge (more socially induced than natural) to display their adornments and sexual charms and this should not be denied altogether.

The Qur'an, therefore, goes on to specify categories of men and women before which a woman can display her adornments and sexual charms. She can do so before her husband whom she has to attract without reducing herself to being an object of lust as the relationship between husband and wife is much above that. It is humane and respectful and much more than sexual. The Qur'an, in fact, describes husband and wife as each other's garments.[82] She can also reveal her adornments before her father who has nothing but love and pride for her. She can be to him anything but a sexual object. Similarly, she can show her charms and creative talent for adornment to all those whom she cannot marry (all those categories mentioned in this verse, before whom she can reveal her charms, are within the prohibited degree of marriage) or those who have not achieved puberty and who do not know anything of sexual secrets ('*awr 'atin 'nisa*') and those who are beyond sexual urge (*ghayru ulil irbati minar rijali*).

Thus all this makes it quite clear that the sole idea is to elevate women above their sexuality, thus giving them dignity and individuality and at the same time not preventing them from displaying their charms before those who would appreciate them without looking towards them as sexual objects. The 'ulama, however, interpreted it differently in their own social context and read this verse in conjunction with those revealed about the Prophet's wives[83] and concluded that women should be veiled and confined to their homes. There also arose a controversy about the words *ill ma zahara minha*, i.e. except what appears thereof. It has not been resolved. Hafiz ibn Kathir, a great commentator on the

Qur'an, says that women should protect their chastity and keep themselves away from exhibitionism. They should not reveal their adornment before other men except those which cannot be hidden from others, for example, the *chador* (a piece of cloth wrapped around the body) or the overall cloth which cannot be hidden anyway. It is said that what is meant by this is the face and hands up to the wrist and the ring. But maybe it is the adornments worn other than those which the Shari'ah has prohibited from display. Hazrat Abd Allah bin Mas'ud (a companion of the Prophet) says that they (women) should not reveal their charms, i.e. the earrings, necklaces, ornaments, etc. He says that adornments are of two types: those which can be seen only by the husband, such as the rings, bracelets, etc and those which can be viewed by all such as the uppers garments. Zahri says that to the relatives mentioned in this verse one can reveal head-coverings, earrings, etc, but before others nothing more than rings.[84]

This clearly shows that the 'ulama and the classical commentators are themselves not sure as to what exactly is meant by the words "except what appears thereof". Different theologians have taken the verse in different senses and hence one cannot say that this or that particular interpretation is binding on us. Tabari, another eminent commentator, says that "the most correct opinion is that the exception relates to the face and hands". As an argument he says that, when praying a women is not required to keep her face and hands covered – hands meaning up to the elbow – while she is required to cover the rest of her body.[85]

The interpretation that the exception relates to the face and hands is based on a Prophet's tradition which we find in *Abu Da'ud*. It says that Asma' bint Abu Bakr came to the Prophet wearing very thin clothes. The Prophet turned away his face from her and said that when a woman reaches the age of puberty she should not reveal (and the Prophet showed through gesture) anything other than her face and hands.[86] But this *hadith* is *mursal* (i.e. not all the narrators' versions are available), as Khalid bin Darik has narrated it from 'A'isha and there is no proof of his having met her. The tradition is therefore at best a doubtful one. If true, it indicates that a woman, on reaching puberty, should not wear thin clothes revealing her bodily charms. This verse also exhorts women to cover their breasts, for in pre-Islamic times they used to go about without covering them. Islam, it must be noted, was born in an urban milieu and hence imposes certain sexual norms which are followed by towns' people. Thus the Qur'an does not put needless restrictions on women but only urges them to wear dignified dress, to cover their bodies properly and to avoid displaying their sexual charms which, after all, militates against the concept of their own dignity. Nothing more should be read into this verse and especially so in our own context.

It is strange that jurists who impose such restrictions on women wish to reserve the right of men to see the faces of their would-be brides before making a marriage proposal. All the four schools of jurisprudence permit a suitor to look at the face and hands of the girl before deciding to marry her, a kind of right to inspect the 'commodity for which he is bargaining. The Hanafi school also permits the inspection of legs.[87] Da'ud al-Zahiri, founder of the now extinct Zahiri school of jurisprudence, even held that the suitor had the right to look at the whole body of a girl, excepting, of course, her private parts, before deciding to marry her.[88] However, no such right was given to a girl by these jurists to have a satisfactory look at her future husband. At best she could cast a fleeting glance towards him. To have a close look at him was considered an act of immodesty.[89]

Also, as for keeping the face and hands open, we have many traditions collected by Muslims, including Nasa'i, Bayhaqi, Ahmad ibn Hanbal, etc. These traditions show that women in the Prophet's time used to come with their faces and hands open for prayers or for consulting the Prophet about their problems. So in no case can veiling of the face be upheld as a qur'anic injunction. One can say it is the opinion of a section of jurists, at the most. Allah wishes no other restrictions placed on women other than those protecting their chastity and dignity. This protection may take different forms but its content has to remain what it is meant to be. In certain extreme conditions, protection through the veil may become necessary but certainly not in a normal situation. We find an instance of an extreme condition in the Qur'an itself. In a related verse the Qur'an says:

> O Prophet, tell your wives and your daughters and the women of believers to draw over themselves their outer garments. This is more proper, so that they may be known, and not be given trouble. And Allah is ever Forgiving, Merciful.[90]

We are told that some mischiefmongers used to harass Muslim women on the pretext that they did not know who these women were and that there was nothing to distinguish them from the slave girls. To take care of this situation it was prescribed by the Qur'an that the believing women while going out of their houses should put on a *jilbab* (an over-all garment) and to draw it over their faces to protect themselves from harassment. Thus Justice Aftab Husain says:

> The use of the *jilbab* was made compulsory to save women from harassment at the hands of persons who among the non-Muslims were profligates. They annoyed women in order to find out those who were sexually available. The *jilbab* thus assumed the role of a symbol of sexual non-availability and chastity.[91]

That the above verse relates to a time-bound situation is corroborated by Muhammad Asad. He says:

> The specific, time-bound formulation of the above verse (evident in reference to the wives and daughters of the Prophet), as well as the deliberate vagueness of the recommendation that women should draw upon themselves some of their garments (*min jalabibihinna*) when in public, makes it clear that this verse was not meant to be an injunction (*hukm*) in general, in the timeless sense of this term, but rather a moral guideline to be observed against the ever-changing background of time and social environment. This finding is reinforced by the concluding reference to God's forgiveness and grace.[92]

However, the orthodox jurists and the 'ulama concluded from the above verse that the women should always go out drawing the overall garment close over their faces whatever the time and circumstance. They even forget the context in which the verse was revealed. Again, related to this question is the question of a woman travelling only in the company of a *mahram*, i.e. a male within the prohibited degree of marriage. Most of the 'ulama maintain that she cannot travel alone. In Saudi Arabia even today a woman cannot go out in the market unaccompanied by a *mahram*. Here also the spirit of the recommendation that a woman should go out in the company of a *mahram* has been lost. The eminent jurist Imam Sahfi'i understood it well and maintained that a woman was required to travel in the company of *mahram* for her own protection and security and to preserve her chastity. If her safety is otherwise vouchsafed there is no harm in her travelling with strangers, men or women. Here one should also keep in mind that in those days travellers were far and few, the roads were not well guarded and the means of communication were slow. In short, a woman travelling alone did not feel as safe as today. Thus while carrying out an injunction, if at all it is an injunction, one has to be very conscious of the circumstances. In other words, it has to be carried out intelligently.

That many *ahkam* clearly relate to specific circumstances is obvious from the way in which the Hanafi jurists later changed their opinion and required women to cover their faces in view of the mounting corruption in society. They began to apply to all believing women what was meant for the Prophet's wives exclusively in the Qur'an.[93] It was in view of these circumstances that they declared that the whole body of a woman was *'aurah* (an object to be concealed) from head to foot. Even her voice was declared *'aurah* and should not be heard by stranger. Can such an injunction be followed in the modern context? Moreover, these were personal opinions, not divine injunctions. It is another matter altogether that many jurists even today insist on following these orthodox opinions mechanically and want to see women veiled from head to foot.

It would be wrong to say that the Qur'an takes a one-sided view and only requires women to be modest and to keep their chastity protected. It also requires men to keep their sights low and not to stare at women. The Qur'an says, "Say to the believing men that they lower their gaze and restrain their sexual passion. This is purer for them."[94] It is to be borne in mind that the verse requiring women to lower their gaze and restrain their sexual passion or protect their chastity follows this verse.[95]

This clearly means that men are the first to be exhorted in this manner. Unfortunately, since most of the interpreters of the Qur'an were men they put more restrictions on women than on themselves.

The injunction that men and women should lower their gaze clearly shows that in those times they used to meet each other in public places, otherwise there would be no point in saying that both should lower their gaze.

The custom of veiling (*purdah*) began during the Umayyad period. A critical evaluation of the Prophet's time would clearly show that women used to pray in mosques with their faces uncovered and hands bare and that they interacted with the Prophet and his male companions in religious and other matters. Later, when foreign influences, especially of Rome and Persia, appeared on the scene, women came under increasing restrictions. The rulers began to maintain large harems, which needed to be strictly guarded from outsiders. Soon the ways of the rulers began to be followed by other members of the ruling classes and, finally, by the people in general. Thus *purdah* became common. Slowly women were even forbidden from attending mosques for public prayers.

It would be interesting to quote Justice Ameer Ali here. He says:

As I have already mentioned, the custom of female seclusion, which was in vogue among the Persians from very early times, (compare the story of Esther, verses 9 and 12), made its appearance among the Muslim communities in the reign of Walid II. And the character and habit of the sovereign favoured the growth and development of a practice which pride and imitation had transplanted to the congenial soil of Syria. His utter disregard of social conventionalities, and the daring and coolness with which he entered the privacy of families, compelled the adoption of safeguards against outside intrusion, which once introduced became sanctified into a custom. To the uncultured mind walls and warders appear to afford more effective protection than nobility of sentiment and purity of heart.

Despite these unfavourable circumstances, women continued down to the accession of Mutawakkil, the ninth Caliph of the house of Abbas, to enjoy an extraordinary degree of freedom. The old chivalry was still alive among men. Byzantine licence and Persian luxury had not destroyed the simplicity and freedom of the desert. Fathers continued to assume surnames after their accomplished and beautiful daughters; brothers and lovers rushed to battle acclaiming the names of their sisters and lady loves. The sophisticated Arab maiden could still hold conversation with men without embarrassment and in absolute unselfconsciousness of evil. To her the beautiful lines of Firdausi were still applicable: "Lips full of smiles, countenance full of modesty, conduct virtuous, conversation lively."

Women entertained their guests without shyness, and as they knew their own worth they were respected by all around them. A well-known author related how on returning from Mecca, he halted at a watering place near Medina. The heat of the sun drove him to seek shelter in a neighbouring house which appeared to be of some pretension. He entered the courtyard and asked the inmates if he might alight from his camel. A lady's voice gave him the sought—for permission. He then asked for leave to enter the house, and receiving permission entered the hall, where he found "a maiden fairer than the sun" engaged in household duties. She bade him to be seated and they conversed, and "words like pearls were scattered from her lips". Whilst they were conversing, her grandmother entered and sat down by their side, laughingly warning the stranger to beware of the witchery of the fair girl.

Another incident related by the father of this author throws further light on the manners and customs of the age. He was proceeding to Mecca, and halted on the way at the house of a friend who asked him if he would like an introduction to Kharika, the famous lady whose praise had been sung by one of the greatest poets of the Omayyad times. On his expressing a desire to meet the beauty, he was taken to her residence, where he was received by a tall and extremely beautiful woman "in the force of age". He saluted her and was asked to sit down. "We conversed for a time", continues the narrator, "when she asked me laughingly, 'Didst thou ever make the pilgrimage?' "More than once," said I "And what then has hindered thee from visiting during the pilgrimage?" "And how is that?" "Hast thou never heard what thy uncle Zu'r Rahma said: To complete a pilgrimage, the caravan should stop at Kharika's (abode) whilst she is laying aside her veil."

Under the early Hakamites flourished Syeda Sukaina or Sakina, the daughter of Husain, the Martyr of Karbala, who was regarded as "the first among the women of her time by birth, beauty, wit and virtue." Her residence was the resort of poets, *faqihs* (jurists) and learned and pious people of all classes. The assemblies in her house were brilliant and animated and always enlivened by her repartee.

Ummal Banin, the wife of Walid I, and sister of Omar II, was another remarkable women of her time. Her influence over her husband was considerable and was always exercised for the good of the people.[96]

Justice Ameer Ali tells us that during the early Abbasid period women continued to enjoy freedom. In the time of Mansur we hear of two princesses going to the Byzantine war clad in mail; in Rashid's time also we see Arab maidens wanting to fight on horseback and commanding troops. The mother of Muqtadir herself presided at the Court of Appeal, listened to applications, gave audiences to foreign dignitaries and envoys. It all continued until the time of Mutawakkil.[97]

Reuben Levy quotes Tabari[98] to show that until the 3rd century of the *hijrah* and even later, women used to pray in mosques along with men. They were not required to be veiled. However, the law books prescribed that the dress to be worn should be in two pieces. The face, hands and upper side of the feet need not be covered, though there is some controversy about the last detail.[99]

Levy also quotes Ibn Batuta[100] who says:

Their women showed no modesty in the presence of men and did not veil. Yet they were assiduous in their prayers. Anyone who wished to marry them could do so, but they would not go on a journey with their husbands. Even if one of them wished it her kinsfolk would prevent her. The women there have friends and companions amongst men who are not related to them. So also the men have friends amongst men who are not related to them. A man may enter his house and find his wife with her friend and yet will not disapprove.[101]

Thus we see that the *purdah* was not always an integral part of Muslim society, much less was it theologically justified. Arab society had known it only in sections of the urban population, not among the Bedouins. Even in later Muslim society, especially after Mutwakkil, when the veil became widely accepted, it was found among sections of urban societies. It was not prevalent among the urban poor nor among the rural women. The Muslim women from poorer families in urban areas and rural women in general had to work outside their homes to make ends meet. In urban areas, too, not all Muslim societies observed *purdah*. Ibn Batuta observed this fact during his period.

In a modern industrial economy women have to play an increasingly greater role. They have to take up jobs to ensure a comfortable family life. As already pointed out, there is nothing in the Qur'an which prevents women from working. On the contrary, it says that whatever she earns (*ma kasabat*) is hers and hers alone. The view that a woman has to look after the home and children is not, strictly speaking, a qur'anic view; it is essentially a juristic view. What is required by the Qur'an is not that she cannot work but that the man has to maintain his wife and in return the wife has to look after the children. This does not deprive a woman of her right to work; it only establishes an equation between wife and husband. The equation, it should be remembered, is not mandatory. The wife can choose to work and establish a different equation according to which both will share family expenses, the upkeep of the house and the bringing up of the children. Whether this will prove to be the best arrangement or not is a different question altogether. One may hold one or the other opinion and prefer one or the other arrangement with mutual consent. But, as far as the Qur'an is concerned, there is no bar on a woman going out of the house and earning, provided she protects her chastity and restrains her sexual urge (*wa yahfizna furujahunna*). The same thing is demanded of men also (*wa yahfuzu furujahum*). Man, in no way, then, is superior to woman in any of these respects.

Notes and References

1. Interview with Riffat Hassan by Betty Milstead, "Feminist Theology and Women in the Muslim World", in *Women Living Under Muslim Laws*, Dossier 4, p. 32.
2. The *Qur'an* 2:282.
3. Muhammad Asad, *The Message of the Qur'an* (Gibralter, 1980), f.n. 273, p. 63.
4. See Manar, vol. III, p. 124f; cf. Muhammad Asad, Ibid.
5. See verse 2:282 above.
6. Verse 2:282.
7. Justice Aftab Hussain, *Status of Women in Islam* (Lahore, 1987), p. 278.
8. The *Qur'an* 5:106.
9. Ibid., 2:228.
10. Ibid., 5:107.
11. Justice Aftab Hussain, op. cit., pp. 279-80.
12. The *Qur'an* 24:6-9.
13. Ibid, 4:15.
14. *Fiqh al*-Qur'an, op. cit., vol. III, p. 79.
15. See Shafai's *Kitab al-Umm*, vol. VII, p. 102; cf. *Fiqh al-Qur'an*, op. cit., vol. III, p. 102.
16. See Jassas, *Ahkam al-Qur'an*, op. cit., vol. I, pp. 596-98.
17. See *Ikhtiyarat al-'Illmiyah al-Matbu 'm' al-Fatwa*, p. 213 and *Al-Tariq al-Hikmiyah fi' al-Siyasat al-Shar'iyah*, p. 142; cf. *Fiqh al-Qur'an*, op. cit., p. 104.
18. Ibn Qayyim, *I'lam al-Muwaqqa'* in (Lahore. n.d), vol. I, pp. 71-7.
19. Ibn Qayyim Jauzi, *Al-Turuq al-Hukmiyyah* (Cairo, n.d.), pp. 68-70.

20. See *Sahih Bukhari* (Lahore, 1980), vol. III, p. 655. Also *Jami'ul Fuwad hadith*, nos. 5231, 5233 and 5234.
21. For a detailed discussion see 'Umar Ahmad Usmani's *Fiqh al-Qur'an*, op. cit., vol. III, pp. 105-12.
22. See Jassas, *Ahkam al-Qur'an*, op. cit., vol. I, pp. 596-8.
23. Justice Aftab Hussain, op. cit., p. 271.
24. *Musannaf 'Abd al-Razzaq* (Beirut, n.d.), vol. VIII, *hadith* no. 15413.
25. Ibid., *hadith* no. 15414.
26. Ibid., *hadith* no. 15415.
27. Ibn Qayyim, Jauzi, *Al-Turuq al-Hukmiyyah*, op. cit., p. 92.
28. The *Qur'an* 4:11.
29. Ibid., 4:12.
30. Fakhruddin al-Razi, *Tafsir Kabir* (Beirut, n.d.), vol. V, p. 210.
31. Ibid.
32. The *Qur'an* 65:6-7.
33. Ibid., 4:4.
34. See *Ikhwanus Safa* (Bombay, 1306 AH)
35. *Dirham* is an Arabian currency prevalent then as now.
36. *Ikhwanus Safa*, op. cit., vol. IV, p. 150; cf. Prof S.T. Lokhandwala, "The Position of Women under Islam", in Asghar Ali Engineer (ed.), *Status of Women in Islam* (Delhi, 1987), pp. 75-6.
37. Parvez, *Matalib al-Furqan* (Lahore, 1981) published in six volumes but still incomplete.
38. Ibid., vol. IV, p. 279.
39. Ibid., vol, IV, p. 280.
40. Ibid.
41. See verses 4:11-12.
42. Maulana Umar Ahmad Usmani, op. cit., vol. VII, pp. 75-6.
43. See Imam al-Jassas, *Ahkam al-Qur'an* (Egypt, 1347 AH), vol. II, p. 598; cf. Umar Ahmad Usmani, op. cit., vol. VII, p. 77.
44. The *Qur'an* 4:8.
45. We will throw more light on maintenance in another chapter.
46. The *Qur'an* 27: 32-35.
47. See *Sahih Bukhari* (Delhi, n.d.), vol. II, p.1053.
48. Justice Aftab Hussain, op. cit., p. 214.
49. See *Fiqh al-Qur'an*, op. cit., vol. III, pp. 293-304.
50. See Dr. Abdul Hamid, *Mabadi Nizam al-Hukm al-Islami* (Cairo, n.d.), Maulana Umar Ahmad Usmani, op. cit., vol. III, p. 279.

51. The *Qur'an* 27:32-35.
52. Ibid., 9:71.
53. See ref. 47 above.
54. See *Imdad al-Fatwa* (Darul Ulum Karangi), vol. V, pp. 99-101.
55. Prof. Abdul Hamid, *Mabadi Nizam al-Hukm al-Islami*, op. cit., p. 876.
56. Ibid., p. 202.
57. Ibid., p. 879.
58. Ibid., pp. 879-82.
59. This tradition has been narrated by Hazrat 'Ali and reported by Ibn 'Asakir. See Rashid, Rida, *Al-Wahi al-Muhammadi*, p. 280.
60. The *Qur'an* 9:71.
61. See *Fath al-Bari Sahih Bukhari* (Cairo, n.d.), vol. VIII, p. 97.
62. Ibid, vol. XIII, p. 47.
63. See *Radd al-Mukhtar 'ala al-Durr al-Mukhtar*, vol. IV, p. 494; Maulana Umar Ahmad Usmani, op. cit., vol. III, pp. 273.
64. Syed Sulaiman Nadvi, *Sirat al-'Aisha* (Azamgarh, n.d.), p. 126.
65. See *Aghani*, vol. XIX, pp. 34-37; cf. Philip. H. Hitti, *History of the Arabs* (New York, 1958), p. 333.
66. See Sayyidna Idris, *'Uyun al-Akhbar*, vols. VI and VII; cf. *Bulletin of Oriental Studies*, 1934, vol. VII, part 2, pp. 317-21.
67. See Asghar Ali Engineer, "Women and Administration in Islam" In *'National Seminar on Status of Women in Islam* (Bait al-Hikmat, New Delhi) p. 25.
68. The *Qur'an* 4:32.
69. Maulana Abul Kalam Azad, *Tarjuman al-Qur'an* (Delhi, 1980), vol. II, p. 191.
70. Ibid.
71. Maulana Said Ansari, *Siyar al-Sahabiyat* (Azamgarh, 1972), pp. 8-9.
72. See Tabqat ibn S'ad, vol. VIII, p. 213; cf. *Siyar al-Sahabiyat*, op. cit., p.10.
73. Usd al-Ghaba, vol. V, p. 398 and *Musnad Ahmad ibn Hanbal*, vol. V, p. 166; cf. *Siyar al-Sahabiyat*, op. cit., pp. 10-11.
74. See Ibn Abd Rabbihi, *Al'lqd al-Farid* (Beirut.1986), vol. VI, p. 83. Also Masudi, *Al-Muruj al-dhahb* (Beirut, 1984), vol. II, pp. 174-5.

75. The *Qur'an* 33:32-33.
76. Maulana Umar Ahmad Usmani, op. cit., vol. III, p. 306.
77. See Asghar Ali Engineer, *The Origin and Development of Islam* (Bombay, 1980), pp. 130-1.
78. Al-Razi, *Tafsir Kabir*, op. cit., vol. XIII, p. 209.
79. The *Qur'an* 33:53.
80. Ibid.
81. Ibid., 24:31.
82. Ibid., 2:187.
83. The verses 33:32-33 and 33:53 discussed above.
84. See Hafiz ibn Kathir, *Tafsir ibn Kathir*, Urdu tr., notes, etc. by Maulana Anzar Shah Kashmiri (Deoband, n.d.), vol. II, section 19, p. 61.
85. *Tafsir Tabari*; cf. Maulana Muhammad Ali, *Holy Qur'an* (Lahore, 1973), p. 685.
86. See *Tafsir ibn Kathir*, op. cit., vol. II, section 19, p. 61.
87. Sha'rani '*Al-Mizanu'l Kurba* (Cairo, 1940), vol. II, p. 108.
88. Sha'rani, Ibid.
89. S.T. Lokhandwala, op. cit., p. 36.
90. The *Qur'an* 33:59.
91. *Status of Women in Islam* (Lahore, 1987), p. 177.
92. Muhammad Asad, *The Message of the Qur'an*, op. cit., p. 651.
93. See Abdul Majid Daryabadi, *Tafsir Majidi* (Karachi, 1953), vol. II on verse 33:32. Maulana Daryabadi says this with reference to Jassas, Mujahid, Qurtubi, etc.
94. The *Qur'an* 24:130.
95. Ibid., 24:31.
96. Justice Ameer Ali, *History of the Saracens* (National Book Foundation, Karachi), pp. 199-202.
97. Ibid., p. 455.
98. Tabari, vol. I, p. 2469; cf. Reuben Levy, *Social Structures of Islam*, p. 126.
99. Levy, Ibid., p. 126.
100. Ibn Batuta, *Voyages*, vol. IV, p. 388.
101. Levy, ibid, p. 127.

5

MARITAL RIGHTS OF WOMEN IN ISLAM

Marital rights are an important indicator of women's general status in a society. In most of the societies and religious systems women have been given no independent right to enter a marital relationship of their own free will. A woman is generally considered incapable of choosing a life partner as her mental capacity is supposed to be inferior to that of a man. However, the Holy Qur'an takes no such view and considers a woman mentally as well as morally equal to a man. Both will be equally rewarded or punished for their good and bad deeds. Thus the Qur'an says: (33:35)

> Surely the men who submit and the women who submit, and the believing women, and the obeying men and the obeying women, and the truthful men and the truthful women, and the patient men and the patient women, and the humble men and the humble women, and the charitable men and the charitable women, and the fasting men and the fasting women, and the men who guard their chastity and the women who guard (their chastity), and the men who remember Allah much and the women who remember—Allah has prepared for them forgiveness and a mighty reward.

Thus it will be seen that the Qur'an equates both the sexes in terms of moral responsibility and rewards and punishments. This is logically extended to the sphere of marriage also. Marriage in Islam, as is well known, is a contract between two equal partners.

A woman as an equal party can stipulate her preferred conditions in the same way that a man, the other partner, can. Men enjoy no superiority in this respect. The *qadi*, or anyone else, who solemnises a marriage, cannot do so without ensuring the approval of the woman concerned and the conditions she wishes to stipulate, including the amount of *mahr* (dower) she wishes to have from the husband to be. These conditions are laid down in the presence of two witnesses who testify before the *qadi*, who then puts them before the bridegroom for his acceptance. When the bridegroom gives his acceptance and approval to marry her, the *qadi* solemnises the marriage.

Thus it will be seen that without the woman's approval, and approval on her conditions, a marriage cannot take place. She is clearly and equal partner in contracting a marriage. There is no concept of marriage as a sacrament in Islam. It is, therefore, possible to dissolve a marriage just as any other contract between two individuals can be terminated. Thus divorce is perfectly legitimate though it is discouraged by the Holy Prophet, as we shall see in the next chapter on divorce. Let us first discuss the marital rights of women in Islam.

First of all, we must bear in mind that sex is no taboo in Islam. It is considered a legitimate activity within the framework of marriage. There is no concept of sin attached to it. It is considered necessary for procreation. The creation of human beings is through the sexual act. The Qur'an says: "So let man consider of what he is created. He is created of water pouring forth, coming from between the back and the ribs." (86:6-7) "Water pouring forth" is nothing but semen which comes from between the back and the ribs. Thus the Qur'an accepts that a sexual relationship between man and woman is necessary for procreation. Hence sex within the marital framework is legitimate and necessary.

Because procreation is necessary for human survival marriage is encouraged in Islam, though it is not made compulsory. Just as slavery was an accepted institution (which of course Islam sought to discourage) in those days, so was marriage: The Qur'an says "And whoever among you cannot afford to marry free believing women, (let him marry) such of your believing maidens as your right hands possess" (4:25). Thus a man should try to marry as far as possible, if not a free woman, then the maiden he owns. However, if he has no capacity even to marry a maiden, let alone a free woman, then one must be patient until Allah makes him capable of marrying. "And let those who cannot find a match", says the Qur'an, "Keep chaste, until Allah makes them free from want out of His grace." (24:33)

These verses from the Qur'an show that though there is no compulsion in the matter of marriage, there is no doubt that the institution of marriage is encouraged so that human progeny is sustained. It is also through this institution that the rights of women, both as wives and mothers, can be safeguarded. While making marriage compulsory could have caused hardship to some, discouraging it would have caused difficulties to many more, particularly to women who would have enjoyed no legal rights. Islam, therefore, preferred a middle way. It encouraged the marital institution while making it clear that those who cannot afford to marry free women should marry the oppressed women (those captured in war or enslaved in other ways) and that if they cannot afford to marry even them, then they should wait till Allah frees them from want.

According to a *hadith* (tradition)' the Prophet did not approve of conduct which merely emphasises the need for praying and fasting but forbids marrying. He is reported to have said, "I fear Allah more than anyone else. I pray and fast and yet I marry women and those who deviate from my practice are not from me."[1] According to another tradition, anyone who has sexual potency should marry.[2] The Prophet is also reported to have said that those who do not have the financial capacity to marry should observe fasts, as fasting reduces sexual desire.[3] But wherever possible one must marry—perhaps even migrating for this purpose—and Allah will reward him according to his intention.[4]

Thus it can be seen that marriage as an institution is encouraged by Islam because family life not only ensures survival of the human race but also guarantees social stability and a dignified existence for both woman and man. According to the qur'anic philosophy, there is nothing wrong with sex if it is used for procreation within the marital framework and not merely for enjoyment and pleasure. The Qur'an specifically forbids sexual relations for "fornicating and receiving paramours".[5] For fornication or receiving paramours cannot impart dignity to women. It would not only reduce sex to mere physical pleasure but would also lead to a much greater exploitation of women. According to the Qur'an, husband and wife are each other's garments (2:187). Thus marriage is not merely a sexual urge which brings woman and man together; it has a higher end, and exalted motive, and is a relationship of love and mutual respect.

Here two important questions arise so far as the practice of orthodox Islam is concerned, namely, polygamy and concubinage. If one carefully studies the Qur'an one learns that it neither encourages the former nor permits the latter. Since polygamy is much talked about we will take it up first. There is no doubt that the Qur'an does permit it. One can marry up to four wives. But it is not enough to say this. There is much more to it which must be critically examined, medieval notions of orthodox Islam notwithstanding. Before we examine the institution of polygamy let us see what the Qur'an says on the matter.

The first verse in this connection is:

> And if you fear that you cannot do justice to orphans, marry such women as seem good to you, two, or three, or four; but if you fear you will not do justice, then (marry) only one or that which your right hands possess. This is more proper that you may not do injustice. (4:3).

This verse expressly and unambiguously permits marriage with more than one woman. However, it cannot be read in isolation. It has to be read in conjunction with the preceding verses, i.e. 1 and 2 of chapter 4. One has also to keep in mind the context of the revelation of this *surah*, i.e. of chapter 4.

The first verse of this chapter talks of the creation of men and women from the same source and thus emphasises equality of the sexes. The second verse exhorts Muslims to give orphans their property and not to exchange their good property with the bad property of their wards. The third verse relating to polygamy also begins with the words: "And if you fear that you cannot do justice to orphans..." First of all, we should note that the very first verse makes it clear that men and women have been created from *nafsin wahidatin* (a single being) and hence they enjoy equal status. The second verse talks of doing justice to the orphans, and the third, concerning polygamy, begins with doing justice to the orphans and goes on to say that if you cannot do so then marry such women as seem good to you, two or three, or four.

Thus it can be seen that the emphasis is not on marrying more than one woman but on doing justice to the orphans. Here it is to be borne in mind that in those days guardians often used to misappropriate their wards' properties and sometimes did so by marrying them without even paying the dower money. The Qur'an wanted to check this malpractice. That is why, according to *Sahih Muslim*, the Prophet's wife 'A'isha understood this verse as meaning that if the guardians of orphan girls feared that by marrying them they would not be able to do justice to them, they should marry other women.[6] Thus the verse is not the general licence for polygamy that it is often taken to be but rather it refers to a clear context in which justice to orphan girls is more central than marrying more than one at a time. This point should not be missed.

Even Hazrat 'A'isha's explanation is not considered final. There are other interpretations. Many of her contemporaries did not subscribe to her understanding of the verse. Thus, according to Sa'id ibn Jabayr, Qatadah and other successors of the Prophet's companions, the purport of the verse is this: "Just as you are, rightly, fearful of offending against the interests of orphans, you must apply the same careful consideration to the interests and rights of the women whom you intend to marry." Tabari, a noted commentator on the Qur'an quotes several variants of this interpretation and gives it his approval.[7]

Thus justice to orphan girls, on the one hand, and the rights and interests of women whom men intend to marry, on the other, receive primary consideration. These cannot be trifled with. Also, it is necessary for a man to do equal justice to all his spouses. If he cannot do so he should marry only one. This also makes it quite unambiguous that justice is the central concept and polygamy cannot be treated as a right or privilege as has unfortunately happened in a male-dominated society. Another important factor to be borne in mind is the contextual revelation of these verses. The commentators agree that these verses were revealed immediately after the Battle of Uhud and were meant to provide guidance to Muslims after that cataclysmic event. In this battle 70 out of 700 men were slain and this carnage sharply reduced the number of Muslim males.[8] Many Muslim women were widowed and girls orphaned. They had to be taken care of and in the prevalent social context this could best be done by allowing Muslim males to marry widows and orphans, up to four in number, strictly on condition that they did justice to all of them and if they were not capable of doing so, they should not marry more than one woman.

It should be noted here that during *jahiliyah* (pre-Islamic period) there was no restriction on the number of women one could marry. Thus restricting the number to four wives was a reform. We see in *Sunan Abu Daud* that Wahab al-Asadi had eight wives before he embraced Islam. After he became a Muslim the Prophet advised him to retain any four of the eight wives and divorce the rest.[9] This reform was introduced in the then prevailing conditions, i.e. the drastic reduction in the Muslim male population following the Battle of Uhud, as pointed out earlier. Marriage with widows and orphans was also encouraged. The Prophet himself married mostly widows to set an example to others. Seen in this perspective, one can understand the real importance of permitting marriage to up to four wives. However, Muslims themselves treated it as a general licence and still insist on retaining it. In today's conditions it should be considered as good as impermissible except in certain highly exceptional circumstances.

There is one more verse about polygamy in the Qur'an (chapter 4, verse 129). It states: "And you cannot do justice between wives, even though you wish (it), but be not disinclined (from one) with total disinclination, so that you leave her in suspense. And if you are reconciled and keep your duty, surely Allah is ever Forgiving, Merciful." Thus in this verse again the Qur'an tells the believers that they cannot do justice, even if they so desire, between wives, so they should refrain from taking more wives than one.

Muhammad Asad makes the following comment on the verse:

> This refers to cases where a man has more than one wife—a waiver which is conditional upon his determination and ability to 'treat them with equal fairness' as laid down in verse 3 of this *surah* (chapter 4). Since a man who is fully conscious of his moral responsibility might feel that he is committing a sin if he loves one of his wives more than the other (or others), the verse provides 'judicial enlightenment' on this point by making it clear that *feelings* are beyond a human being's control; in other words, that the required equality of treatment relates only to outward behaviour towards and practical dealings with one's wives. However, in view of the fact that a man's behaviour towards another person is, in the long run, almost inevitably influenced by what he feels about that person, the above passage—read in conjunction with verse 3, and especially its concluding sentence—imposes a moral restriction on plural marriage.[10]

Commenting on the plurality of wives, Parvez, a noted commentator on the Qur'an, says:

> It would be seen that the permission for more than one wife is contingent on two conditions: (1) If there is an excess of single or husbandless women in society and there is no other reasonable solution possible, then exception could be made to the rule of monogamy and one would marry these (husbandless) women. (2) This permission is also conditional on justice being done to all individuals in the family. Also, it should be possible for an individual to bear the burden of all the children begotten by the wives. It should not become an unbearable burden on him.[11]

Parvez maintains that the first wife's permission is necessary for just and equal treatment of all wives without which equal treatment is not possible. He also feels that it should be for the state—and not an individual—to decide whether such social conditions exist which could necessitate taking more than one wife at a time. Thus it is for the state to allow or disallow polygamy through enactment of laws, keeping social conditions in view.[12] If such conditions do not exist then there is no question of permitting more than one wife. He also maintains that the verse on polygamy itself begins with the words *wa in Khiftum*, that is, if you fear (that you cannot do justice), how can polygamy be considered a general rule?[13]

There is one very interesting tradition (*hadith*) of the Prophet narrated by Bukhari. The Prophet said that one who works hard for the sustenance of widows is like one who wages war in the way of Allah or one who prays at night or fasts during the day.[14] If this *hadith* is seen in the light of the qur'anic verse 4:3 permitting polygamy, the emphasis laid on marrying widows and orphan girls becomes clearer. If working and earning for widows and orphans is like *jihad*, marrying them in times of distress would amount to maintaining and protecting them and would be a meritorious act. Thus this *hadith* makes it clear that marrying more than one wife is to help widows and orphans and not to satisfy one's lust. The whole intent is to establish social justice.

It is to be noted that marriage should not be treated merely as a means of satisfying one's lust; love and procreation are two of its important motives. The Qur'an does not approve of sex for pleasure or for fornication (musafahah); marriage has a purpose. Thus the Qur'an says:

> And so are (lawful) the chaste from among the believing women and the chaste from among those who have been given the Book before you when you give them their dowries, taking them in marriage, not fornicating nor taking them for paramours in secret.(5:5)

The word for fornication used in the Qur'an is *musafahah* which literally means shedding water mutually, i.e. ejaculation. So marriage even in the normal course is much more than the satisfaction of lust. When it is permitted with more than one woman at a time, it has hardly anything to do with sexual lust; it is only to fulfil some social obligation which has arisen out of an abnormal situation like war or pestilence. Thus, looked at from whatever angle, polygamy is not a general permission for men to marry up to four wives in all circumstances as it was made out to be in male-dominated medieval societies, and it is this received tradition which has acquired the status of a Divine Law for Muslims today.

Concubinage

Another controversy in Islamic law is about concubinage or the permissibility of sexual intercourse with slave girls or women captured in war without marrying them. The words used for such women are *milk-i-yamin*, generally translated as those whom your right hand possesses, i.e. those whom you possess as war booty or otherwise. The orthodox Muslims consider it as lawful to have sexual relations with women captured in war or purchased in the market. However, many modern scholars and commentators feel that such a relationship is not legal and has not been permitted by the Qur'an. We would like to discuss this question at some length as it has been the subject of a great controversy.

There are several verses on *milk-i-yamin* in the Qur'an. Let us consider the following verse:

> And whoever among you cannot afford to marry free believing women (*muhsanat*), (let him marry) such of your believing maidens as your right hand possesses. And Allah knows best your faith—you are (sprung) the one from the other. So marry them with the permission of their masters, and give them their dowries justly, they being chaste, not fornicating, nor receiving paramours; then if they are guilty of adultery when they are taken in marriage, they shall suffer half the punishment for free married women. This is for him among you who fears falling evil. And that you abstain is better for you. And Allah is Forgiving, Merciful.(4:25)

The above verse clearly speaks of marrying a slave girl or a *milk-i-yamin* if one cannot marry a free believing woman (*muhsanat*). If one is required to marry a *milk-i-yamin* in case one cannot marry a free woman, how can he be permitted to have sexual relations with a *milk-i-yamin* when one is already married to a free believing woman? The Qur'an wants a man to marry a slave girl if he does not have enough to spend on a free believing woman so that he does not go astray and resorts to fornication, thereby reducing sex to mere lust. If the Qur'an permits one to have sexual relations with slave girls without marriage, one can possess any number of slave girls (there is no limit fixed in law for this) and have intercourse with them, turning sexual relations into mere lust. This would be in clear contradiction to the qur'anic purpose of sex.

Here it would be quite appropriate to quote a *hadith* from the Prophet as regards the slave girls. The Prophet was not in favour of retaining slavery, let alone permitting sex with slave girls without marriage, as thought by later theologians. According to this *hadith*, reported by Bukhari, anyone who has a slave girl, and gives her the necessary education, teaches her proper discipline and then marries her after manumitting her, would be doubly rewarded.[15] Thus the Prophet, far from permitting sex with slave girls, wanted them to be educated, disciplined and freed before being married to their former masters. However, the orthodox 'ulama went by the legal technicalities instead and advocated the right of masters to have sex with those whom their right hand possessed. These are instances wherein the Prophet said that manumission of slave girls was her dower (*mahr*). Malik bin Ans says that the Prophet emancipated Safiyah and that became her dower.[16]

Thus we see that the Prophet was very kind to the slave girls and did everything possible to improve their lot. He advocated their manumission, their education and marriage. One could hardly find a parallel to this in the history of other religions and societies and yet unfortunately, orthodox practice sanctioned sex with slave girls without marrying them. Maulana Muhammad Ali says:

> I do not find any verse in the Holy Qur'an or any instance in the Prophet's life sanctioning what is called *concubinage* (emphasis in the original). On more occasions than one, when establishments of

conjugal relations with slave girls is mentioned, their taking in
marriage is clearly laid down as a condition as in verse 3, verse 24,
and this verse (verse 25). Here marriage with those taken prisoner in
war is allowed under certain circumstances, the first of these being
that they should be believing women or Muslims.[17]

It is true that slavery was prevalent in those days. It is also
true that men were permitted to regard women as their
possessions, as war booty. But the Prophet never encouraged it,
though for various social constraints he could not abolish it
altogether. But it was no less a radical measure to ask free men to
marry them after manumitting them and to provide a double
reward for doing so. The only superiority a master could claim
over a slave girl was to marry her without permission from anyone
else. Normally, permission from her father, grandfather or elder
brother was needed. But in this case no such permission was
needed. If he so desired he could marry her either in bondage or
after manumitting her. Thus no one should be in any doubt that
concubinage was not allowed in Islam. It is true that most of the
orthodox 'ulama and commentators on the Qur'an have held for
long that one could have sexual intercourse with women captured
in war or with slave girls without marrying them, but this is
obviously an erroneous view. When the Prophet clearly says that
one should educate and train slave girls and then manumit and
marry then how could he approve of concubinage?

Many modern commentators, including Muhammad 'Abdahu
(a highly learned theologian and scholar), Maulana Muhammad
Ali (an Ahmadi theologian from Lahore) and several others, hold
that nowhere has the Qur'an permitted concubinage or intercourse
with slave girls without marrying them.[18]

Nikah and the Role of the Guardian

Nikah, as pointed out in the beginning of this chapter, is
contractual in Islam. In other words, both the bride and the
bridegroom can stipulate conditions for marriage. It implies that
women are free to enter or not to enter a marriage contract.
However, traditionally, the woman herself is not allowed to

negotiate her marriage. She is given into marriage by her guardian (*wali*), who generally happens to be her father. In his absence her grandfather or brother acts as the guardian. During *jahiliyah* it was the *wali* who gave her into marriage. Of course, the *wali* does so with her consent and consent is given in the presence of two witnesses. But coercion in such cases cannot be ruled out. In fact, during the medieval period it was the father, grandfather or brother who decided her marital fate. However, as far as the Qur'an and Islamic Shari'ah are concerned, her right to accept or refuse a marriage proposal is untrammelled. Neither her father nor anyone else can coerce her into accepting a proposal.

The Islamic jurists have distinguished in matters of marriage between a *bakirah* (a young unmarried girl) and a *thayyibah* (a widow or divorcee). A *bakirah* is required to appoint a marriage guardian (*wali*) which is not necessary in the case of a *thayyibah*. The reason for this could be that as a young unmarried girl is not experienced enough in matters of marriage, it is best for her to leave them to her elders who could make the right decision, though finally it is she who would approve or disapprove it. Widows or divorcees acquire experience in such matters and hence they can rely on their own judgement. Thus, we find a *hadith* according to which, although a *bakirah* cannot be given into marriage without her approval, her silence on being asked could be taken as her approval.[19]

A *thayyibah* has the right to make her own decision and she can refuse to accept a *nikah* even if solemnised on her behalf. According to a *hadith*, a *thayyibah* was given into marriage by her marriage guardian without her consent. When the Prophet came to know of it, he cancelled the *nikah*.[20] In fact, even for a *bakirah* there is no mention of a *wali* or marriage guardian in the Qur'an. It is a pre-Islamic practice which was incorporated into Islamic jurisprudence later. It would be interesting to understand how Islamic jurisprudence developed in order to understand certain practices which are not mentioned in the Qur'an but which are an integral part of Islamic Shari'ah today. It is in this light that certain concepts and practices of Islamic marriage have to be understood.

Schacht writes:

Muhammadan law came into existence through the working of
Muhammadan jurisprudence on the raw material which consisted of
the popular and administrative practice of late Umaiyad times and
was endorsed, modified or rejected by the earliest lawyers. These
lawyers and their successors were guided by a double aim: by the
effort to systematise...and by the tendency to 'Islamise', to
impregnate the sphere of law with religious and ethical ideas, to
subject it to Islamic norms, and to incorporate it in the body of
duties incumbent on every Muslim.[21]

What Schacht says gives us an insight into the formation of
Islamic law which came to be known later as the Islamic Shari'ah.
Many practices from *jahiliyah* were continued either because they
were not injurious to Islamic values or because they were
Islamised. Islam undoubtedly gave a new outlook and new values
to Muslim society, but an ideology, religious or political, never
succeeds in transforming an entire society, lock, stock and barrel.
The old practices creep in the new forms and new practices are
ritualised, thus robbing them of their revolutionary potential.

Islam gave women a new status; it wanted to create a *new
woman* as much as a new man. However, the old ethos soon
robbed the woman of that status and set back her position. A close
study of the Qur'an would reveal that she was given full autonomy
in matters of marriage. Her marriage depended on her approval
being given under her own conditions. However, the *jahiliyah*
practice of contracting marriage by her *wali* (marriage guardian)
on her behalf reestablished itself and her approval was reduced to
a mere nod or silence. From playing an active role in her own
marriage she came to be relegated to a passive position.

However one has to keep in view the prevailing social
structure while discussing the evolution of a law. Arab society as
we have seen, was essentially a patriarchal one. In such a society
women are protected beings dependent completely on their
menfolk for their existence. Naturally, in such a society it is for
the parents, grandparents or brothers to look after the welfare of a
woman, she herself being incapable of doing so. Thus it became

necessary for a *wali* to intervene on her behalf in contracting marriage, her business being to either nod or to keep silent.

According to the Qur'an, any believing man can marry a believing woman without any consideration of social status. The Qur'an makes a normative statement in this respect. However, in Shari'ah we find that the concept of the social status of a woman is an important factor in her marriage with a man. The question is whether a man wishing to marry a woman enjoys a higher or lower status. Technically this is called the concept of *kafa 't* which literally means equality (between man and woman). Thus we find in *Hedaya*:

> In marriage regard is had to equality, because the Prophet has commanded, saying, 'Take care that none contract women in marriage but their proper guardians and that they be not so contracted by save with their equals; and also, because the desirable ends of marriage, such as cohabitation, society, and friendship, cannot be completely enjoyed except by persons who are each other's equal (according to the customary estimation of equality), as a woman of high rank and family would abhor the society of and cohabitation with a mean man; it is requisite, therefore, that regard be had to equality in respect of the husband; that is to say, that the husband be the equal of his wife; but it is not necessary that the wife be the equal of the husband since men are not degraded by cohabitation with women who are their inferiors.[22]

Further, it is said in *Hedaya*:

> It is proper to observe, in this place, that one reason for attending to equality in marriage is that regard is had to circumstances in confirming a marriage and establishing its validity; for if a woman should match herself to a man who is her inferior, her guardians have a right to separate them, so as to remove the dishonour they might otherwise sustain by it. [23]

Thus we see that the concept of *kafa 't* (equality of status) has been introduced by the Islamic jurists in the Shari'ah though it is not at all mentioned in the Qur'an. From this one can easily infer that the Qur'an makes normative statements whereas the Shari'ah lays down social practices. It could not have been otherwise. The people practise norms in certain concrete social contexts. No legal system, let alone the Islamic Shari'ah, can ever ignore the concrete social context while framing a law. Thus for a realistic student the distinction between law as a norm and law as a sociological application is important. If we ignore any of these aspects, the balance would be lost.

The male-dominated Islamic society in the Middle East and elsewhere made social status rather than individual choice supreme. But as far as the Qur'an is concerned, it is without doubt that the individual choice is more important. However, social status may not be laid down as a criterion, though it is this kind of marriage which is invariably encountered in society. People prefer social status to individual choice and hence the Islamic jurists had to consider *kafa't* as a criterion for marriage though this may not exactly be in keeping with the qur'anic spirit. This clearly shows that absolute norms are not socially acceptable. Society is unable to keep pace with divine justice.

Child Marriage

In the Holy Qur'an there is no concept of child marriage as such. The Qur'an mentions only the concept of *nikah* irrespective of age and, as pointed out above, status. Its main concern is marriage as union between woman and man for procreation and for solace for each other[24] and not when and with whom. It would be too much to try to prove that the Qur'an allows child marriage. Some 'ulama argue that verse 65:4 of the Qur'an does talk of marriage with a girl who has not reached the age of puberty. The verse is as follows: "And those of your women who despair of menstruation, if you have a doubt, their prescribed time is three months, and of those too, *who have not had their courses*." (emphasis added). From, *"who have not had their courses"* (*walla'i lam yahidne*) the 'ulama infer that those who have not reached the age of menstruation can also marry. But the words *lam yahidne* do not necessarily mean those who have not reached the age of menstruation. On the other hand, these may mean those who do not menstruate for any physiological reasons whatsoever.[25]

In a trenchant criticism of these 'ulama, Maulana 'Usmani says that they failed to consider that the Qur'an does not require *iddah* (period of waiting) to be observed in cases of divorce without sexual intercourse; all the theologians agree on this. If this is so then these 'ulama should also uphold sexual intercourse, with those girls who are yet to menstruate, as the question of *iddah* arises only where there is the Qur'an permit such intercourse?[26] Maulana 'Usmani also tries to prove that the age of the Prophet's wife Hazrat 'A' isha was not six years at the time of *nikah* as popularly believed, but at least 16 or 17 years.[27]

Thus this shows that the Prophet's *Sunnah* also does not permit child marriage. The 'ulama often cite the Prophet's example to legitimise child marriage. This is a highly controversial issue and arouses much passion but there is evidence to show that the Prophet's marriage with 'A' isha at the age of six seems quite improbable.[28] Child marriage came to be practised in Islam under the influence of those times rather than due to the Qur'an or the *Sunnah*. Hence, there is no need to justify it today as times have changed.

However, it must be said that the 'ulama who advocate child marriage do not impose the father's decision on the girl when she grows to adulthood. Instead, she is given 'the option of puberty' technically known as *khiyar al-Bulugh*, according to which the girl who has been given in marriage in her childhood by her *wali* (marriage guardian) has the option of accepting or rejecting the marriage on reaching adulthood. This right of her's is absolute and no one can interfere with it, not even her father or any other female or male relative. Thus Fyzee says, "If a Muslim minor has been married during minority by a guardian, the minor has the right on attaining majority to repudiate such marriage."[29] Thus we see that while permitting child marriage the rights of adult women have been safeguarded by the Muslim jurists.

Concept of Mahr in Islam

Mahr or dower money is an essential part of Islamic marriage. Without *mahr* a *nikah* cannot be said to have been properly solemnised. Dower money must be paid or fixed before the solemnisation of a marriage and it is the exclusive preserve of the woman or the bride to determine the amount. Also *mahr* belongs to the wife alone. Neither her father nor husband can claim it. She can spend it the way she likes. However, the Qur'an does not use the word *mahr*, but either *saduqatun* or *ujurun*. *Saduqatun* is derived from *sadaqa* which means truthfulness, sincerity and a gift given as an act of virtue. It is not something to show off one's social or financial status.[30]

Thus it would be seen that according to the Islamic concept the bridegroom must pay to the bride some amount as a token of his love, truthfulness and sincerity. No doubt its origin is pre-Islamic and tribal and it is essentially a bride-price but Islam elevated it from being merely a bride-price to being a token of love, truthfulness and sincerity. Another word used for dower in the Qur'an is *nahlah*. *Nahlah*, according to Raghib, is something given without any expectation in return, i.e. purely out of love and regard.[31] *Nahlah* is derived from *nahl*, which means honey. Thus *nahlah* is something sweet yielded by the honeybee without any expectation in return. Similarly, *mahr* is what is given purely for love, not for any return. Thus the concept of *mahr* was greatly refined by the Qur'an.

The Qur'an repeatedly exhorts men to give *mahr* to the women they intend to marry. It says: "And give women their dowries as a free gift. But if they of themselves be pleased to give you a portion thereof, consume it with enjoyment and pleasure."[32] Thus, the *mahr* should be a free gift and the husband can enjoy it only if the *wife* permits it, not otherwise. This verse makes it quite clear that it is the wife who fully owns the amount or *mahr* and it is for her to allow her husband to enjoy part of it if she agrees to remit it.

Also, the Qur'an does not specify any *mahr*. It is right of the bride to demand as much as she desires. It could be nominal or it could be quite substantial. Where the husband has no capacity to pay, it could be as nominal as an iron ring or teaching.[33] Also, it could be quite substantial if the woman insists on it. There is no limit to it. It could be, as the Qur'an says, even a heap of gold.[34] No ceiling could be fixed for *mahr*. When the second Caliph and a close companion of the Prophet tried to fix a ceiling on *mahr*, a woman stood up and recited this verse from the Qur'an: And if you wish to have (one) wife in place of another and you have given one of them a heap of gold, take nothing from it. Would you take it by slandering (her) and (doing) her manifest wrong?"[35] Hazrat 'Umar on hearing this had to withdraw the proposed ceiling.

The husband thus cannot take back the dowry which he has given to his wife at the time of divorce. It can be taken back only if the wife wishes to have a divorce called *'Khula'*, which we will discuss at an appropriate place in the next chapter. If, however, divorce takes place before the consummation of the marriage, the husband need not pay the entire amount agreed to by way of *mahr* but only half of it. Thus the Qur'an says: "And if you divorce them before you have touched them and you have appointed for them a portion (pay) half of what you have appointed unless they forgo or he forgoes in whose hand is the marriage tie. And it is nearer to dutifulness that you forgo. Nor neglect the giving of free gifts between you.

This verse not only says that the husband has to pay half the amount of dower if marriage is not consummated, but it also exhorts him to forgo that half too, if he has paid the entire amount to his wife before consummation of the marriage. It also says that even if no dowry has been agreed upon and divorce takes place before consummation, the husband must show consideration to his divorced wife and give her some gifts. Thus we see that the Qur'an shows maximum consideration to women and tries to safeguard their rights in every possible manner. Some 'ulama even maintain that even if marriage has not been consummated and husband and wife spend some time together, the husband will have to pay the full dower amount. Imam Malik holds this view. According to Imam Abu Hanifah, even a moment spent together would necessitate full payment of the dower.[36]

Thus even if a person is impotent but spends some time with his wife he has to pay the full amount of the dower. Of course, his impotency will become a ground for obtaining divorce, as we will see in the next chapter. Also, if *mahr* has not been fixed in advance the *qadi* can do so in keeping with her status or in keeping with the *mahr* given to other women in her family. It is known as *mahr-i-mithl* (an equivalent amount of *mahr*). Here too the underlying idea is that she should not suffer and should get due.

According to *Hedaya*, contracting a marriage without mention of *mahr* is valid. Thus it says:

> A marriage is valid, although no mention be made of the dower by the contracting parties, because the term *nikah*, in its literal sense, signifies a contract of union, which is fully accomplished by the junction of man and woman; moreover, the payment of dower is enjoined by the law merely as a token of respect for its object (the man), wherefore mention of it is not absolutely essential to the validity of a marriage and, for the same reason, a marriage is also valid, although the man were to engage in the contract on the special condition that there should be no dower; but this is contrary to the doctrine of Malik.[37]

I think it is not only contrary to the doctrine of Malik, but it is also contrary to the doctrine of the Qur'an itself. The Qur'an is very specific about *mahr* being an integral part of a marriage that no contract will be valid without *mahr* ultimately being paid, though it may not be mentioned at the time of the contract. That is why the 'ulama evolved the concept of *mahr-i-mithl'* as mentioned above. If no *mahr* has been fixed or mentioned at the time of marriage *mahr-i-mithl* will have to be paid by the husband. Also, part of the mahr could be paid at the time of *nikah*, which is known as *mahr-i-mu'ajjal* (immediately paid portion of the *mahr*) and part of it could be paid at a later date or at the time of divorce. This is known as *mahr-i-muwajjal* (deferred portion of the *mahr*). Generally, at the time of *nikah* both the portions of *mahr* are separately specified. *Mahr* also often acts as a security against divorce though it is not its original intent, as specified above.

Conditions in Marriage

Since marriage is contractual in Islam either side can validly lay down certain conditions. It is technically known as *khayar al-Shart* (choice to put conditions). However, the option to annul the marriage is not mentioned as a condition *per se* in the contract.

That which is mentioned as a condition in this case is a particular quality—such as the bride's virginity or the groom's possessing a university degree—in a manner that if the said quality is not found to exist the other party shall have a right to annul the contract.[38] There is a difference of opinion about the validity of a contract if its conditions are not fulfilled. The Maliki, the Shafi'i, the Imamiyyah and the Hanbali schools have said: "The condition is valid and if not satisfied, results in the spouse laying the condition acquiring the option of either unfolding or annulling the contract".[39]

Muta' Marriage

Muta' marriage is a temporary contract of marriage and is valid only among the Ithna 'ashari' Shi'as, also known as the Imamiyyahs. In a *muta'* marriage the period of the validity of the contract is mentioned, after which the marriage stands automatically annulled. The Imamiyyahs maintain that the validity of *muta'* marriage is mentioned in the Qur'an in chapter 4 (verse 24). However, other Muslims reject this interpretation of the words *'famastamt' atum 'bihi'*. A Shi'a commentator says:

> This timed alliance or a temporary marriage or wedding was current in the time of the Holy Prophet during the Kalifate of Abu Bakr and also for some time during the regime of Omar, who later at his own choice against the sanction of the Holy *Qur'an,* which is always and in all matters irrevocable and which position was respected even by Abu Bakr and even by himself for half the term of his own regime as the Kalif, revoked *muta'* by mounting the pulpit and declaring: 'Two *mutas'* as were in force during the time of the Holy Prophet. I decree now both of them as unlawful and will punish those who practise them.[40]

The same commentator adds:

> That it (i.e. muta') is an inferior form of marriage is admitted. See the discourse of the divine Hisham or this in 'Kafi'. It is thus not desirable unless there exist special reasons and circumstances calling for it and making the normal permanent marriage undesirable. Such circumstances do arise, everyone knows.

Thousands of persons are obliged to remain for long periods away from home and are forced for various reasons to leave their wives at home. To deny a temporary marriage to them is either to force them to celibacy or to drive them to clandestine practices.[41]

The noted commentator Zamakhshari also discusses *muta'* marriage while dismissing verse 24 of chapter 4. Defining *muta'* marriage, he says it is a marriage for a known period of time, say, a night, or two, or a week or more; the man fulfils his desire and then releases the woman. It is called *muta'* as he benefits or enjoys (*muta'* literally means enjoyment).[42] Zamakhshari also says that it might mean the benefit which women derive in return. He notes that it is said that this verse was revealed when Mecca was conquered. It remained valid for three days and was then abrogated. He also quotes from the *Holy Prophet* to the effect that 'I had permitted you to practice *muta'* but Allah has prohibited it until the day of judgement'. He goes on to quote Ibn 'Abbas (who was the Prophet's companion) who maintained that the above verse was never abrogated; he used to recite the verse as *"famastamt 'atum bihi minhunna ila ajalin musamma* (take benefit of these women for a specified time). He, however, reports that Ibn, 'Abbas recanted from this view and held before his death that *muta'* was not permissible.[43] Thus we see that there are contradictory positions on this temporary form of marriage.

An Iranian Shi'a scholar compares the *muta'* marriage with Bertrand Russell's concept of temporary marriage and quotes him from his book *Marriage and Morals* at length, concluding:

That which Judge Lindsey and Russell call 'companionate marriage', though it is a little different from temporary Islamic marriage, clearly shows that thinkers like them have gone to the root of the problem and are satisfied on the point that the usual permanent marriage is not itself sufficient for social requirements.[44]

According to the Shi'a scholar, it is necessary to procreate as far as the *muta'* marriage is concerned. Its sole purpose seems to be fulfilment of sexual desire. He says: As far as we know, the Church forbids birth control but according to Islam, if the husband and wife prevent the birth of a child at the point of conception it is permissible. When the pregnancy has already begun, Islam, in no case allows abortion. When the Shi'ite jurists say that the aim of permanent marriage is to have children, and the aim of temporary marriage is gratification and satisfaction of the sexual instincts, they mean the same thing.[45]

Thus we see that the *muta'* marriage has no common acceptability in the Islamic world. It is legitimised only by the Shi'ites of the Imamiyyah persuasion. Just as Bertrand Russell's concept of temporary marriage did not find many takers in the Western world, the acceptance of the *muta'* marriage also remained quite limited in the Eastern world.

Maintenance of the Wife

The Qur'an puts the entire burden of maintenance of the wife on the husband whatever her own wealth and income. She is not obliged to give her husband anything from her income. Even if a husband is poor and she is wealthy, the husband has to give her maintenance according to his capacity. There are different verses on maintenance of the wife in the holy book. Thus it says:

> Let him who has abundance spend out of his abundance, and whoever has his means of subsistence straitened to him, let him spend out of that which Allah has given him. Allah lays not on any soul a burden beyond that which he has given it. Allah brings about ease after difficulty. (65:7).

Thus a man who has abundant means must spend abundantly on his wife and if his means are scarce he should spend accordingly but he must maintain his wife.

It is to be noted that maintenance includes food, residence and clothing. About residence the Qur'an says:

> Lodge them where you live according to your means, and injure them not to straiten them. And if they are pregnant spend on them until they lay down their burden. Then if they suckle for you, give then their recompense, and enjoin one another to do good; and if you disagree, another will suckle for you. (65:6)

Thus we see from the above verse that the Qur'an broadened the concept of the wife's maintenance. The husband will have to spend extra, if necessary, to maintain her during her pregnancy. Not only that, she should be paid recompense for suckling the child. If she does not agree either because of inadequate recompense or for other reasons he should employ a wet nurse. I think this is the ultimate in the concept of the maintenance of a wife. No other scripture or system of law has provided so much for the wife by way of maintenance. It may seem odd that the mother should be paid for suckling her own child. But for suckling she needs extra energy which can come only from better and richer food and hence she should be compensated by her husband. Along with this the Qur'an also uses the words "to enjoin one another to do good". This is to exhort both husband and wife that they should not view their relationship only in material terms but in the human and moral dimensions as well.

For food and clothing the Qur'an asks the husband to provide for the mother of his children. It says: "And maintenance and their clothing must be borne by the father according to usage (or in a fair manner)." (2:233) Thus it can be seen that in the above qur'anic verses all aspects of maintenance have been covered quite comprehensively. We would like to throw some more light on the concept of maintenance in Islamic Shari'ah.

Maintenance of the wife is obligatory for the husband as well as that of his parents and children. As far as the wife is concerned, she is not obliged to spend on her husband but she can do so of her own free will if she possesses the means of doing so. However, it is obligatory for the husband to maintain his wife whatever his means, abundant or scarce. Maintenance, as pointed out above, includes the provision of food, clothing and shelter. However, food does not mean raw food but cooked food. She is not obliged to cook food. Similarly, it is not enough to give her a piece of cloth; she should be given sewn clothes or her husband should bear the sewing charges. And as for residences, she can demand a separate house to live in and is not obliged to live with her husband's parents. However, if he cannot provide a separate house, he is obliged to provide a separate portion of it with separate access to it.[46] Maintenance also includes apart from food, clothing and housing, items like soap, oil, water, medicines and other things necessary for her comfortable living.[47]

It should be noted that maintenance in Islamic Shari'ah is obligatory on the husband when the wife begins to live with him and allows physical intimacy after marriage, provided of course she is capable of it. He has to pay for her maintenance when she is living with her parents and the husband has not invited her to live with him or has no good reason for not inviting her to live with him.[48] Also, if the husband has not paid the *mahr mu'ajjal* (the immediate amount of *mahr* to be paid) and if for this reason the wife refuses to go to live with him then it will be obligatory for him to pay her maintenance because basically it is his fault and hence he must pay for her maintenance. Thus he must do even if he had no physical intimacy with her.

Even if the wife becomes old or is struck with madness or falls sick and is not capable of intimacy, it will be obligatory for the husband to pay her maintenance. However, if she falls sick before coming to the husband's house and is not capable of sexual intercourse, her maintenance will not be obligatory for the husband. If she is imprisoned for a crime committed by her the husband will not be responsible for her maintenance, but if the husband is imprisoned for no fault of hers, it will be obligatory for him to maintain her. Also, if the wife refuses to comply with conjugal obligations (*nashizah*) and leaves her husband's house without any reason or turns out her husband from the house (if it belongs to her), then the husband will not be obliged to maintain her. But if she turns *nashiza* and does not live in her husband's house and does not allow him sexual intercourse, even then she would be entitled to maintenance. Also if it is proved that separation between her and her husband has taken place on account of her fault, she would not be entitled to maintenance.[49]

A woman has the right to demand maintenance dues from her husband.[50] If the husband is absent she can take a loan for her maintenance and her husband will be obliged to pay it back provided court has fixed the amount of maintenance. This is so according to the Hanafis. But the Hanbalis, the Malikis and the

Shafi'i is give her this right without her having to go to court. She can take a loan in her husband's name without obtaining any court decree.[51] It is also laid down in the Shari'ah that any agreement with the wife that the husband will not be bound to pay her maintenance will not be valid and the husband will have to pay her maintenance despite any such agreement.

These are some of the aspects of the maintenance of a wife that we have considered here. We have not gone into more detail as the intention here is only to show how much consideration is shown for her conjugal rights in the Qur'an and the Islamic Shari'ah.[52] We will deal with maintenance of a divorcee in the next chapter.

Notes and References

1. *Sahih Bukhari* vol. III (Lahore, 1980), *Babun Nikah,* p. 67.
2. Ibid., p. 67.
3. Ibid.
4. Ibid., pp. 68-9.
5. The *Qur'an.* 4:25.
6. See f.n. 535 on p. 187 of Maulana Muhammad Ali's *Holy Qur'an* (Lahore. 1973)
7. See f.n. 3, p. 101 of Muhammad Asad's *The Message of the Qur'an,* Dar al-Andalus (Gibraltar, 1980).
8. Maulana Muhammad Ali, op. cit., p. 187.
9. *Sunan Abu Da'ud,* vol. II (Karachi. n.d.), Bab 153, p. 193.
10. Muhammad Asad, op. cit., p. 130, f.n. 147.
11. Parvez, *Matalib al-Furqan* (Lahore, 1979), vol. III, p. 345.
12. Ibid., p. 346.
13. Ibid.
14. *Sahih Bukhari,* op. cit., vol. III, p. 165.
15. Ibid., vol. III, p. 72.
16. Ibid., vol. III, p. 73.
17. Maulana Muhammad Ali, op. cit., p. 197, f.n. 561.
18. Maulavi Chiragh Ali, *A 'azamul Kalam fi irtiqa' 'Al-Islam,* vol. II, p. 21; *Tafsir al-Manar,* vol. IV, p. 350; cf. Hafiz Muhammad Sarver Qureshi, *Namus-e-Rasul* (Kauhat, Pakistan, 1979), pp. 42-3.

19. *Sahih Bukhari*, op. cit., vol. III, p. 92.
20. Ibid.
21. J. Schacht, *Origins of Muhammadan Jurisprudence* (Oxford, 1950), pp. 283-4.
22. *Hedaya* (*Commentary on Islamic Laws*), Eng tr. by Charles Hamilton (Delhi, 1987), p. 40.
23. Ibid.
24. The *Qur'an* 30:21.
25. See Muhammad Asad, *The Message of the Qur'an,* op. cit., p. 873, f.n. 1.
26. Maulana Umar Ahmad 'Usmani, *Fiqh al-Qur'an* (Karachi, 1980). vol. I, p. 533.
27. Ibid., pp. 531-32.
28. See Abu Tahir Irfani, *Saiyyidah 'A' isha Siddiqah ki 'Umr* (Bombay, n.d.).
29. Asaf A.A. Fyzee, *Outline of Muhammadan Law* (Oxford University Press, 1974), 4th edition, p. 94.
30. See *Al-Munjid* (Beirut, 1956), under '*sadaqa'*.
31. Raghib, *Al-Mufradat fi Gharib al-Qur'an* (Beirut, n.d.), p. 485.
32. The *Qur'an* 4:4.
33. *Sahih Bukhari,* op. cit., pp. 95-6.
34. The *Qur'an* 4:20.
35. Ibid.
36. Maulana 'Umar Ahmad Usmani, *Fiqh al-Qur'an*, op. cit., vol. I, p. 550.
37. *Hedaya*, op. cit., p. 44.
38. *Al-Tawhid*, Tehran, vol. IV, no. 4, July-September 1987, p. 43.
39. Ibid., p. 44.
40. S.V. Mir Ahmad Ali, *The Holy Qur'an: Full Commentary* (Karachi, 1977), vol. I, p. 537.
41. Ibid., p. 538.
42. Zamakhshari, *Al-Kashshaf* (Beirut, 1977), vol. I, p. 519.
43. Ibid.
44. Murtada Mutahhari, *The Rights of Women in Islam* (Tehran, 1981), pp. 33-4.
45. Ibid., p. 42.
46. *Fatwa 'Alamgiri* (Kanpur, Matba' Muhammadi, n.d.), vol II, *Kitab al-Nikah*, p. 147. See also 'Ubaid Allah bin Mas'ud, *Shar*

al-Wiqavah. Urdu tr. (Karachi, 1959), p. 491; also *Fatwa Qazi Khan* (Delhi.n.d.) vol. I, p. 196.

47. *Fatwa 'Alamgiri,* op. cit., vol. II, p. 144.
48. See *Quduri* (Karachi, n.d.) p. 173 and Ibn Nujaym, *Bahr al-Ra iq* (Cairo 1311 AH), vol. IV, p.194.
49. See Dr. Tanzil–ur Rahman, *Majmu'ah-e-Qawanin-e-Islam* (Islamabad, 1981), vol. I, pp. 312-13.
50. Here it should be noted that the Hanafis do not give her the right to past maintenance but all other schools – the Sahfi'i the Hanbali, the Maliki, etc. – do so.
51. See *Bahr al-Ra'iq,* op. cit., vol. IV, p. 214.
52. Ibid., vol. IV, p. 203.

6

WOMEN AND DIVORCE IN ISLAM

Divorce is permissible in Islam as marriage is considered to be a contract, which can be dissolved either by mutual consent or by either party to the contract. Contrary to popular belief, Islam also allows women the right to divorce. A woman can repudiate her marriage under a form of divorce known as *'Khula'*.

Divorce, it is true, ruins the relationship between two human beings and hence it is something to be avoided as far as possible. However, in certain circumstances, it becomes absolutely necessary. Marriage cannot always be treated as an indissoluble tie. When marriage is treated as a sacrament, as in Hinduism or Christianity, it becomes indissoluble and hence divorce is not, strictly speaking, possible. But when marriage is treated as a contract, its dissolution and hence divorce become a natural concept. Though divorce can often be misused by the stronger party—and by men in a male-dominated society—its total absence can also become problematic when the relationship between husband and wife gets strained beyond any possibility of reconciliation. This often happens, between modern day couples who are highly conscious of their rights. In medieval times, women were subordinate to men's authority and hence remained submissive to them and the possibility of divorce seldom arose.

However, this was not so in the Arabian society of pre-Islamic days. The women, though under the overall authority of men, did retain a degree of independence. The concept of marriage was contractual, which Islam retained as it ensured a more equitable partnership in the marital relationship. However, it did improve upon the woman's overall status and gave her greater dignity and a sense of freedom possible within that societal framework. It permitted divorce, but at the same time, it described it as *abghaz al-Mubahat* (most disliked of permissible acts).[1] It should be noted that marriage or *nikah* has been described by the Qur'an as *mithaq-i-ghaliz* (a strong covenant).[2] It should not be taken lightly and should not be dissolved except in extraordinary circumstances. The Holy Qur'an discourages divorce. About the dissension of Zayad (the Prophet's manumitted slaved and adopted son) with his wife Zayanab the Qur'an says, "And when thou said to him to whom Allah had shown favour and to whom thou had shown a favour: Keep thy wife to thyself and keep thy duty to Allah."[3]

Here in this verse, it is to be noted, the concept of *taqwa* (piety, to be dutiful to God) has been associated with non-approval of divorce. Again, in verse 4:19 the Qur'an discourages taking recourse to divorce. "And treat them kindly. Then if you hate them, it may be that you dislike a thing while Allah has placed abundant good in it."[4] The Qur'an also strongly disapproves of slandering one's wife just to divorce her and to take back from her the dower money given to her. It says: "If you desire exchange of a wife in place of a wife, and you have given one of them a treasure (*qintar*), do not take anything thereof. Would you, perchance, take it away by slandering her and committing a manifest sin? And how could you take away after you have given yourselves to one another, and she has received a most solemn pledge from you."[5]

Thus it would be seen that the Qur'an not only discourages divorce and charging one's wife by false accusations but also condemns taking back the dower money paid to the wife at the time of marriage. It is unethical. The Qur'an says that when there is a rift between husband and wife, an attempt should be made to appoint a *hakam* (arbitrator). And if you fear a breach between the two, appoint an arbiter from his people and an arbiter from her people. If they both desire an agreement, Allah will effect harmony between them."[6]

Here the question arises as to the role of these arbiters. Will their decision be binding on both sides or will it be only recommendatory? There are differing opinions: Imam Sahfi'i maintains that the decision will be binding while Imam Abu Hanifah thinks otherwise. Imam Sahfi'i take his one from Hazrat 'Ali who enforced the decision of the arbiters.[7]

Maulana Muhammad Ali, commenting on this verse, says:

> This verse lays down the procedure to be adopted when a case for divorce arises. It is not for the husband to put away his wife; it is the business of the judge to decide the case. Nor should divorce cases be made too public. The judge is required to appoint two arbiters, one belonging to the wife's family and the other to the husband's. These two arbiters will find out the facts but their objective must be to effect a reconciliation between the parties. If all hopes of reconciliation fail, a divorce is allowed, but the final decision for divorce rests with the judge who is legally entitled to pronounce it. Cases were decided in accordance with the directions contained in this verse in the early days of Islam.[8]

Here it should be noted that the Qur'an does not ignore the woman's interests. It requires a *hakam* to be appointed to represent her side. She is accorded an equal status with her. This was a revolutionary step judged by the standards prevailing at a time when women were totally subjugated in society. If we keep in mind the fact that among the ancient Romans as well as among the Athenians the husband's right to repudiate the wife was absolute, the privilege to the Muslim women to appoint her own arbiter in a dispute with her husband appears to be far more significant.

However, Arab women had privileges even in the pre-Islamic era. Perron in his *Femmes Arabs* says that in a few instances women of nobler families would, before marriage, reserve to themselves the power of divorcing their husbands; when they wished to exercise the power they divulged the fact of separation by merely changing the positions of their tents, indicating that the marriage had been repudiated.[9] Islam also gave the right of *talaq-*

i-tafwid (delegated right to divorce) to women but without any consideration of social status. Whatever their status, high or low, they could exercise the right of delegated divorce. Thus in matters of divorce Muslim women could not only appoint arbiters but could also exercise that right to delegated divorce. There was no distinction of caste, creed or class as far as legal rights were concerned. It was indeed a very significant aspect of the Islamic legal system.

Before we proceed further one would like to throw some light on the etymology of the word *talaq* used for divorce in the Qur'an. *Talaq* literally means untying a knot, being released from a covenant. It is a derivative of *itlaq*, which means sending away or untying the knot of marriage. The latter is the technical meaning. This word was in use during the *jahiliyah* period.[10] Thus *talaq* essentially means coming out of the marital knot and becoming free. *Itlaq* also means leaving, giving up.

The Qur'anic Method of Talaq

What is the qur'anic way of obtaining divorce? It is quite simple, and is described in Chapter 2 of the Qur'an. It says:

> Divorce may be (pronounced) twice; then keep (them) in good fellowship or let (them) go with kindness. And it is not lawful for you to take any part of what you have given them, unless both fear that they cannot keep within the limits of Allah. Then if you fear that they cannot keep within the limits of Allah there is no blame on them for what she gives up to become free thereby. These are the limits of Allah, so exceed them not; and whoever exceeds the limits of Allah, these are the wrongdoers.[11]

Here it is made clear that divorce can be given twice, not any number of times. This divorce, it should be noted, is a revocable type of divorce. In the waiting period after pronouncing divorce reconciliation can be effected. Here the question arises as to why "divorce may be pronounced twice". It has to be understood against the background of the pre-Islamic period during which the Arabs used to divorce their wives and take them back, something that might be repeated a thousand times. Thus they always had this threat hanging over them. Islam did not approve of such a practice, which was essentially designed to keep women under men's control. The Qur'an, therefore, clearly lays down that divorce could be pronounced only twice and that a third pronouncement would result in irrevocable divorce after which marriage with the woman would not be possible unless she married someone else and happened to be divorced by him. Only then could she marry her former husband again. This was done to prevent the abuse of divorce.

Divorcing a woman thrice at one sitting is considered as the last and final divorce. However, there is controversy whether three divorces could be pronounced in one sitting or such pronouncements could occur on three different occasions. According to the established practice among Muslims it could be pronounced thrice in one sitting after which a woman could not be taken back unless she married someone else who divorced her after establishing a conjugal relationship. In that case she could remarry her former husband after observing the period of *iddah*. Thus we find a *hadith* in *Bukhari* to this effect. A person divorced his wife thrice; she then married another person who also happened to divorce her. The Holy Prophet was asked whether she could marry her former husband. The Prophet said not until her latter husband had physical intimacy with her as the former husband had.[12]

Now let us take up the question of three divorces in one sitting. As pointed out before, this practice among the Sunni Muslims is very widespread and it has legal validity. Even then the jurists call it a *talaq al-aid'ah* (innovative form of divorce). Imam Abu Hanifah and Imam Malik, two great jurists of Islam, maintain that three divorces in one sitting is *bid'ah* (an innovation) and that this form of divorce is not permissible. Imam Ahmad Hanbal concurs with this view. However, Imam Sahfi'i the fourth great Imam and jurist, thinks that this form of divorce is permissible and is the husband's right.[13]

It is true that during the Prophet's lifetime and during Abu Bakr's reign and in the first two years of Hazrat 'Umar's *khilafah*, there was no practice of pronouncing three divorces in one sitting.

Even if someone pronounced three divorces in one sitting, it was treated as one.[14] However, according to 'Allama Hajar 'Asqalani 'Umar, the second Caliph enforced three divorces in one sitting in the later part of his reign as the people were impatient and did not want to wait to obtain divorce.[15] Nasa'i narrates a *hadith* according to which the Prophet, when told of a person who had divorced his wife thrice in one sitting, stood up in anger and said. "You make fun of Allah's book and I am still there among you."[16]

As we have said earlier, Imam Abu Hanifah, Imam Malik and Imam Hanbal considered three divorces in one sitting as *bid'ah* and not permissible, yet they felt that a divorce, once pronounced thrice in one sitting, would be effective. But it is said that Imam Ahmad bin Hanbal had revised his opinion in this respect and had come to the conclusion that a close study of the Qur'an reveals that there is no place for three divorces in one sitting in the holy book; it permits only *talaq-i-raj'i* (revocable divorce). He maintained that one cannot permit three divorces in one sitting or *talaq-i-battah* (irrevocable divorce). According to him, even if three divorces are pronounced they should be treated as one. The husband will have the right to revoke the divorce and enter into *nikah* with the wife again. Ibn Taymiyyah has thrown much light on this issue in his *fatwa* (religious edicts).[17]

Many eminent companions of the Prophet like 'Abdullah bin Mas'ud, 'Abdal-Rahman bin 'Awf, and Zubayr bin al-'Awam have concurred with this view.[18] Nor do the Ithna' 'Asharis and the Isma'ilis accept three divorces in one sitting. Muhammad ibn Maqatil (who is a prominent Hanafi jurist of the third generation) maintains that Imam Abu Hanifah took the position that it would be treated only as one *Raj'i* (revocable) divorce even if pronounced thrice in one sitting. However, he also agrees with the other well-known position (that it would be treated as an irrevocable divorce.)[19]

Thus it will be seen from the above discussion that except for Imam Sahfi'i no other prominent *faqih* (jurist) considers three *talaqs* in one sitting as legitimate and in accordance with the intention of the Holy Qur'an. However, Imam Abu Hanifah and Imam Malik maintain that, permissible or not, once pronounced thrice in one sitting the divorce would be valid and would result in *talaq-i-battah* (irrevocable divorce). Imam Ibn Taymiyyah, a prominent jurist of the 14th century, maintains that such a divorce will have no legal validity. Imam Taymiyyah shows that this was the position of Imam Ahmad Ibn Hanbal.[20]

Maulana 'Umar Ahmad 'Usmani maintains that according to the Qur'an and the *Sunnah*, one can give only one divorce at a time, this being the meaning of the words *Al-talaqu marratan*[21] (divorce may be pronounced twice...). The word *marratan* (twice) clearly shows that there has to be a time gap between the two divorces; it cannot be pronounced twice at the same time. Divorce can be given once at a time and the wife taken back, if so desired, by performing *nikah* afresh. This can occur once more before a man has to decide whether to retain her in good fellowship or release her in kindness. There is no question of a third divorce; it does not exist in the Qur'an. Maulana 'Usmani is not in favour of one *talaq*, each in one *tuhr* (beginning of purity after menstruation), until the third period of *tuhr* (which is called *talaq-i-hasan* or *talaq-i-Sunnah*). *Talaq* once pronounced takes place. There is no need to repeat it three times in three months (at the end of each menstrual period). After divorce is granted a woman has to observe *iddah* (three months or three menstrual cycles), after which she is free to contract another marriage, if she so desires. Thus *talaq* can be pronounced only once at a time and no more than twice after a certain time has elapsed. This is the correct qur'anic position, according to Maulana 'Usmani.[22]

The question arises as to why Hazrat 'Umar, the second Caliph, enforced *talaq-i-battah*. Muhammad Husain Haykal, the noted Egyptian Islamic scholar, says that it was done in view of the extraordinary conditions prevailing at the time. During wars of conquest many women from Syria, Egypt and other places were captured and brought to Medina. They were fair complexioned and beautiful and the Arabs were tempted to marry them. But these women were not used to living with co-wives and often made a condition that the men divorce their former wives thrice so that they could not be taken back. Little did they know that according to the Qur'an and the *Sunnah* three divorces were treated only as one divorce. The Arabs would pronounce three divorces to satisfy these Syrian and other women but later took their former wives back, giving rise to innumerable disputes. To overcome these difficulties, Hazrat 'Umar thought it fit to enforce three divorces in one sitting as an irrevocable divorce.[23]

Since then this form of divorce has become an integral part of Islamic Shari'ah among the Sunni Muslims. It is widely practised throughout the Islamic world. We have dealt with this form of divorce at length as it has been causing a great deal of concern among Muslim women. It is the most arbitrary and non-qur'anic form of divorce, and has made the lives of thousands of women most miserable. If the husband says divorce thrice, even in a state of anger or inebriation, or just for fun, the woman is irrevocably divorced and the husband, even after coming to his senses, cannot help because his pronouncement of divorce thrice has made it legally valid. No one can help the wife either. The husband cannot take her back, even if he repents. Often husbands use this form of divorce to punish their wives for not submitting to their authority.

It is very unfortunate that although Islam intended to give a woman equal status not only in marital contracts but also in matters of divorce, jurists, either enamoured by speculative reason or dictates of old traditions, or influenced by male domination, or swayed by temporary considerations, undermined the woman's position, enforcing arbitrary rules of divorce which went against her interests. She came to depend on the mercy of her husband in matters of divorce. This was so under *jahiliyah*. Islam had rejected *jahiliyah* practices which militated against the dignity of women. Hazrat 'Umar had altered the rules under the pressure of events. It was more in the nature of an ordinance by a ruler to meet a specific situation rather than a divine injunction. It is most unfortunate that it is being enforced as a Divine Law, causing a great deal of injustice to women today. It has become a man's prerogative to divorce his wife as and when he desires, the woman having no say in the matter.

As we saw: the Holy Qur'an requires arbitration before a divorce can take place and Hazrat 'Ali ruled that the decision of arbiters should be binding. That means the *qadi* or the court should have the final say in the matter. However, the prevalent practice is very different, and divorce has become the exclusive presence of the husband who, at any time, in any state of mind, can just pronounce the words *talaq, talaq, talaq*, thus sealing the wife's fate forever. She is left with no legal redress against this pronouncement. At best, she can claim the deferred amount of her *mahr*. Most of the divorces among Muslims, at least in India, take place in this manner. A sizeable number of women are suffering from its effects. However, as pointed out above, this is not the qur'anic way of divorce; it is an unfortunate innovation.

According to *hadith*, divorce must be given in a state of *tuhr*, a state of purity after menstruation. When Ibn 'Umar divorced, while his wife was in a state of menstruation, the Prophet ordered him to take her back as the divorce given in that state was not valid. The Prophet ordered Ibn 'Umar either to retain her or divorce her in a state of purity.[24] The reason for making it obligatory to divorce in a state of purity is obvious. In that state a man can cohabit with a woman and hence would be tempted to retain her. In the state of menstruation the man has to stay away and hence would be more inclined to divorce her. This may not be a very humane way of thinking, but it certainly provides a strategy to prevent divorce, taking human nature into account.

The Holy Qur'an also hints at it thus: "O Prophet", It says, "when you divorce them for their prescribed period, calculate the period."[25] It is also hinted that the period should be properly counted. During this waiting period men can take their wives back, if they desire reconciliation. Thus the Qur'an says:

> And the divorced women shall undergo, without remarrying, a waiting period of three monthly courses: for it is not lawful for them to conceal what God may have created in their wombs, if they believe in God and the Last Day. And during this period their husbands are fully entitled to take them back, if they desire reconciliation; but; in accordance with justice, the rights of the wives (with regard to their husbands) are equal to the (husbands') rights with regard to them, although men have precedence over them (in this respect.)[26]

We can draw certain conclusions from this verse. A woman has to wait for three months after divorce is pronounced for two reasons: if she has conceived, this fact would be known for sure within three months. Also, it gives sufficient time to the husband to takes her back if he desires reconciliation. Thus this verse also makes it quite clear that *talaq-i-batta* (irrevocable divorce in one sitting) is not permissible. Allah requires men to divorce their wives for the waiting period, i.e. for three months or three menstrual periods so that reconciliation can be effected during that time.

It is said in the verse that women have rights equal to those of men, making it clear that women may refuse to go back to their husbands if they so desire and that they cannot be forced against their will. It is also said in the verse that men have precedence over women as they are the breadwinners and are responsible for the maintenance of their wives. They were given the first option to take back the divorced wives but with the provision that the latter can refuse to go back to live with the husbands as they have equal rights *vis-a-vis* their husbands. But if a wife is willing to go back or wishes to marry her former husband even after the lapse of the waiting period, she should not be coerced into refusal by her father, brother or other family members. The Qur'an makes this clear when it states: "And when you divorce women and they end their term, prevent them not from marrying their husbands if they agree among themselves in a lawful manner."[27] It is said that this verse was revealed when the sister of Ma 'qil bin Yasar was divorced and after her *iddah* period wished to remarry her husband.[28] Thus it would be seen that either way a woman's right to go back to her former husband or refuse any such move on the part of her former husband is protected. She cannot be coerced. In every respect her rights should prevail.

Since in those times, men had an upper hand over women in many respects, they were exhorted in almost every verse on divorce to keep them kindly or to release them kindly.[29] The Prophet is addressed in verse 65:1 and told not to turn them out of their houses, nor should they (the wives) leave their husbands' houses unless they commit an act of open indecency. Thus a divorcee cannot be turned out of her husband's house until her case is finally decided. She simply cannot be thrown out of her home. Even after her period of waiting is over and reconciliation is not possible she should be released with kindness and when she is finally divorced, two persons should be made witnesses thereof.[30] These witnesses should be pious and truthful and should protect the interests of the weak, i.e. the wife.

Even after her husband's death the wife should not be removed from the house. She should be allowed to stay there at least for a year. Thus the Qur'an says:

> And those of you who die and leave wives behind should make a bequest in favour of their wives of maintenance for a year without turning (them) out. Then if they themselves go away, there is no blame on you for what they do of lawful deeds concerning themselves.[31]

It should be noted here that among the Arabs, marriage was not only contractual but widow remarriage was also common. Widows found other husbands without any difficulty. Often they found another husband immediately after the period of *iddah*, which was four months and ten days in the case of a widow. That this was so is hinted at by the Qur'an also.[32] A man can speak with a widow during her period of *iddah* about his intended marriage to her. This shows that widows were courted within the period of *iddah*. Thus it was quite possible that the husband's relatives would pressurise the widow to leave her husband's house after *iddah* and seek another man's hand. That is why the Qur'an exhorts the husband to make a special bequest before his death for retaining her in the house for at least a year and for her maintenance and all other benefits (in addition to her usual inheritance as a wife from a husband's property, her portion being one-eighth). Thus if this verse is read in the perspective of social conditions then prevailing, it would be seen that special care was taken to protect women's rights.[33]

The divorcees have also been taken care of. Naturally, a woman, when divorced, feels quite hurt. Something must be done to assuage her feelings if divorce becomes inevitable after the failure of all attempts to save the marriage. Thus the Qur'an says that not only should she be released from marital ties in kindness but also that provision should be made for her in kindness. The qur'anic verse states: "And the divorced women, too, shall have (a right to) maintenance in goodly manner. This is a duty for all who are fearful of God." Maulana Muhammad Ali, commenting on this verse, says, "Note that this provision (*mata'a* is in addition to the dowry, *mahr*) which must be paid to them. Just as in the previous verse, the widow is given an additional benefit; here a provision in addition to her dowry is recommended for the divorced woman. This shows the injunctions of the Holy Qur'an regarding women."[34]

Another commentator, Muhammad Asad, says: "This obviously relates to women who are divorced without any legal fault on their part. The amount of alimony payable—unless and until they remarry—has been left unspecified since it must depend on the husband's financial circumstances and on the social conditions of the time."[35] Here it must be noted that the well-known Shah Bano controversy revolved around the interpretation of this verse. The Supreme Court of India, in its judgement on Shah Bano's appeal for maintenance against her husband, upheld her right to maintenance under section 125 of the Criminal Procedure Code. The Supreme Court relied on 'Allama Yusuf 'Ali's translation of this verse in order to reinforce its judgement on maintenance. 'Allama Yusuf 'Ali translates the verse thus: "For divorced women maintenance should be provided on a reasonable scale. This is a duty of the righteous."[36]

'Allama Yusuf Ali makes it quite clear that divorced women are entitled to reasonable maintenance and that payment of this maintenance is incumbent upon the divorcing husband. The Indian Muslims fiercely opposed this judgement on the grounds that maintenance for a divorcee could not be paid beyond the period of *iddah*, which is three months or three menstrual cycles. Any maintenance beyond that period would be illegal. Thus the Supreme Court judgement was considered an interference in the Muslim personal law. Hundreds of thousands of Muslims agitated and ultimately succeeded in compelling the Rajiv Gandhi government to enact a law to annul the Supreme Court judgement. The enactment was known as the Muslim Women (Protection of Rights on Divorce) Bill, 1986.[37] Muslim sentiment could be mollified only after the passing of the bill. There were many reasons for the massive support the Muslim leadership received from the Muslim masses on this question. However, the agitation was politically motivated. It is true that in Hanafi law a divorcee is entitled to maintenance only for the period of *iddah* whereafter she is free to remarry or to revert to her parents or in their absence to other relatives.

There is nothing in this law to prevent anyone from paying maintenance beyond three months or the period of *iddah*. The argument that Muslims could not be compelled to pay beyond *iddah* was a very sound one. With the change in social circumstances the application of the law could be changed as well. It is a well-known principle pronounced by the eminent jurist Ibn Taymiyyah that the *shar'i ahkam* (injunctions) changes with the times, i.e. *zaman*. A renowned example is that of Hazrat 'Umar's enforcing *talaq-i-thalatha* (three divorces in one sitting), referred to above, which was not permissible during the Holy Prophet's lifetime and during Hazrat Abu Bakr's reign. Hazrat 'Umar enforced it in the changed circumstances. Similarly, Hazrat 'Umar had also suspended the punishment of amputation of hands during a prolonged period of famine. It also shows that laws cannot be applied in the abstract without concrete conditions having been taken into account.

The Qur'an has not fixed any time limit for maintenance. Neither the amount of maintenance nor the period has been mentioned.[38] There are two key words in the verse pertaining to maintenance: *mata'a* and *m'aruf*. These have been translated differently by the exegetists. 'Allama Yusuf 'Ali translates *mata'a* as maintenance but *m'aruf* as reasonable (scale).[39] Muhammad Asad also translates *mata'a* as maintenance but *m'aruf* as goodly manner.[40] Muhammad Pickthall interprets *mata'un bill-m'aruf* as provision in kindness.[41] A noted Indian theologian, Maulana Ashraf Ali Thanavi, translates it into Urdu as *kuch kuch fa'idah pahunch-na-qa'ide ke muwafiq*.[42] Imam Raghib defines it as something from which we benefit at home or anything from which we benefit. But while referring to verse 2:241 of the Qur'an he defines *mata'a* as something which is given for the period of *iddah*.[43]

Thus we see that scholars and exegetists have interpreted these two key words in the verse differently. Most jurists of the classical period interpreted them to mean maintenance of the period of *iddah*. And because the Supreme Court of India awarded Shah Bano maintenance beyond the period of *iddah* the Indian Muslim leaders and office bearers of the Muslim Personal Law Board decried it as an interference in the Divine Law. However, what is divine is verse 2:241 and the words *mata'a* and *bil m'Iaruf*, not their interpretation. In fact, the verse neither sets down any time period nor specifies any amount. It has been left to human understanding and the requirements of the changing times.

Some scholars of early Islam also thought that *mata'a* does not imply any time period. Imam Hasan Basri, a great scholar, a tabi'i (a follower of the companions of the Prophet), maintains that "there is no time limit regarding payment of maintenance. It should be paid according to one's capacity. His actual words are *laysa fiha shay'un muwaqqatun. Yamutta'uha 'ala qadri maysarah*."[44] Similarly, *Lisan al-'Arab*, a classical and widely accepted Arabic lexicon says, "It (*mata'a*) has no time limit, for Allah has not fixed any time limit for the fare. He has only enjoined the payment of maintenance."[45]

A Pakistani scholar, Prof. Rafiullah Shihab, in his article published in *Pakistan Times* argues that according to the principle laid down by the Hanafite jurist, "If a husband does not maintain his wife properly she can get her maintenance allowance fixed through a court. This fixed maintenance allowance will not only be paid to her as a wife but also after divorce." He goes on to cite 'Allama Nujaym, a famous jurist of the Hanafite school, who has discussed this issue in great detail in his book *Al-Bahr al-Ra'iq*. He says there is a difference of opinion among the Hanafite jurists. According to Imam Muhammad, the husband is not required to pay maintenance to his divorced wife. Imam Abu Yusuf feels differently. He is of the opinion that the husband will have to pay this amount even after divorcing her. Imam ibn Nujaym, who has cited these conflicting reports, is himself of the view that the argument over stopping the maintenance allowance of the wife after divorce is a weak one. He agrees with the consensus of the jurists that a woman not maintained properly by her husband can knock at the door of a court and get her maintenance allowance fixed by it. The husband is bound to pay this fixed amount to the wife regularly. It he refuses to do so he will be put behind bars. *If it were possible for the husband to save his skin by divorcing his wife, he would have preferred to do so.* But Islamic law does not allow him to do so (emphasis added). He will have to pay this amount even after divorcing her.[46]

The Qur'anic Verses on Divorce

Before we proceed further it would be appropriate to quote various verses on divorce from the Qur'an. This will help us understand the concept of divorce in the holy book as well as all related matters. The verses are as follows:

1. "If you fear a breach between the two appoint an arbiter from his people and an arbiter from her people. If they both desire an agreement, Allah will effect harmony between them." (4:35)

2. "If a woman fears ill usage from her husband or desertion no blame is on them if they effect a reconciliation between them. And reconciliation is better. And avarice is met within (men's) minds. And if you do good (to others) and keep your duty, surely Allah is ever Aware of what you do." (4:128)

3. "But if they separate, Allah will render them both free from want out of His ampleness. And Allah is ever Ample-giving, Wise." (4:1300)

4. "Divorce may be (pronounced) twice; then keep them in good fellowship or let (them) go with kindness. And it is not lawful for you to take any part of what you have given

them, unless both fear that they cannot keep within the limits of Allah. Then if you fear that they cannot keep within the limits of Allah there is no blame on them for what she gives up to become free thereby. These are the limits of Allah, so exceed them not; and whoever exceeds the limits of Allah, these are the wrongdoers." (2:229)

5. "So if he divorces her (the third time), she shall not be lawful to him afterwards until she marries another husband. If he divorces her, there is no blame on them both if they return to each other (by marriage), if they can keep within the limits of Allah. And these are the limits of Allah which He makes clear for a people who know." (2:230)

6. "O Prophet, when you divorce women, divorce them for their prescribed period, and calculate the period: and keep your duty to Allah, your Lord. Turn them not out of their houses—nor should they themselves go forth—unless they commit an open indecency. And these are the limits of Allah. And whoever goes beyond the limits of Allah, indeed he wrongs his own soul. Thou knowest not that Allah may after that bring about an even," (65:1)

7. "So when they have reached their prescribed time, retain them with kindness or dismiss them with kindness, and call to witness, two just ones from among you and give upright testimony for Allah. Such is the admonition given to him who believes in God and the Last Day. And for those who fear God, He (ever) prepares a way out."

8. "And when you divorce women and they reach their prescribed time, then retain them in kindness or set them free with kindness and retain them not for injury so that you exceed the limits. And whoever does this, he indeed wrongs his own soul. And take not Allah's messages for a mockery, and remember Allah's favour to you, and that which He has revealed to you of the Book and the Wisdom, admonishing you thereby. And keep your duty to Allah, and know that Allah is the knower of all things." (2:31).

9. "And those of your women who despair of menstruation, if you have a doubt their prescribed time is three months, and

of those, too, who have not had their courses. And the pregnant women, their prescribed time is that they lay down their burden. And whoever keeps his duty to Allah, He makes his affair easy for him." (65:4)

10. "O you who believe, when you marry believing women, then divorce them before you touch them; you have in their case no term which you should reckon. But make provision for them and set them free in a goodly manner." (33:49).

11. "Lodge them (during *iddah*) where you live according to your means, and annoy them not to restrict them. And if they are pregnant, spend on them until they lay down their burden. If they suckle for you, give them their recompense, and enjoin one another to do good; and if you disagree, another will suckle for him." (65:6)

12. "Let him who has abundance spend out of his abundance, and whoever has his means of subsistence straitened to him, let him spend out of that which Allah has given him. Allah lays not on any soul a burden beyond that which He has given it. Allah brings about ease after difficulty." (65:7)

13. "There is no blame on you if you divorce women while you have not touched them, not appointed for them a portion, and provide for them, the wealthy according to his means, and the straitened according to his means, a provision according to usage. (This is a duty on the doers of good." (2:236)

14. "And if you divorce them before you have touched them and you have appointed for them a portion, (pay) half of what you have appointed unless they forego or he foregoes in whose hand is the marriage tie. And it is nearer to dutifulness that you forgo. Nor neglect the giving of free gifts between you. Surely, Allah is Seer of what you do." (2:237)

15. "For divorced women maintenance (should be provided) on a reasonable scale. This is a duty of the righteous." (2:237)

We have presented above whatever has been revealed in the Holy Qur'an about divorce and related matters. First of all, divorce is discouraged. The Qur'an says that even if there is a breach between husband and wife (*shiqaq baynakum*) efforts should be made to patch it up, failing which two arbiters from both sides should be appointed. If they fail to bring about reconciliation, there may not be any blame in divorcing. Second the Qur'an says that if the husband has to divorce his wife he should not take back from her whatsoever he has given her even if it be a heap of gold (*wa ataytum ihdahunna qintaran*) (4:20). This is in case the marriage has already been consummated.

In case the marriage has not been consummated and divorce becomes inevitable (there certainly can be such situations for various reasons), the husband can demand only half of the dower which he had given to his wife. The Qur'an, however, exhorts him to forego that portion too, saying it is righteousness to do so. As of right he can demand half of what he had given but it is better if he does not do so. In case the marriage was not consummated and nothing was fixed by way of dower, it is the duty of the husband to make some provision according to usage, the rich giving according to their means and the poor according to theirs. But some provision must be made. Even where consummation has taken place and the husband has to give half of the dower he should give something more by way of free gifts. The husband is exhorted to keep his wife in kindness and release her (when it becomes necessary) in kindness. If he decides to take her back it should not be with the intention of causing physical or emotional injury to her but to keep her in kindness and with due honour and dignity. Also, if he decides to divorce his wife, she should be kept in his own house during the period of *iddah* and in the same way as he keeps himself and according to his status. If she is pregnant she should be kept with the husband until she delivers and after delivery the husband should not neglect to pay for the care of the child.

Thus we see that maximum provision has been made in the Qur'an for the divorcee so that she does not suffer, as far as possible, physically; since emotional suffering cannot always be avoided. Emotional suffering is sought to be minimised by advising the men to release her in kindness. It is very unfortunate that there is a wide gap between the ideal and the practice. Muslims themselves are to be blamed for this. What is needed is to import the qur'anic education on a much wider scale to Muslim women so that they become conscious of their qur'anic rights and the struggle to achieve them. This is not an easy enterprise, though it is quite a worthwhile one.

It would be interesting to know something of the laws made by Islamic countries on arbitration between husband and wife before a divorce takes place. In Egypt, arbitration has been provided for in the *Text of Egyptian Family Law 1920-1929*. Article 25 states: "Arbitration shall be undertaken by two persons eligible to act as witnesses under the Islamic law of evidence, one each either from the families of the spouses or from amongst persons knowing their circumstances, and possessing the ability to effect a reconciliation." The law requires that "the arbitrators shall be bound to make all enquiries into the causes of discord and to take all possible measures to effect a reconciliation." The arbitrators are required to report their award to the *qadi* who shall pronounce judgement on the basis of the award.[47]

The Ottoman Law of Family Rights, 1917, makes provision for arbitration in its Articles 130 and 131. This is, it must be noted, in accordance with the Maliki school of jurisprudence. If there is a dispute between husband and wife and either of them approaches the court, an arbiter from both sides will be appointed. Outsiders can also be appointed if suitable persons from the husband's and the wife's families are not available. This is known as a "Family Council". It hears the parties' grievances, closely examines them and makes all possible efforts to effect a reconciliation. And if reconciliation is not possible and the fault lies with the husband, he will be asked to divorce his wife; where the wife is found to be at fault she will be granted *'Khula'* in lieu of part or all of the dower. If the arbitrators cannot agree then either other arbitrators from the respective families shall be appointed or help sought from an impartial umpire whose decision would be binding on both the parties.[48]

In Pakistan under the Muslim Family Laws Ordinance, 1961, an arbitration council has been provided for. The "arbitration council means a body consisting of the chairman and a representative of each of the parties to a matter dealt within."[49] This Ordinance provided that where any party fails to nominate a representative within the prescribed time, the body formed without such a representative shall be the arbitration council. The Ordinance further lays down that "within thirty days of the receipt of notice under sub-section (1) the chairman shall constitute an arbitration council for the purpose of bringing about a reconciliation between the parties, and the arbitration council shall take all necessary steps to bring about such reconciliation."[50]

In Iran major changes were introduced in 1967 in the Family Protection Laws known as *Qanun-i-Khanwadah-i*. Amongst other decisions it laid down that:

1. All family disputes could be referred by the courts for settlement to arbitrators;
2. Every divorce, in whatever form, must be preceded by an application to the court for the issuing of a certificate of 'irreconcilability' (*gawahi-i-adam imkani sazish*) which has been exhausted:
3. The court could grant a certificate of 'irreconcilability' and a decree of *faskh* (annulment) to a petitioner on the grounds of the other party's imprisonment for five years, addiction to dangerous habits, bigamous marriage, desertion or conviction for an offence repugnant to the status of the family.[51]

However, after the Islamic revolution all previous laws and amendments were declared null and void and it was laid down that only the Islamic laws in accordance with the Ja'fari Ithna 'Ashari school would be recognised and that those who follow other schools of Islamic law like the Hanafi, the Maliki, the Sahfi'i and the Hanbali would be judged accordingly.

'Khula' (woman's right to divorce)

Now we would like to throw some light on a woman's right to divorce. Islam is probably the first religion in the world to have recognised such a right. It is called *'Khula'* which literally means to disown or to repudiate, for a woman can repudiate her marriage. It has been referred to in the Qur'an in the following words: "Then if you fear that they cannot keep within the limits of Allah, there is no blame on them for what she gives up to become free thereby."[52] It should be noted that the wife's right to *'Khula'* is absolute and no one can prevent her from exercising it.

The case of Jamilah, the wife of Thabit ibn Qais, reported by numerous authorities, goes to prove this. She was quite dissatisfied with her marriage though there was no quarrel between husband and wife. She plainly stated to the Prophet that she did not find any fault with her husband on account of his morals or his religion; it was just that she hated him. The Prophet allowed divorce provided she returned to her husband the orchard which he had made over to her as her *mahr*.[53] We also learn of repudiation of marriage by a woman called Burairah who had married Mughith. When she decided to obtain *'Khula'*, Mughith wept bitterly, tears rolling down his cheeks into his beard. The Prophet addressing ibn 'Abbas, his companion, said, "don't you wonder about Mughith's passionate love for Burairah and her equally passionate hatred for him?" The Prophet asked Burairah whether she could take him back. Burairah thereupon asked the Prophet, "Are you ordering me?" He said, "No, I am only recommending Mughith's case to you. Burairah thereupon said. "I do not need him." She persisted in asking for *'Khula'*.[54] Thus it was that Burairah turned down even the Prophet's recommendation and insisted on her right to repudiate her marriage.

Of course, there is a difference of opinion among the jurists as to whether *'Khula'* is divorce or *faskh*, i.e. simply annulment of marriage. Some feel that it is divorce in as much as the husband has to pronounce it after the wife returns the dower, in part or full, as agreed upon. Others maintain that it is only *faskh* (repudiation) and occurs soon after the wife returns the dower and sits at her home. There is no need, according to this view, for the husband to pronounce divorce (*yanfasakhun nikah min ghayri tatliq*, i.e. the *nikah* is repudiated without pronouncement of divorce.[55] That it is *faskh* and not divorce is also proved by the fact that the Prophet ordered the wife of Thabit ibn Qais to observe *iddah* of one menstrual period only, whereas in divorce a woman is required to observe *iddah* for three menstrual periods.[56] It is also said that it is divorce in words though *faskh* in reality.

Conditions Governing *'Khula'*

A wife can initiate *'Khula'* and win judicial dissolution of her marriage on account of any physical defect in her husband, of ill-treatment and of legal cruelty. The charges of legal cruelty (*darar*) are numerous and vary from locality to locality, though uniform guidelines are found regarding this in Shari'ah legal manuals.[57] The inability or unwillingness of the husband to consummate the marriage on account of life imprisonment, mutilation or sentence of death will constitute *darar*. Not only that; if the man becomes unable to fulfil his marital obligations, such as providing shelter and maintenance, the woman may be entitled to *'Khula'*.[58]

What the woman needs to do in these circumstances is to sue for *'Khula'* in a court and produce witnesses to establish her case. If the evidence is in her favour, she wins a judicial divorce from the court; if otherwise, the court may dismiss her case.[59] However, according to another school of thought, a woman needs no particular grounds and the court has to agree to *'Khula'* or the *qadi* will order it. When the wife of Thabit took up her *'Khula'* case with the Prophet she was only requested to return her *mahr*, which was an orchard. She did so and won *'Khula'*.[60] The question arises whether she will be entitled to maintenance, as in any other form of *talaq* during the *iddah* period. It is maintained that as long as *'Khula'* is repudiation of the *ba'in* category[61] the woman is not entitled to maintenance during the *iddah* except when she is pregnant. She is also not entitled to clothing during this type of *iddah* but she has a right to accommodation. She may, however, lose any of these entitlements if she chooses—in seeking *'Khula'*—to redeem herself of any of them.[62]

There may be an element of uncertainty about the *'iwad* (refund or compensation for the *'Khula'* agreed to). The *'Khula'* will be valid despite this element of uncertainty. For example, a woman redeems herself through an agreement that she will finance her child's education up to the university level. Should the child fail to gain admission into a university, or if it dies in infancy, the woman will gain some amount of money which otherwise should have been spent on the child's education. In either of the two cases, the husband is not required by law to seek refund of such money gained from the divorced wife. But if the woman should be deducted from her estate as a debt before distributing the residue passes to her heirs.[63] The legal manuals also deal with cases where a pregnant woman seeks *'Khula'* by agreeing to maintain the baby she is expecting and then gives birth to twins.

Divorce by a Sick Person

Another interesting matter that is dealt with is that of divorce by a sick person and a woman's right to inheritance. Here also Islamic law has been quite meticulous in defining and protecting the divorce's rights. The four schools differ though on the rights of a woman who is divorced irrevocably by her sick husband who dies from the same sickness. The Hanafis entitle her to inherit as long as she is in *iddah*, provided the husband is considered attempting to bar her from inheritance and the divorce takes place without her consent. In the absence of any of these two conditions she will not be entitled to inherit. The Hanabalis maintain that she will inherit from him as long as she does not remarry, even if her *iddah* terminates.[64]

The Malikis are of the view that will inherit from him even after marriage. *Al-Shafi'i* has given three different opinions, one of them being that she will not inherit even if he dies while she is observing *iddah*. This is the harshest provision against women.[65] It is to be noted that except for the Imamiyyah the other schools speak of a divorce by a sick person only if it is irrevocable. But the Imamiyyah observed that if he divorces her while he is sick, she will inherit from him, irrespective of the divorce being irrevocable or revocable, on the realisation of the following four conditions:

1. That the husband's death occurs within a year of the date of divorce. Thus, if he dies a year after the divorce, even if only by an hour, she will not inherit from him.
2. That she does not remarry before his death. If she does and he dies within a year (of the divorce), she will not inherit.
3. That he does not recover from the illness during which he divorced her. Thus if he recovers and then dies within a year, she will not be entitled to inherit.
4. That the divorce does not take place at her request.[66]

Talaq-i-Tafwid (Delegated Right to Divorce)

This is also something in favour of women. It protects their rights. In this form of divorce a man, at the time of marriage, can delegate his right to divorce his wife, and she can exercise it when any of the conditions of the marital contract are violated. However, this would not deprive the husband of his own right to divorce his wife under certain circumstances.[67] *Tafwid-e-talaq* (delegation of the power to divorce) means to give the right to divorce to one's wife. A woman can include this as a condition of her marital contract, saying she would exercise the right to divorce herself on his behalf. The personal law in Syria has also accepted this right of the husband to delegate the power of divorce to his wife.[68]

If a woman has the right to divorce, delegated to herself either before or after marriage, she can separate herself from her husband by divorcing herself. This divorce would be considered as valid as if the husband himself has given it. It is to be noted that after having delegated this right to his wife, the husband cannot revoke it because after delegation it is the wife, who owns this right on his behalf.[69]

This right to delegate divorce can prove very useful to the wife if the man takes another wife without her consent or if he neglects her or deserts her or violates any other marriage condition or does anything which the wife disapproves. If it is, no doubt, a novel concept, which does not exist in any other legal system, and it undoubtedly provides extra security to a married woman. She can stipulate it as one of the conditions of marriage. From this it can be seen that in addition to the Holy Qur'an

Muslim jurists have also taken care to protect women's rights and interests.

Divorce Under State of Intoxication

There are differing opinions about the validity of a divorce granted under a state of intoxication. Imam Abu Hanifah feels that if one is intoxicated and one has entered the state of intoxication at one's own will and pronounces divorce in this condition, the divorce should be valid.[70] However, according to Imam Malik, such a divorce is invalid. Imam Sahfi'i agrees with him. According to another report, Sahfi'i accepts divorce under intoxication as valid. Even Imam Ahmad bin Hanbal disapproves of divorce under the influence of liquor, especially when the man is so intoxicated that he cannot distinguish between good and bad.[71] Neither the Zahiris nor the J'afaris accept the validity of a divorce in a state of inebriation.[72] Nor does Imam ibn Taymiyyah.[73] Pronouncement of divorce by a man under threat is not recognised as valid either. It is called *talaq-i-mukrah*. If a person has no intention to divorce and yet does so under threat to his life or some other threat, such a divorce will have no validity. Imam Malik, Imam Hanbal, and Imam Sahfi'i do not accept the validity of this type of divorce. But *talaq-i-mukrah* acquires validity if the husband has the intention of doing so.[74] This protects the interests of women. If a divorce pronounced under threat is recognised it will go against their interests. So care has been taken to see that such a divorce is not recognised.

Muslim women have also been given the right to obtain divorce on grounds such as the disappearance of the husband (*mafqud al-khabar*), non-payment of maintenance, imprisonment of the husband for a long term, impotency, etc. This right is separate from her right to *'Khula'* because in *'Khula'* it is her dislike of the husband which makes her repudiate the marriage, for which she has to return all or part of the *mahr* or any property given her by her husband. But if she asks for divorce on the above grounds, it will be divorce by the husband obtained through the *qadi* and she will not be obliged to return the *mahr* and it will be without prejudice to her other rights. In the case of the disappearance of the husband, the latter will be taken as dead after a reasonable period of time has elapsed, ranging from four years to the average life span of a man; this varies according to the schools of jurisprudence. She will be allowed to remarry after observing *iddah* which she would otherwise have observed on the death of her husband.[75]

Clearly women's interests have been taken into account as far as possible in matters of divorce, even by the classical jurists of Islam in the formulation of Shari'ah injunctions.

Notes and References

1. Imam Hajar al-'Asqalani, *Bulugh al-Maram* (Benaras, 1982), p. 312.
2. The *Qur'an* 4:21.
3. Ibid., 33:37.
4. Ibid., 4:19.
5. Ibid., 4:20-21.
6. Ibid., 4:35.
7. Al-Razi, *Al-Tafsir al-Kabir (Dar al-Fikr*, Beirut, 1981), vol. V, section X, p. 96.
8. Maulana Muhammad Ali, *Holy Qur'an* (Lahore, 1973), p. 200, f.n. 573.
9. See Shukri Ahmad, "Muhammadan Law of Marriage and Divorce" (New York, 1977), p. 93, cited in Dr. Zeenat Shaukat Ali, *Marriage and Divorce in Islam* (Bombay, 1987), p. 165.
10. Hajar 'Asqalani, op. cit., *Bab al-Talaq*, p. 312.
11. The *Qur'an* 2:229.
12. See *Sahih Bukhari*, op. cit., vol. III, p. 134. *Bab al-Talaq*
13. See Maulana 'Umar Ahmad 'Usmani, *Fiqh al-Qur'an*, op. cit., vol. II, p. 204.
14. See Imam Hajar *Al-Asqalani, Bulugh al-Maram*, op. cit., p. 314.
15. Ibid.
16. Ibid., pp. 314-15.
17. See *Fatwa ibn Taymiyyah* (Cairo, n.d.), vol. III, p. 22.
18. See also Al-Shaukani, *Nayl al-Awtar* (Egypt, n.d.), vol. VI, pp. 25-57.
19. *Ighathat al-Lahfan* (Egypt, 1961), vol. I, p. 308.

20. See *Fiqh al-Qur'an*, op. cit., vol. II, p. 209.

21. The *Qur'an* 2:29

22. See *Fiqh al-Qur'an*, op. cit., vol II, pp. 220-1. See also Muhammad Hussain Haykal, Al-Faruq 'Umar (Cairo, 1364 AH), vol. II, pp. 225-85.

23. See Al-Faruq 'Umar, op. cit., vol. II and also 'Umar Ahmad 'Ummani, op. cit., vol. II, pp. 237-9.

24. *Bulugh al-Maram*, op. cit., p. 313. It has also been reported by Bukhari, op. cit., Bab al-*Talaq*.

25. The *Qur'an* 65:1.

26. Ibid., 2:228.

27. Ibid., 2:232.

28. See Maulana Muhammad Ali, *Holy Qur'an*, op. cit., p. 100, f.n. 306.

29. See verses 65:1-2, 6-7 of The *Qur'an*.

30. The *Qur'an* 65:2.

31. Ibid., 2:240.

32. Ibid., 2:235.

33. Ibid., 2:241.

34. Maulana Muhammad Ali, op. cit., p. 104, f.n. 318.

35. Muhammad Asad, *The Message of the Qur'an*, op. cit., p. 54, f.n. 231.

36. Abdullah Yusuf Ali, *The Holy Qur'an* (Hyderabad, n.d.), vol. I, p. 63.

37. See Asghar Ali Engineer, ed., *The Shah Bano Controversy* (Bombay, 1987) for details of the Bill.

38. See verse 2:241 above.

39. Abdullah Yusuf Ali, op. cit., vol. I, p. 63.

40. *The Message of the Qur'an* op. cit., p. 54.

41. See Mohd. Marmaduke Pickthall, *Holy* Qur'an (Delhi, 1980), p. 44.

42. See the *Holy Qur'an,* op. cit., vol. I, p. 63. This edition has an English translation by Abdullah Yosuf Ali and Urdu translation by Ashraf Ali Thanavi.

43. Imam Raghib, *Mufradat al-Alfaz al-Qur'an* (Tiras, Iran, 1343 AH), p. 461.

44. See Ibn Hazm, *Muhalla*, vol. X, p. 248, cited by C.N. Ahmad Maulavi in his article "On Maintenance for the Divorce, circulated in the form of a pamphlet published from Calicut, Kerala, India.

45. See *Lissan al-Arab*, cited by C.N. Ahmad Maulavi, op. cit., p. 2.
46. Ibn Nujaym, *Al-Bahr al-Ra'iq*, vol. IV, pp. 189-90, cited by Prof. Rafiullah Shihab, " Islamic Shari'at and the Shah Bano Case", *Pakistan Times*, Lahore, 9 January 1986).
47. See Tahir Mahmood, *Family Law Reform in the Muslim World* (Delhi, 1972) pp. 61-2.
48. Ibid., p. 46.
49. Tahir Mahmood, *Personal Laws in Islamic Countries* (Delhi, 1987), p. 224.
50. Ibid., p. 246.
51. Ibid., pp. 215-16.
52. The *Qur'an* 4:229.
53. See *Bulugh al-Maram* op. cit., p. 311. Also see Maulana Muhammad Ali, *Holy Qur'an*, op. cit., p. 98. f.n. 301.
54. See *Sahih Bukhari*, op. cit., vol. III, p. 142.
55. See f.n. 1069 in *Bulugh al-Maram*, op. cit., pp. 311-12.
56. Ibid.
57. Musa Ali Ajetunmobi, "The Concept of *'Khula'* and Examination of its cases in Nigerian Courts of Shari'ah Jurisdiction" *Islam and the Modern Age*, vol. XIX, no. 4, November 1988, p. 265.
58. Ibid., p. 266.
59. Ibid.
60. We have referred to this event above.
61. *Talaq-I-ba'in* an irrevocable form of divorce which is immediate and final.
62. See Musa Ali Ajetunmobi, op. cit., p. 267.
63. Ibid., p. 269.
64. Allamah Muhammed Jawad Maghniyyah, "Divorce According to the Five Schools of Islamic Law", part 2, *Al-Tawhid*, Tehran, vol. VI, no. 2, December 1988, February 1989, p. 50.
65. 'Allamah Maghniyyah, Ibid.
66. Ibid., p. 51.
67. Dr. Tanzil-ur-Rahman, *Majumu 'a-e-Qawanin-e-Islam* (Islamabad, 1984), 3rd edition, vol. II, p. 392.
68. See *Qanun al-Ahwal al-Shaksiyah*, Syria, section 88, cited by Dr. Tanzil-ur-Rahman, op. cit., p. 392.
69. *Fatwa* 'Alamgiri, op. cit., vol. II, p. 67. Also Tanzil-ur-Rahman, op. cit., vol. II, p. 393.

70. See Ibn Human, *Fath al-Qadir* (Egypt, 1356 AH), vol. III, p. 41.
71. Ibn Qadamah Muqaddisqi, *Al-Mughni* (Egypt, 1347 AH), pp. 115-16.
72. Ibn Hazm, *Al-Muhalla* (Cairo, 1352 AH), vol. X. Also for J'afari Fiqh see Shaikh Muhammad Idris, *Al-Sara'ir* (Iran, n.d.) p. 237.
73. Ibn Taymiyyah, *Al-Ikhtiyarat al-'Ilmiyyah* (Egypt, n.d.), p. 150.
74. See *Majmu 'ah-Qawanin-e-Islam*, op. cit., vol. II, p. 445.
75. For details see Ibid., pp. 676-715.

7

ISLAM AND THE INDIVIDUAL DIGNITY
OF WOMEN

The Holy Qur'an makes it abundantly clear that women have their own individual status and are not to be treated as an adjunct of their fathers, husbands or brothers. They enjoy all their rights as individuals, not merely by virtue of being a mother, wife or daughter though such status would be considered for purposes of their inheritance. Unlike in some other religions, a woman in Islam enjoys respect not because she happens to be a mother or one who gives birth to children, but because she is a complete human being. Being a mother is incidental to her existence as an individual.

Motherhood for a woman is undoubtedly a noble calling but even more important is her individuality. The Qur'an, while recognising this fact: does not compromise with her individual rights.[1] In verse 2:23 it observes:

And mothers shall suckle their children for two whole years, for him who desires to complete the time of suckling. And their maintenance and their clothing must be borne by the father according to usage. No soul shall be burdened beyond its capacity. Neither shall a mother be made to suffer harm on account of her child, nor a father on account of his child; and a similar duty (devolves) on the (father's heir). But if both desire weaning by mutual consent and counsel, there is no blame on them. And if you wish to engage a wet nurse for your children, there is no blame on you so long as you pay what you promised according to usage.

In the above verse it would be seen that a mother's individual right as a woman has been emphasised by saying that' "Neither shall a mother be made to suffer harm on account of her child, nor a father on account of his child." Thus the Qur'an very clearly recognises a woman's individuality. The Qur'an expresses it differently when it says, "For men is the benefit of what they earn, and for women is the benefit of what they earn."[2] This too is a clear enunciation of a woman's individuality, dignity and rights. Even if there are certain contextual statements in the Qur'an indicating that men have a slight edge over women, in the socioeconomic sense it does not, in any sense, detract from the woman's individuality. If she has more income than her husband or father, she has a right over it and is not obliged, in the legal sense, to hand it over to her husband or father. If her husband is poor and she is rich, she is least obliged to spend anything on him. If the husband himself has given her something by way of dower (*mahr*) it is hers and he cannot take anything from it, except with her consent. Thus the Qur'an says, "And give women their dowries as a free gift. But if they of themselves be pleased to give you a portion thereof, consume it with enjoyment and pleasure."[3]

The Qur'an, in order to leave no doubt about the individuality of women, declares that women will be judged on their merits and men on theirs. If women earn religious merit, they will be duly rewarded for it and if men earn it, they will be justly rewarded for it. The Qur'an puts it as follows:

Surely the men who submit and the women who submit, and the believing men and the believing women, and the obeying men and the obeying women, and the truthful men and the truthful women, and the patient men and the patient women, and the humble men and the humble women, and the charitable men and the charitable women, and the fasting men and the fasting women, and the men who guard their chastity and the women who guard their chastity, and the men who remember Allah much more and the women who remember—Allah has prepared for them forgiveness and a mighty reward.[4]

It can be seen from the above verse that the Qur'an does not make the slightest discrimination between women and men in any respect. Both are promised "mighty rewards" for their religious and secular virtues. How then can anyone say that women are in any respect inferior to men? To maintain such a position would be totally injurious to the spirit of the Qur'an. In creation, too, men and women are of the same kind. They spring from *nafsin wahidatin*, i.e. from one being. In Arabic the word *nafs* means either soul or essence and whatever meaning is taken here, it would indicate the same source of origin for both men and women.[5] Also, unlike the Bible, the Qur'an does not maintain that Eve was born of the rib of Adam, which implies the inferiority of women. Thus, in creation, too, women, according to the Qur'an, are in no way inferior to men.

However, it must be noted that what is stated above is the qur'anic position. The Muslim theologians, on account of the social prejudices of their times, deviated considerably from it. In many instances they not only held women to be inferior to men, but they also showed contempt for them. The *hadith* literature is full of such instances. One of these traditions maintains that a nation which has assigned its reign to a woman can never prosper. We find this tradition in *Al-Ghazzali's Ihya al-'Ulum*, a noted work in the world of Islam. According to another tradition reported by Bukhari, the celebrated traditionalist, a woman is like a crooked rib: it will break if you try to straighten it. Women have also been described as a source of evil, lust, etc who lead men to hell.

These traditions must be taken with a pinch of salt. Just because they have been reported in some traditional works is no guarantee of their authenticity. It should be borne in mind that social prejudices prevalent at certain times play a very important role in personal narrations even by truthful persons. If something is in keeping with our prejudice we tend to accept it with an uncritical attitude. Traditions which are supposedly passed on from one narrator to another over a very long span of time (more than a century) cannot remain unaffected by the distortions of changing social prejudices, not to mention the distortions of memory.

The Prophet was the repository of the qur'anic wisdom and value orientations. He could not have made statements which were injurious to the qur'anic spirit even if he was considering the practical situation in his times. He must have made certain statements which seem rather unacceptable to the feminist consciousness today. But we cannot judge our past in the light of our present consciousness. The Prophet, who was also a great social reformer, could not have altogether ignored the social situation of his days. A reformer cannot succeed if he becomes idealistic in an abstract sense. He has to strike certain acceptable compromises in a way which does not injure the basic spirit of his reforms, or his vision.

However, the pronouncements regarding women found in *hadith* literature appear to be rather dubious. The Prophet had great sympathy for women, whom he considered to be the weaker section of society. He behaved very kindly towards them, and personally he was even inclined to give them the right to retaliate against their husbands. He did react in this manner when a daughter of his companion came to him complaining that her husband had slapped her unjustly. The Prophet gave her the right to retaliate but he was restrained by a subsequent revelation, as his personal inclination was too radical for his times. However, it is certainly indicative of the Prophet's approach towards the woman's plight. Even in his last sermon delivered at the time of *Hajjat al-wada'* (the last pilgrimage) he said. "Treat the women kindly. They are your helpers and are not in a position to manage their affairs themselves. Fear Allah concerning women, for verily you have taken them on the security of Allah and have made their persons lawful unto you by words of Allah.

Here some readers may object to the Prophet's words, "(women) are not in a position to manage their affairs themselves", but these must be seen, as pointed out above, in their socioeconomic context. The Prophet considered women as incapable of managing their affairs not because of their female sexuality, but because in his time there was no concept of women taking part in public life or undertaking enterprises, which were considered to be the man's domain. In the context of his situation, he wanted to treat women kindly. In the true spirit of the Qur'an, he never said anything which would prevent their upward social mobility. The Qur'an had already declared the doctrine of equitable treatment of women in ringing words: *"lahunna mithlul ladhi 'alayhinna"*[6] (their rights are equal to their obligations). It is this doctrine which makes their social status in Islam quite unambiguous. Once this status was conceded to the women by Allah, no one could, in theory at least, take it away from them. However, it was a normative pronouncement. The social conditions were far from congenial for the enactment of this revolutionary doctrine. Male prejudice proved to be far more stronger than the normative force of the ideal contained in the doctrine.

Though there is nothing in the Qur'an to the effect that women must remain subservient to their husbands and do everything to please them, this became the norm in later Islamic society.

According to a medieval writer:

An ideal woman speaks and laughs rarely and never without a reason. She never leaves the house, even to see neighbours of her acquaintance. She has no women friends, gives her confidence to nobody, and her husband is her sole reliance. She accepts nothing from anyone, excepting her husband and her parents. If she sees her relatives, she does not meddle in their affairs. She is not treacherous, and has no faults to hide, nor bad reasons to proffer. She does not try to entice people. If her husband shows his intention of performing the conjugal rites, she agrees to satisfy his desire and occasionally provokes it. She assists him always in his affairs, and is sparing in complaints and tears; she does not laugh or rejoice when she sees her husband moody or sorrowful, but shares his troubles, and wheedles him into good humour, till he is quite content again. She does not surrender herself to anybody but her husband, even if abstinence would kill her. Such a woman is cherished by everyone.[7]

Such a woman was considered perfectly virtuous in medieval Islamic society. The qualities attributed to her were considered Islamic virtues. But nothing could be more untrue. Islam, as shown above, recognises a woman's individuality and does not regard her as a mere adjunct of her husband. She is not expected to submit uncritically to her husband but can assert her rights as a free individual. As we have seen in the chapter on divorce, the Prophet even granted a woman a divorce just because she did not approve of her husband's looks. There was no other reason. Similarly, for every marital obligation, she has been given conjugal rights which are enforceable in any Islamic court. She does not have to meekly submit to her husband nor does she have to seek his pleasure at the cost of her personal dignity. She is not made into a mere instrument of sexual pleasure for her husband. Of course, she has marital obligations towards her husband; she must allow him his conjugal rights but against this she can also demand the same treatment from her husband. Her husband, having taken her as his wife, cannot deprive her of her sexual satisfaction. If he neglects her, or if he turns out to be impotent she can, if she so desires, seek divorce. She can also seek divorce if he fails to provide her with a reasonable amount of maintenance.

As we have seen above, the Qur'an allows a woman to refuse to suckle her child in the event of divorce. This might appear rather unmotherly behaviour but rights are to be seen strictly in the light of legality. A legal concept has its own logic and it cannot be judged in the light of any other category. Though motherhood has its own appeal and should not be downgraded, individual rights transcend such considerations. Islam allows a woman to assert her right even at the cost of her motherhood.

As for custody of children, known as *hidanah* in Islamic terminology, a woman has her well-defined sphere of rights. It should be made clear that Islam basically follows a patriarchal pattern of society. In a patriarchal structure, the child is considered to belong to the father. It is for this reason in a way that the father has to pay not only for the child's maintenance but also for its suckling. In the absence of the father, this obligation falls on a paternal relative. The rights of *hidanah* should also be seen in this light. However, maternal rights must not be ignored either. After all, the woman carries the child in her womb for several months and bears all kinds of hardship. The Qur'an acknowledges this when it says, "And we have enjoined on man concerning his parents—his mother bears him with faintings upon faintings and his weaning takes two years—saying: Give thanks to Me and to thy parents."[8] In another verse it is said:

And We have enjoined on man the doing of good to his parents. His mother bears him with trouble and she brings him forth in pain. And the bearing of him and the weaning of him is thirty months. Till, when he attains his maturity and reaches forty years, he says: My Lord, grant me that I may give thanks for Thy favour, which Thou hast bestowed on me and on my parents, and that I may do good which please Thee; and be good to me in respect of my offspring...[9]

It will be seen that in both these verses mothers come in for special mention as they bear children with trouble and pain. The children owe gratitude especially to their mothers. Fathers bear no such pain in bringing forth children. Thus though the Qur'an addresses itself to a patriarchal society it does not ignore the mother's role. It makes special mention of it. Though the Qur'an does not clearly mention whom the children should go to in the event of separation or divorce, it accepts the father's right over them and hence jurists deduced that ultimately the children should revert to their father in the event of divorce or to paternal relations in the event of death of the father.

However, a mother can retain her child up to a certain age. But this does not mean that the father has an absolute right over the child. Ultimately what matters is not the right of the father or of the mother, but rather the welfare of the child. In general, the mother will have the right to custody of a daughter up to the age of puberty and that of a son up to the age of seven, subject to the child's best interests.[10] There is unanimity on the issue of the right of the mother to rear the child. All other relatives, including the father, come later. However, there is a difference of opinion regarding the age up to which the mother has priority over the child.

According to Imam Abu Hanifah, when a boy is capable of eating and dressing himself and can perform *istinja* '[11] the right of rearing shifts from mother to father. Some jurists like 'Allamah Khassaf consider that the age of seven or eight years is appropriate for a male child to attain this competence. For the female child the mother should have the right to look after her until she attains the age of puberty. This is what Imam Abu Yusuf (an eminent Hanafi Imam) maintains. But, according to another Hanafi Imam, Imam Muhammad, the mother should have the right over the girl until the onset of sexual desire.[12]

According to Imam Malik, the mother can retain the male child until he begins to talk and the female child until she marries. But, according to Imam Sahfi'i and Imam Ahmad Hanbal, the mother can bring up children only up to the age of seven whereafter they will be given the option to choose between one of the parents.[13] In a way this seems to be a more progressive position. It takes care of the rights not only of the parents but also of the children. One might argue that the children may not be able to make up their mind at the early age of seven, but that is a different matter. To be sure, the age limit can be further extended by a couple of years.

The Shi'i position is not very favourable to the mother. According to the Shi'i jurists, the mother can retain the male child up to the age of two and the female child up to the age of seven. After the children attain these ages, the father has to take them away from the mother.[14] However, this position is quite unfair to the mother and she may not wish to surrender her children at such a tender age. It also seems unfair to the children because before they achieve self-sufficiency and confidence, they will be deprived of motherly love.

Thus there is no clear injunction in the Holy Qur'an about the custody of children, and the jurists have given their opinions according to their own inclinations. Some jurists have used the qur'anic verse "And mothers shall suckle their children for two whole years, for him who desires to complete the time of suckling " in support of the argument that the children should be allowed to spend their formative years in the custody of the mother. Some jurists have used certain traditions, to reinforce their case. According to one such tradition' the Prophet was once going out when the daughter of Hamzah called him out. 'Ali meanwhile caught hold of her hand and told his wife Fatima to look after the uncle's daughter. Fatima lifted her up to take her away. However, Zayd, Ja'far and 'Ali quarrelled over her possession. Zayd said she was his brother's daughter while Ja'far maintained that her maternal aunt (*khalah*) was his wife and hence he had a greater claim over her. The Prophet decided in favour of the maternal aunt as she (the maternal aunt) should take the place of the mother.[15]

The Prophet preferred the maternal aunt, who can give a mother's love to the child, over his own daughter Fatima, who was the wife of 'Ali. Thus, in the matter of custody of children the Prophet's preference was clearly for the mother. There is yet another *hadith* according to which a woman came to the Prophet and said, "I have a son for whom my womb was like a vessel, my breasts like a water-bag to drink from and my lap a refuge for him and now his father has divorced me and wants to take away my son from me." Thereupon the Prophet replied, "You have a greater right over him (than his father) and hence you keep him until you remarry,"[16]

This *hadith* clearly indicates the Prophet's inclination to give the child to the mother. The way the mother put it to the Prophet also shows that she was highly conscious of her motherhood and of what she had done for the child. The Prophet did not disappoint her. She, as a mother, was given custody of her child. According to another tradition, a woman approached the Prophet telling him that her husband had embraced Islam while she had refused to do so, adding that her daughter was being deprived of her mother's milk as her father was taking her away. The Prophet made the child sit between mother and father and said both of them should call her. The child would go to whoever she chose. The child responded to the mother. The Prophet prayed to Allah to guide the child and the child then chose the father and hence Rafi (the father) took the child.[17]

Here perhaps the Prophet was keen that the father should take the child as he had embraced Islam while the mother had refused to do so. Of course 'he had given the child the right to choose between mother and father. This shows that the Prophet did not want to decide the case arbitrarily.

It is quite possible that since the child first decided in favour of her mother the Prophet might have agreed to it. Later the Prophet prayed and Allah guided the child to choose the father, or perhaps what is narrated in the tradition is entirely true.

According to Abu Hurayrah, a well-known narrator of traditions, a woman came to the Prophet and said that her husband desired to take away her child from her. The father also came and put forward his claim. The Prophet addressed the child and said, "This is your father and this is your mother. You can choose, my boy, anyone you like. The child chose the mother and the Prophet handed him over to her.[18] In this narrative the Prophet respects both the mother's sentiments and the child's right to choose. This is as it should be, even in our own day.

Thus it can be seen that in the matter of custody of children too, women's rights have been fully protected in Islam. This despite the fact that the basic concept of society in the Holy Qur'an is patriarchal. 'Allama Qadamah Maqdisi, the author of *Kitab al-Mughni*, maintains that a mother has a greater right over a child after she is divorced. The reason given by him for holding this opinion is that the mother is closer to the child and loves it with greater intensity than anyone else, including the father. He also says that the matter of custody can be decided only on grounds of the welfare of the child and nothing that harms the child and its religion can be permitted by any law.[19]

Imam Sahfi'i holds a similar opinion when he says that the mother has a greater right over her child and that it is a question of the welfare of the child and is not merely one of the parent's right over it.[20]

From all this we conclude that in the matter of custody of children the primary consideration is the welfare of the child; and since the mother is more capable of looking after it, she has a greater right over the child. Each case will have to be decided on its merits. In certain cases it may be the father who is in a better position to ensure the child's welfare and thus is entitled to have custody. This is especially so when the woman remarries after divorce or after the death of her husband. In the latter case it may be in the interest of the child to be handed over either to the deceased father's relatives or the mother's relatives, whoever can better ensure its welfare. If the child by himself/herself can make a choice, then he or she will have to be given the right to do so.

It can be seen from the traditions cited above that the Prophet kept all this in view while deciding the cases of custody. Naturally, his sympathies lay with the mother. If the child's welfare lies in handing it over to the mother even after her remarriage, then it should be done. Imam Hasan Basari held that a mother, on account of her remarriage, does not automatically lose her right of custody of her children.[21] Judge Kekaus of Pakistan even held that if the mother does not have enough resources to look after the child it does not deprive her of the right to custody of the child as Islamic law does not regard this as incompetence on her part as far as her right to *hidanah* is concerned.[22]

In the case of Umar Ilahi vs. Rashidah Akhtar, Justice Akhlaq Husain decided that a woman does not forfeit her right to custody merely by virtue of her second marriage. Her preferential right is affected, however, if after she remarries there is some other relative of the child who can be relied upon to look after it better. Then the mother cannot claim custody of the child as the child's welfare is likely to be affected at the hands of a man whom its mother marries. But, on the other hand, if she is looking after the child properly and the child also prefers to stay with her, the child's father or the father's relatives cannot claim the child just because she has remarried. The welfare of the child is the main consideration.[23]

Thus it would be perfectly legitimate to maintain that the rights of women in Islam have been well protected and that, except in some minor respects, the Qur'an concedes women near parity with men. But what appears so disparaging to women is more contextual than normative and must be seen as such.

Notes and References

1. The *Qur'an* 65:6.
2. Ibid., 4:32.
3. Ibid., 4:4.
4. Ibid., 33:35.
5. Ibid., 4:1.
6. Ibid., 2:228.
7. See Shayekh Nefzawi, *The Perfumed Garden*, tr. Richard F. Burton (New York, 1964), p. 97.
8. The *Qur'an* 31:14.
9. Ibid., 46:15.
10. See Dr. Tanzil-ur-Rahman, *Majmu'a-e-Qawanin-e-Islam*, vol. III, (Islamabad, Pakistan, 1985), p. 87.
11. *Istinja'* is the ritual cleaning of one's private parts.
12. Dr. Tanzil-ur-Rahman, op. cit., pp. 877-8.
13. Ibn Qadama, *Al-Mughni* (Egypt, 1367 AH), vol. VII, pp. 614-16.
14. See Najmuddin Ja'far, *Sharai' al-Islam* (Tehran, n.d.), vol. II, pp. 1-2.
15. See Bayhaqi, *Sunan al-Kubra* (Hyderabad, Deccan, n.d.), vol. VIII, p. 5.
16. Ibid., p. 405.
17. See *Abu Da'ud* (Karachi, n.d.), vol. I, p. 305.
18. See *Nasa'i* (Karachi, n.d.), vol. II, p. 93.
19. See 'Allamah Maqdisi, *Kitab al-Mughni*, op. cit., vol. VII, pp. 613-14.
20. See Shafi'i, *Kitab al-Umm* (Egypt, 1381 AH), vol. VIII, p. 235.
21. See *Kitab al-Mughni*, op. cit., vol. VII, p. 619.
22. See PLD 1953, Lahore, p. 73, quoted by Dr. Tanzil-ur-Rahman, op. cit., vol. III, p. 898.
23. Ibid., p. 899.

8

MUSLIM PERSONAL LAW:
THE NEED FOR REFORM

In the preceding chapters we have seen in detail what rights Islam has given to women in respect of marriage, divorce, inheritance, property, custody of children, maintenance, etc. Islamic laws, as far as the Qur'an is concerned, seem to be reasonable and quite close to the modern approach to the subject. However, there is a strong demand from a section of Hindus and Muslims and others for a change in the Muslim personal law as it operates in India. Some of them demand enactment of a common civil code so that there is no discrimination between different religious groups in matters of laws relating to marriage, divorce, inheritance, maintenance, etc. It is argued that a secular society must have common, and not religiously discriminatory, laws. The argument seems to be quite plausible on the face of it and needs to be examined carefully. We shall do so in the following pages. Before we proceed to examine the arguments for and against a common civil code we would like to state the case of those who desire certain essential changes in Muslim laws as practised in India today.

Those who desire change in Muslim personal law argue that on the whole Muslim law in respect of women tends to be quite progressive. Marriage is a civil contract with equal rights for both the parties to stipulate conditions; a marital contract would be valid only on fulfilment of those conditions. Thus women may always stipulate conditions which would protect them from whimsical behaviour on the part of their spouses. A woman can always stipulate that the husband shall not take a second wife at all or without her previous consent. Both these conditions will be Islamically valid. She can also delegate to herself the right to divorce on behalf of her husband (known as delegated right to divorce or *talaq-i-tafwid*) in her *nikah-nama* (marriage contract). Some *nikah-namas* have also been devised to include these conditions in a standard form.

The main areas of reform in the Muslim personal law are: 1. polygamy, 2. arbitrary divorce, and 3. maintenance after divorce. Though the incidence of polygamy among Muslims in India is not very high, it does pose a legal problem. Some surveys in Mumbai, Marathwada and Delhi show that the incidence of polygamy, which may be illegal or couched in the form of a *maitri qarar* (friendship agreement) is higher among the Dalits, Jains, caste Hindus and others. Muslims were found to be the least polygamous of other religious and caste groups. However, the fact remains that among Muslims it is legally permitted and some Muslims do take advantage of it by taking more than one wife. Here legality and not the incidence of its occurrence is the main problem.

The reformists argue that taking more than one and up to four wives is not generally allowed in the Holy Qur'an. Permission was granted in specific circumstances when more than one-tenth of the Muslim population had been wiped out in wars with the unbelievers. There were many widows and orphans to be taken care of. Both the verses in the Qur'an on polygamy reveal this context. They emphasise the need for a man to treat all his wives justly and state that if this cannot be done he should stick to one wife only. The words of one of the verses on polygamy are: "And if you fear that you cannot do justice to orphans, marry such women as seem good to you, two or three, or four, but if you fear that you will not do justice then (marry) only one or that which your right hand possesses. This is more proper that you may not do injustice." (4:3)

The spirit of this verse is quite clear. In the *Holy Qur'an* Maulana Muhammed Ali observes: "*This passage permits polygamy under certain circumstances; it does not enjoin it, nor even permit it unconditionally* (emphasis in the original)." It can be seen that the main emphasis is on justice for women in general, and for widows and orphans, in particular. In order to explain the full import of the verse, I would like to quote Maulana Muhammad Ali's comment on it:

> It is admitted that this chapter was revealed to guide the Muslims under the conditions which followed the battle of Uhud, and the last chapter deals with the battle. Now in that battle 70 men out of 700 Muslims had been slain, and this decimation had largely decreased the number of males, who being the breadwinners were the natural guardians and supporters of the females. The number was likely to suffer a still greater diminution in the battles which had yet to be fought. Thus many orphans would be left in the charge of widows, who would find it difficult to procure the necessary means of support. Hence in the first verse of this chapter the muslims are enjoined to respect the ties of relationship. As they all came from a single ancestor, a breadth is introduced in the idea of relationship, inasmuch as they are told that they are all in fact related to each other. In the second verse the care of orphans is particularly enjoined. In the third verse we are told that if they could not do justice to the orphans, they might marry the widows, whose children thus would become their own children; and as the number of women was much greater than the number of men they were permitted to marry, even two or three or four women. It would thus be clear that the permission to have more wives than one was given under peculiar circumstances of the Muslim society than existing, and the Prophet's action in marrying widows, as well as the example of many of his companions, corroborates this statement. Marriage with orphan girls is also sanctioned in this passage, for there were the same difficulties in the case of orphan girls as in the case of widows, and the words are general.[1]

From the above discussion it becomes abundantly clear that permission to marry more than one wife should be seen strictly in the context of the prevailing circumstances and that even if a situation compels a man to marry more than one woman, justice in treatment cannot be dispensed with. The element of justice in the form of equal treatment is so essential that in its absence the qur'anic verse requires men not to take more than one wife. Situations warranting polygamy should be treated as an exception rather than as the rule and such situations, as the qur'anic verse stresses, require a very delicate balance in doing justice to one's first wife as well as to the orphans and widows who, in such exceptional situations, should not be left to fend for themselves. The Qur'an tries to achieve this cautious balance. According to the Qur'an, polygamy is contextual whereas monogamy is normative. We should bear in mind that the Qur'an had prescribed monogamy as normative in the 7th century of the Christian era and pleaded emphatically for justice for the weaker sections of society. Women were oppressed in society as were orphans and widows, the latter more so.

It is very unfortunate that later theologians and Muslims treated this highly restricted permission as a general license for marrying more than one wife. The position of women in medieval feudal society further deteriorated when men became dominant and supreme. Even highly just laws were so interpreted as to favour men. The restricted law of polygamy in Islam was no exception. Gradually, under feudal influences women totally lost out to men and in the new power equation that emerged men held women in total subjugation, relegating the principle of gender justice in Islam to the background. Polygamy became the rule rather than an exception. Arguments began to be advanced that men had a much greater sexual potential and could not restrain themselves when their wives were undergoing the menstrual period or giving birth to children. During these intervals, they must have more than one wife so that they do not feel the need for extramarital sex.

It is to be noted that none of these arguments are advanced either by the Qur'an or by the Prophet's traditions. The qur'anic spirit in permitting polygamy is very clear— to help widows and orphans and not to satisfy men's extra-sexual urge. The Prophet himself never advanced such arguments about men's sexual needs. It was only in the 19th century that reformers like Muhammad Abduh of Egypt began to advocate the real qur'anic spirit in respect of polygamy and advanced arguments on these lines. Thus Muhammad 'Abduh, a great late 19th century theologian of Egypt says:

> Polygamy, although permitted in the Qur'an is a concession to necessary social conditions which was given with the greatest reluctance, inasmuch as it is accompanied by the provision that a man may take more than one wife only when he is able to take equal care of all of them and give to each her rights with impartiality and justice. The Shari'ah has, in requirement of circumstances, permitted the legality of four contemporaneous marriages with great reluctance. Since the proviso immediately following —if you fear that you cannot be equitable and just with all then (marry) only one—is given so much stress that the permission to contract four contemporaneous marriages becomes practically ineffective.[2]

After quoting Muhammad Abduh, Mahmadul Haq remarks:

> Like other modernist interpreters Abduh invokes the immediately following proviso of this verse restricting freedom of polygamy and then underlines his concept that the ideal form of marriage in Islam is monogamy. He emphasised the point that the Qur'an allowed polygamy under exceptional circumstances prevailing in Muslim society at the time of the Prophet. It neither enjoins polygamy nor even allows it unconditionally. Abduh also says that the welfare of a society is superior to the satisfaction of sensual desire of its individuals. Since the condition to treat them with perfect equality is most difficult, he argues, it is clear that the Qur'an's recommendation is towards monogamy.[3]

Thus it can be seen that an eminent theologian like Muhammad Abduh feels that in the Qur'an monogamy is the rule and polygamy is an exception. It could not have been otherwise since the Qur'an is so fundamentally concerned with gender justice. It could not have left women subject to the arbitrary decisions of men to take up to four wives just to satisfy their lust. However, in the male-dominated society of those times this was treated as a general privilege. Thus it is necessary that taking a second wife may be subjected to the decision of a court and such permission could be granted only in exceptional circumstances such as the medically certified barrenness of the first wife or that she might have contracted an incurable disease. This has been done in almost all Muslim countries. Although, as pointed out above, the incidence of polygamy among Muslims in India is not very high, it would be very desirable if permission were required for a second marriage since it would remove a great deal of misunderstanding among the non-Muslims who seem to think that the muslims are a privileged community permitted to marry up to four wives.

Such a step would help contain communalism, to some extent. It would also uphold the true Islamic spirit of justice towards women. The non-Muslim should also understand that though, as per Muslim personal law, a Muslim man is permitted to take up to four wives, it is simply not possible to do so even if desired by every Muslim, as the sex ratio among Muslims, as among other Indians, is quite adverse. For every 1000 males among the Muslims there are no more than 940 females. Thus even if every Muslim wants to take only one wife he would not be able to do so. Four factors have been identified for this low sex ratio: (1) sex ratio at birth, (2) sex differentials at mortality, (3) sex differentials in migration, and (4) sex differentials in population enumeration. It is generally agreed that it is sex differentials in mortality that have caused this low ratio in India's population.[4] Even if the ratio becomes even, and that will take quite some time, one Muslim male will be able to marry only one Muslim woman. The Muslims also have to understand that the Holy Qur'an, as pointed out above, permits polygamy not because it is man's nature to be polygamous but because of imbalances in the sex ratio in the population as a result of war. Now that the number of males far exceeds that of females this reason no longer exists and monogamy should be the norm.

Also, at that time women's consciousness was not what it is today. Women had internalised their subjugation to men as the latter were the breadwinners. Since then women have become quite conscious of their new status. They are co-partners with men in earning a livelihood and looking after their families and thus they refuse to be subjugated to men as before. Polygamy is thus becoming difficult to practise. In view of all this, monogamy should be accepted as a norm, which anyway was the qur'anic intention, too. The Prophet, we recall, forbade his son-in-law, 'Ali to take a second wife as long as his daughter Fatima was alive.

The other major problem is that of triple divorce in one sitting. This form of divorce has indeed caused a lot of misery to a large number of Muslim women in India. What is worse, it is still in practice although the Prophet himself disapproved of it. The Qur'an does not mention it at all. The qur'anic divorce not only requires two arbiters, one from the wife's side and one from the husband's side, but also two reliable witnesses for pronouncing divorce. Thus the Qur'an says, "And if you fear a breach between the two, appoint an arbiter from among his people and an arbiter from among her people. If both desire agreement, Allah will effect harmony between them. Surely Allah is ever Knowing, Aware."[5] In another verse it is said: "So when they have reached their prescribed time, retain them with kindness or dismiss them with kindness, and call to witness two just ones from among you, and give upright testimony for Allah. With that is admonished he who believes in Allah and the latter Day."[6]

The two verses read together make divorce far from the arbitrary affair brought about by triple divorce in one sitting. First, one should try to bring about a reconciliation between husband and wife through mediation by two arbiters. The intention of appointing arbiters should be to bring about a reconciliation, as is clear from the words "and if they both desire agreement, Allah will effect harmony between them". The second verse exhorts men to keep them with kindness or dismiss them with kindness. Thus the intention should be to be kind and not to dismiss them with the sudden threefold pronouncement of the word *talaq*.

The *Holy Prophet* had strongly disapproved of the pronouncement of triple divorce in one sitting. We have a *hadith* from Mahmud bin Labid that tells us that when the messenger of Allah came to know that a person had pronounced triple divorce in one sitting he stood up in anger and said, " Do you ridicule the Book of Allah when I am amongst you?" This tradition has been narrated by Nasa'i and other reliable reporters.[7] Then also we have the tradition of Abu Rukanah in which the Prophet asked him to take back his wife even after the pronouncement of three divorces in one sitting.[8] The triple divorce in one sitting was prohibited until the early period of Hazrat 'Umar, who enforced it again. It was a temporary measure, an ordinance to meet a particular situation. It cannot be taken as a permanent measure.

However, 'ulama and the jurists in the male-dominated society of those days reduced divorce to an arbitrary action on the part of men. This is totally alien to both the qur'anic spirit and early Islamic culture. The Prophet called divorce the most disapproved of actions of all that is permissible. The marital bond is a sacred bond uniting two souls. It cannot be dissolved unless cohabitation by husband and wife has become almost impossible and all efforts to reconcile them have failed. And, if after all, a woman is to be divorced she should be divorced in kindness, as directed by the Qur'an and not in anger and with a feeling of hurt. The triple divorce in one sitting, on the other hand, is valid even if pronounced in a state of anger, or worse, in a state of inebriation. There is no question of treating the wife in kindness at the time of divorce. Thus triple divorce does not meet with any of the qur'anic conditions and must be abolished forthwith. Moreover, in modern times it has become highly incongruous as it does not add even an iota of justice to the divorce. However, in India it continues to be the predominant form of divorces. The irony of it is that it is practised in the name of Divine Law. No arbitrary action can be attributed to Allah. It cannot be divine and has rightfully been described as a sinful form of divorce.

It is high time the 'ulama and the members of the Muslim personal law Board take the initiative to dispense with this unjust form of divorce which has caused a lot of suffering to many Muslim divorcees. This is among the most desirable and most urgent of reforms that should be introduced without delay. Unfortunately, no member of the Muslim Personal Law Board seems to have the courage to campaign for it. Muslim theologians had shown a sense of urgency in 1939 when they recommended dissolution of the Muslim Marriages Act as many Muslim women were converting to Hinduism. Why cannot they show the same sense of urgency now? Divorce should never be made easy and arbitrary. If this urgent piece of reform is enacted much misunderstanding about women's treatment in Islam will be removed. As shown in these pages, Islam has been most fair to women. No other religion has so concretely defined the rights and privileges of women, and yet there is a widespread impression that Muslim women are treated most unfairly. Who is responsible for this? Islam or Muslim men? Certainly, Muslim men. Whether it is polygamy or divorce, men have considered these as their male privileges and practised them most arbitrarily. Thus Muslim men should own up to their responsibility and change their attitude.

Often the rigid attitude of Muslims towards their personal law causes communal tension, though, or course, Muslims alone cannot be blamed for this. We saw how close to communal confrontation we came during the Shah Bano agitation in 1986. There was no need to take a rigid attitude towards the award of maintenance beyond the *iddah* period. After all, the Qur'an talks of kindness towards the divorcee so as not to hurt her feelings and of provision being made to support her economically. The agitation against the Supreme Court judgement forcing the Government to enact a separate law for Muslim women depriving them of maintenance beyond the *iddah* period was not, strictly speaking, in the qur'anic spirit. Moreover, the agitation created a strong impression in the minds of non-Muslims that Islam is highly oppressive towards women, which is totally wrong.

While it may nòt be possible to scrap Muslim personal law altogether, the Muslims should adopt certain necessary changes in it, such as abolishing triple divorce in one sitting and introducing the qur'anic form of divorce or *talaq al-Sunnah*. Some reasonable restrictions should be put on polygamy, making the permission of a law court necessary for anyone wanting to take a second wife. The court of law, or a family court set up for the purpose, should be the competent authority to decide whether or not a man should be allowed to take a second wife. Such a flexible attitude would not only relieve Muslim women of many problems but would also go a long way in easing communal tensions in India.

Many eminent Muslims of the subcontinent, like Syed Amir Ali, Maulvi Chiragh Ali, Sir Syed, Sir Mohd. Iqbal and several others have advocated reforms in Muslim personal law and called for greater justice for women. Mohd. Iqbal, an eminent poet, philosopher and intellectual, welcomed the reforms brought about in Turkey which were much more thoroughgoing. He observed:

> Passing on to Turkey, we find that the idea of *ijtihad*, reinforced and broadened by modern philosophic ideas, has long been working in the religious and political thought of the Turkish nation. This is clear from Halim Sabit's new theory of Muhammadan law, grounded on modern sociological concepts. If the renaissance of Islam is a fact, and I believe it is a fact, we too one day, like the Turks, will have to reevaluate our intellectual inheritance. And if we cannot make any original contribution to the general thought of Islam, we may by healthy conservative criticism, serve at least as a check on the rapid movement of liberalism in the world of Islam.[9]

Iqbal fully endorses the Turkish poet Ziya's advocacy of radical changes in "the family law of Islam as it is understood and practised today." He quotes Ziya's views on women when he says:

> There is the woman, my mother, my sister, my daughter; it is she who calls up the most sacred emotions from the depths of my life. There is my beloved, my sun, my moon and my star; it is she who makes me understand the poetry of life. How could the Holy Law of God regard these beautiful creatures as despicable beings? Surely, there is an error in the representation of the Qur'an by the learned?... As long as the full worth of the woman is not realised national life remains incomplete. The upbringing of the family must correspond

with justice. Therefore equality is necessary in three things – in divorce, in separation, and in inheritance.[10]

We have seen in an earlier chapter that a daughter inherits from her father half of what her brother gets. This has been considered iniquitous by many. It has been suggested that her share be raised to be on a par with her brother's. It is argued by those who uphold an equal share for daughters that they, on getting married, received *mahr* and that they have no obligation towards maintenance whereas men, on getting married, not only pay a substantial amount by way of *mahr* but also have an obligation tọ maintain the family. Thus, in effect, the woman, it is argued, is at an advantage, on the whole. There is no doubt that there is some truth in this. But some scholars argue that a daughter gets half the share only if her father dies intestate. However, the Qur'an does not stop a man from making a will and giving his daughter as much as his son, or even more, if he so wishes.

Parvez, a Pakistani commentator on the Qur'an, who has written a commentary on the Holy Qur'an in several volumes, maintains that the Islamic law of inheritance applies to what someone leaves behind after making a will. According to him, the Qur'an requires every person to make a will for whatever he/she is leaving behind. He/she should indicate how his/her property will be distributed and the qur'anic law of inheritance shall apply to that which will remain after fulfilling his/her will. A man can thus give more to his daughter, if he so desires, so as to bring her on a par with her brothers. Parvez says that if he wills away the whole of his property and nothing remains thereafter, others (including his children) will get nothing.[11] However, it is true that the Muslim personal law, as it applies to Muslims today, gives a daughter a half share and generally Indian Muslims think that they cannot make a will and that their properties can be distributed among the inheritors according to the Shari'ah law and not as they like. So either no will is made or a will is made, if at all, in keeping with the shares fixed by the Shari'ah.

The words of the Holy Qur'an are very clear that the relatives will receive the proportion enjoined by Allah "after (payment of) a bequest he may have bequeathed or a debt" (*min-b'adi wasiyyatin yusi biha*).[12] These are very clear words which unambiguously indicate that anyone can make a bequest and certainly can do so in favour of his daughter, giving her an equal share, if so desired. The Qur'an awards a half share to the daughter from whatever is left without a bequest by the deceased. This is not unfair in view of the fact that a daughter has neither to spend anything by way of maintenance nor to pay any dowry according to the Islamic law of marriage. But her share gets reduced if she does not receive a substantial amount of dowry from her husband – which happens in many cases – if she decides not to marry, as happens in certain other cases. In these cases the father has to take care of her share by making provision for her in his bequest.

Common Civil Code

Many people argue that there should be a common civil code in the country as we have opted for a secular polity and the Directive Principles of the Constitution under Article 44 require that the state shall endeavour to secure for the citizens a uniform civil code throughout the territory of India. However, this has remained the most tricky question and no government since independence has been able to take any step in that direction. There are historical reasons for it. The Congress gave an assurance to the Muslims during freedom struggle that it would not interfere with their personal law and that they would be free to practise their religion as they understood it. When some members of the Constituent Assembly raised a demand for a uniform civil code, its Muslim members opposed it, but, ultimately, it was included among the Directive Principles of the Constitution.

Is a common civil code very desirable and should it be enacted at any cost? Let us examine this question in some detail and arrive at a conclusion, if possible. There are three categories of people who are demanding the enactment of a common code: (1) The secularists, (2) The feminists, and (3) The Hindu communalists. Also, there are three categories of people who oppose its enactment: (1) average Muslims, (2) fundamentalist and communalist Muslims, and (3) non-Muslims who are sensitive to the identity problems of minorities.

Let us examine the arguments of those supporting enactment of a common civil code. Let us start with the secularists, whose arguments are based on genuine secular convictions, not on any anti-Muslim bias, that is, in a secular country like India, we cannot have separate religious codes for different religious groups. There should be a common law applicable to all citizens. Separate laws amount to discrimination on grounds of religion and that is unconstitutional. When all citizens enjoy common rights, without any discrimination on the basis of religion, caste, sex or creed, why cannot they be subjected to common civil laws too, without any discrimination whatsoever?

Moreover, they further argue that all citizens are governed not only by a common criminal code but also by common civil laws in all spheres other than that of personal laws, and so why not remove this, discrimination too? This would bring about uniformity as well as great unity and integrity in the country. Different personal laws perpetrate discrimination on grounds of caste, sex and creed, as do different religious identities which are not in keeping with the secular ethos. All citizens should have a common identity, that is, a national identity. It is only when this sense of common identity develops that secularism will become strong and we will have a viable polity based on the national interest.

It is also argued that under a secular constitution all citizens should be equal before the law. If personal laws are allowed to be practised, then there will be not only sexual inequality between men and women of one community but also inequality between women of one religious community and those belonging to another religious community. For example:

1. The Muslims are polygamous, and the Hindus, Christians and Parsis are monogamous.
2. The Muslims are allowed extra-judicial divorce, but the Hindus, Christians and Parsis can effect divorce only though a court of law.
3. A wife married under the Muslim law can be divorced by her husband on a whim, but a wife married under the

Hindu, Christian or the Parsi law can be divorced by the husband only on certain grounds specified in those laws.

4. Under the Muslim law, a husband's apostasy from Islam results in automatic dissolution of a Muslim marriage, though a wife's apostasy does not.

5. Under the Hindu law, apostasy from Hinduism, by either of the spouses, does not affect a Hindu marriage, though it confers on the non-apostate spouse a right to sue for divorce.

Under the Parsi law also, a spouse's ceasing to be a Parsi Zoroastrian would only entitle his or her partner to sue for dissolution, but would not otherwise affect a Parsi marriage.

Under the Christian law, a change of religion by one or the other spouse has no effect on a Christian marriage except where the apostate husband has married again, in which case the wife would be entitled to sue for divorce.

Under the Muslim law, a divorced wife is not entitled to any maintenance except during the period of *iddah*. But the other personal laws allow a divorcee post-divorce alimony in perpetuity.

6. Under the Muslim law, a daughter inherits half the share of a son; but under the Hindu law, a daughter shares equally with a son (it may be noted, however, that under the Indian Succession Act governing the Parsis and also others who are neither Hindus, Muslims, Buddhists, Sikhs nor Jains, the position is the same as under the Muslim law).

7. Under the Muslim law, a person cannot dispose of more than one-third of his property by will; there is no such restriction in the other personal laws.

8. The Muslim law confers on a person the right to preempt any property in respect of which he is a co-sharer, or a participator in appendages or immunities or an adjoining owner. The other personal laws do not confer any such right.[13]

These differences, it is argued, militate against the spirit of the Constitution and hence must be removed by enacting a common civil code. The enactment of such a code is long overdue. Already 56 years have passed since India became independent and 53 years since the Constitution was enacted without there being any sign of the enactment of a common civil code.

These arguments are advanced by genuine secularists who bear no ill against the Muslims. The second category of supporters of a common civil code are those who feel strongly about injustice against women. They consider all personal laws as being oppressive of women. Their view is not without justification. Whatever the spirit of this or that religion, in practice personal laws have been quite unjust to women. These injustices can be overcome only when a comprehensive, common civil code, which gives women equality of status with men and treats women of all communities on the same footing, is enacted. These arguments are made with a genuine concern for the plight of women of the forefront of feminist movements. They must be taken seriously, but it is not our intention to cause offence to any religious community in particular. Every attempt should be made to improve the lot of women in India, whatever community they might belong to. There is no religious community which does not oppress women. This criticism does not apply to any particular religious community and must be taken in that spirit. It is a gender conflict rather than an inter-communal one. Gender justice is overdue in our country. Common civil code, or no common civil code, gender justice must be done in every way.

The third category is that of Hindu communalists, who are very vocal in demanding a common civil code. One must be wary of them, for their concern for the plight of women, let alone that of Muslim women, is not genuine. They argue that if changes can be made in the traditional Hindu law, then why not in the Muslim personal law? They indulge in propaganda arguing that the "Muslim population is fast increasing because Muslim men are allowed to take four wives. "They forget that there are only *940 Muslim women for every 1,000 Muslim men* and hence it is not possible for the majority of Muslims to take more than one wife. Also, field surveys have shown that the incidence of polygamy is lower among the Muslims than in other communities. The Muslim population, moreover, is not increasing as fast as is generally believed. The increase is marginally higher and the reasons for this have been explained by demographers. Polygamy is certainly not one of them. These communalists have neither a genuine concern for women's rights (as they are instrumental in oppressing women in their own communities) nor are they really enamoured by secularism. Their arguments, therefore, cannot be taken seriously at all. Hindu communalist propaganda is doing great harm to the cause of a common civil code by building up more resistance to it among Muslims.

Opposition to the Common Civil Code

Those opposed to having a common civil code can also be divided into three categories. The first category comprises of fundamentalist and communalist Muslims. They want to follow their religion blindly, caring nothing for its true spirit. They have turned a blind eye to the newly emerging realities. According to them, the medieval jurists resolved these matters once and for all and there is no need to have a fresh look at any of these laws formulated in their time. They do not want to take into account the fact that the great jurists of classical Islam differed among themselves on practically every important issue. There were numerous schools of jurisprudence, of which six have survived. They also completely ignore the progressive principle of *ijtihad* (the creative reinterpretation of law.)

What is worse, these fundamentalists, quite opportunistically, use Islam as a political weapon. For them, Islam is less a spiritual and more a political entity. They are hardly concerned with the plight of women and other weaker sections of society. Their sole concern is a soulless, spiritless, feudalised Islam. They are more concerned with ritual piety than with the spirit of justice. Any talk of justice for women infuriates them, and they feel Islam is under attack from its enemies. Muslim women have suffered terribly because of such a rigid attitude. Notwithstanding a common civil code, these fundamentalists do not allow even the slightest reinterpretations in the framework of Islam. Within the limits of God (*hudud* Allah) they do not allow any freedom of action. For these fundamentalists and communalists the only 'Muslim problem' in India is to ensure the perpetuation of the Muslim personal law, as if Muslims have no other problems. It is this exploitation of religious sentiment which is doing great harm to the Muslims themselves. The fundamentalists have singled out emotional problems for easy political exploitation. Any political party which seeks the votes of Muslims has to assure these leaders that it will not amend the Muslim personal law.

The second category of opponents of a common civil code comprises Muslims who are neither communalists nor fundamentalists; it includes the Muslim intelligentsia. For them a common civil code is not acceptable for reasons other than religious ones. For them it is more a question of identity and security. They feel the Hindu communalists' campaign, demanding a common civil code, has been an aggressive one. They also feel that nothing is being done to check the frequent occurrence of communal riots in India, in which hundreds of Muslims perish. Those who are concerned with a common civil code on grounds of secularism should be more concerned about these riots, as they question the very existence of Muslims. It is not merely a question of doing justice to their women. And what about women who become widows in riots, and women who are raped?

After all, most of the civil laws are common to all communities. When in 1949 Article 44 of the Constitution directed that the state shall endeavour to secure for the citizens of India a uniform civil code, there were uniform codes of law covering almost all legal relationships except for those matters in which we were governed by personal laws, e.g. laws of contract, of transfer of property, of sale of goods, partnership, companies and negotiable instruments, and of civil procedure. Arbitration and limitation of crimes and criminal procedure and a host of other statutory laws were uniform civil codes applicable to all throughout the country. During the debates in the Constituent Assembly on the draft Article 35 (subsequently enacted as Article 44), Dr. Ambedkar observed that the only provinces which was not covered by a uniform civil code was marriage and succession. It was the intention of those who enacted Article 44 of the Constitution to bring about such a change.[14]

Thus personal laws are the only marks of identity that were omitted, argue the Muslim intelligentsia, and hence should not be touched. After all, it is not the intention of a democratic society to bring about uniformity, though it may desire unity. If personal laws are not protected, tribal religious identity will lose all its meaning. Every effort should be made to retain distinctive identities. Muslims are very conscious of their minority status and would not agree to any tampering with their personal law. There may be a debate about the desirability of reform but there is no need for a common civil code which does away with the distinctive laws of marriage, succession, etc.[15]

The last category of supporters of personal laws comprise non-Muslims who also feel that a uniform civil code should not be enacted in a hurry. They feel that we must view the question in the concrete conditions which obtain in India. We should not merely think of secular ideals. Practical situations are always far from ideal ones. A uniform civil code may be desirable but is certainly not practicable at this stage. Unless the Muslims themselves are prepared to accept it, we cannot impose it upon them. To do so would be undemocratic, even if it were a secular act. It would be construed by some as a totalitarian measure. Change, to be acceptable, must be brought about in a democratic manner. The community most affected by it should be the first to be taken into confidence. What would be more desirable at this stage would be to codify the Muslim law and enact a comprehensive bill. And since many communalist Hindus have been pressing for such a measure the Muslims have come to resent it. Moreover, successive central governments have also given assurances to Muslims that a common civil code would not be enforced unless the Muslims are ready to accept it.

What is Desirable?

As there are divergent views on the subject of a common civil code, what should be done? Should we enforce such a civil code with or without the agreement of the Muslims? Should we perpetuate the *status quo*? Should we go in for gradual reforms? A common civil code, if enforced from above, is likely to disturb communal harmony and the unity of the people. We saw during the Shah Bano agitation how a simple question of maintenance could bring thousands of protesting Muslims out on the streets. The pressure was so intense that the government had to capitulate and enact a separate law for Muslim women in respect of maintenance. All such questions get politicised and no one is prepared to examine them on their religious merits, let alone on their secular merits. The communal temperature rose sharply during the Shah Bano agitation. What would happen if a uniform civil code is enacted is anyone's guess. After all, one has to give priority to communal harmony over uniformity of laws. Thus a common civil code, even if desirable, cannot be on our agenda in the near future. Also no democratically elected government would dare adopt such a measure.

Should we, then, perpetuate the *status quo?* The answer is certainly no. The government can take steps to enact an optional common civil code. The Rajiv Gandhi government had committed itself to bringing in such a code at the time of their enacting the Muslim Women (Protection of Rights on Divorce) Bill, 1986. Muslim leaders had assured him that they would not object to it. However, nothing came out of it. It is worth pursuing the matter. Moreover, in enacting an optional code we will at least have a draft code before us. If such a draft code is placed before the public, one can debate its merits and demerits.

There is a great deal of misunderstanding among Muslims on the subject of a common civil code. An average Muslim is often made to believe that a common civil code means the imposition of Hindu law and the jettisoning of all Islamic principles. This is not true. Islamic law is much more progressive and any common civil code is bound to contain many features of Islamic law. It is, therefore, necessary to formulate a common code at the earliest, and throw it open for discussion. Some such attempts have been made but they were not well publicised at the time and so made little impact.

If one registers one's marriage under the Special Marriages Act one is not governed by one's personal law, but by the Indian Succession Act and other common laws. It is, for all practical purposes, an optional common code and people belonging to various religions, Hindus, Muslims, Christians, Parsis, etc. register their marriages under this Act and avail themselves of the common laws of the country. In the case of inter-caste and inter-religious marriages, one resorts, more often than not, to the Special Marriages Act so that no legal complications arise later due to the applicability of different personal laws of husband and wife.

The Muslim intelligentsia should work within their own community for progressive reforms and the codification of Islamic laws. Islamic law is basically quite progressive though in practice it has suffered many deviations from the early spirit of Islam. Ibn Taymiyyah, the great jurist thinker of the 14th century, tried to infuse this early spirit by opposing triple divorce in one sitting, etc but did not succeed. Since the 19th century many eminent Muslim theologians, jurists and social thinkers have pleaded for reforms. It is necessary to revive this spirit of reform and remove the injustice being done to Muslim women, not so much because of Islamic law but because of social prejudice and male domination. Islam allows *ijtihad* (creative interpretations). However, in the Indian subcontinent *taqlid* (unthinking imitation) has reigned supreme and there have been very few instances of *ijtihad*. It is high time that Indian Muslims used the provision of *ijtihad* in secular India.

To live in a secular country is a new challenge for Muslims. They have not only to preserve their identity and culture but also to find a creative expression of their religious beliefs in a secular environment, both socially and politically. It must not be mere adjustment. It is unfortunate that the challenge has not even been properly understood, let alone be creatively met. The reasons are not far to seek. The Indian Muslims are socially, educationally and economically quite backward and hence under the influence of orthodox theologians. Unless they make progress in these spheres it will not be easy to free them from this influence. The task is difficult but not impossible. It requires courage, patience, endurance and perseverance.

One cannot expect the political leadership to show these qualities. The politicians are more interested in the pursuit of power than in bringing about progress. It is the intellectuals who do not have political ambitions and who can be expected to give a lead in this respect. Their success will depend on the flowering of secularism in India. This is what is lacking in India today. Hindu fundamentalism is becoming more and more aggressive, intimidating the minorities. Minority fundamentalism also grows in proportion to majority fundamentalism; minority fundamentalism, in turn, feeds majority fundamentalism. Nobody knows how to break this vicious circle. The secular and progressive elements in both communities must strengthen each other. This will lead to a more congenial atmosphere for the introduction of reforms.

Notes and References

1. See Maulana Muhammad Ali, *The Holy Qur'an* (Lahore, 1973, f.n. 535, p. 187.
2. See Muhammad 'Abduh, Tarikh, vol. II, quoted in Dr. Mahmudul Haq, *Muhammad 'Abduh: A Study of a Modern Thinker of Egypt* (Aligarh, 1970), p. 50.
3. Quoted in Dr. Mahmudul Haq, *Muhammad 'Abduh* (Aligarh 1970), p. 51 from 'Abduh's *Tafsir,* vol. IV, pp. 349, 350, 366 and *Al-Manar,* vol. VIII.
4. See S. Anantha Ram, "Declining Sex Ratio in India", *J.N.U. News,* June 1990, p. 20.
5. The *Qur'an* 4:35.
6. Ibid., 65:2.
7. See Imam Hajar, '*Asqalani Bulugh al-Maram min Adillah al-Ahkam* (Benaras, 1982), *Bab al-Talaq,* pp. 314-15.

8. Ibid., p. 315.
9. Dr. Sir Muhammad Iqbal, *The Reconstruction of Religious Thought in Islam* (Lahore, 1960), p. 153.
10. Ibid., p. 161.
11. See Parvez, *Matalib al-Furqan* (Lahore, 1981), vol. IV, p. 280.
12. The *Qur'an* 4:11.
13. See Justice A.M. Bhattacharjee, *Muslim Law and the Constitution* (Calcutta, 1985), pp. 171-3.
14. Ibid., p. 169.
15. This is the gist of the discussion I had with several educated Muslims throughout India, both men and women.

9

MUSLIM WOMEN ON THE MOVE

There is widespread perception that Muslim women are among the most backward, illiterate and oppressed in the world. In media they are always shown clad in burqa or wrapped in *hijab* (veil). They are also perceived to be confined to the four walls of their homes totally cut off from the outside world. While partly it is true but reality is much more complex and also not static. Generally we tend to oversimplify and assume reality to be static. In a fast changing world reality cannot be taken to be static. We should always pay attention to the changing and emerging reality.

What happens in the Muslim world is usually blamed on Islam. The underlying assumption is that Muslim behaviour is always determined by religious belief and since Muslim women are backward and do not enjoy rights like other women it is because of Islamic teachings. This impression is further reinforced by the pronouncements of some orthodox 'ulama who want to see Muslim women wrapped in *hijab*.

It has to be borne in mind that firstly all Muslims do not behave according to what theologians or 'ulama say or even according to the teachings of Islam; secondly, social customs, traditions and social milieu exert their own pressure. It is difficult to ignore all this. Thirdly, there are multiple interpretations of Qur'an. Fourthly, modern world-view also plays an important role in determining one's point of view as well as behaviour.

The question of Muslim women, their social status and rights cannot be understood without keeping the following things in mind. First of all it must noted that Qur'an makes clear pronouncement in favour of equal rights for both sexes (2:228). However, this vision of Islam for sexual equality could not find practical implementation for number of reasons. Those who embraced Islam, however sincere they might have been, were product of a fiercely male-dominated society. The qur'anic pronouncement on the other hand, was an ideal which required very different cultural milieu. From sociological viewpoint it was not immediately implementable.

The scriptural understanding is always mediated through culture. The Arab culture was patriarchal and had set its own understanding of women's position. Thus the qur'anic pronouncement of sexual equality was understood and implemented through mediation of Arab culture. What is worse, Islam spread through deeply feudal societies like those of Iran, parts of Roman empire and India. The 'ulama certainly could not transcend cultural norms of these societies. Thus Shari'ah formulations came into existence mainly in Iraq, Egypt and of course Medina. Iraq and Egypt were confluence of ancient cultures with age-old traditions of their own. These milieux greatly influenced the Muslim theologians in their understanding of the qur'anic pronouncement of sexual equality.

To meet the demands of their societies they selectively used the qur'anic verses and certain sayings of the Holy Prophet (PBUH) to formulate Shari'ah approach to women problem, their status and rights. This became medieval religious heritage, which no one could question. However, under pressure from modern social norms these qur'anic pronouncements are being rediscovered by modernists and a debate is raging in the Muslim world today about rights of women in Islam.

Meanwhile the Muslim women are on the move in Muslim countries. In every Muslim majority country and countries with considerable Muslim population like India education is spreading fast among Muslim women. This certainly brings increased awareness among women themselves and they press for their rights, both Islamic as well as secular. There are both types of movements among Muslim women in Islamic world. In some Muslims countries women theologians have emerged with thorough knowledge of the Qur'an, Islamic theology and Shari'ah. Like Fatima Merssini from Morocco, Amina Wadood and Riffat Hassam from USA and several others. Also there are women's organisations like 'Sister-in-Islam' from Malaysia.

These Muslim women theologians and organisations are questioning the traditional interpretations of the Qur'an in respect of women's rights and are developing new feminine-oriented theology, ensuring equal rights for men and women. Sisters-in-Islam from Malaysia is challenging the orthodox 'ulama from Malaysia. They are even trying to get the concept of 'marital rape' accepted as a valid law.

As pointed out above, reality is not static in Muslim women's world. The women in orthodox society as that of Kuwait are demanding right to vote which is being denied to them by the Kuwait ruling elite. It is hoped they will win this right sooner than later. In Pakistan the women agitated in early fifties itself against the Pakistani prime minister when he married his secretary and took her as his second wife. The agitation continued until Ayub Khan who had captured power in 1958 brought Muslim Family Ordinance in 1961, which put certain restriction on polygamy and oral divorce. This ordinance could not be undone even during Zia-ul-Haq's period when the orthodox 'ulama were closest to state power in Pakistan.

The Pakistani society, despite its ups and downs, as far as project of 'Islamisation' is concerned, is on the move in changing women's social status. Recently seven Pakistani women diplomats have been appointed ambassadors. An official of Pakistani foreign ministry said that it is for the first time so many women have been appointed ambassadors in important world capitals. They are all career diplomats and have been posted to European capitals. One woman Asma Aneesa, who was ambassador to one of the Central Asian countries, has been appointed on directing staff of National Defence College. This is no mean achievement.

Bangladesh, though otherwise quite poor and backward, is not far behind. There recently twenty female officers have completed two year gruelling military training and passed out from Bangladesh Military Academy (BMA). This training was for the post of second lieutenant and their passing out ceremony was attended by Bangladesh Prime Minister Khaleda Zia.

The Saudi society too is by no means as static as we think of. The Saudi women too are facing complex choices. There is no doubt compared to other Muslim countries that they are subjected to stricter traditions. But there is no reason to assume that they are passive and inert to modern changes in the society. The Saudi society as a whole is conceived as governed by purely traditional Islam and totally shut out to modern world. The Saudi society is undergoing pangs of modern change and this is causing social convulsions and these social convulsions occasionally assume violent forms. This is subject of another article and cannot be discussed here.

We will discuss here only other issues related to women in Saudi Arabia. The women in Saudi Arabia are taking modern education. The princess called Umm Abdul Aziz, for example, said (see www.amanjordan.org) "We have our own traditions, but they do not prevent women seeking education." Though there are obviously separate educational institutions for women and there is no coeducation in Saudi Arabia. They strictly follow the tradition of sexual segregation.

The newsletter of Pakistani women's organisation *Shirkatgah* of April 2003 says about changes among Saudi women, "Trying to balance the challenges of modernity with the demands of traditional past has meant that change is cautious and slow, but women insist that change is afoot." Mona Megalli says in her article "Saudi women face complex choices" in the above newsletter, "Saudi women now outstrip men as graduates and other specialised colleges, making up 58 per cent of a total of nearly 32000 students in 2000." The female students listen to male instructors through closed circuit video, an audio system.

There are many restrictions Saudi women have to grapple with. Women are not taught engineering and law, for example.

They have to compete in touch job market in Saudi society. Similarly though women own 40 per cent of private wealth and thousands of businesses from retail to heavy industry, they face frustrating legal and cultural restraints and they have to rely on male agents to deal with government offices.

It is also encouraging news from Jordan that it has amended law to give women equal rights. This was announced by Queen Rania. She made this announcement on the opening day of 'Arab First Ladies' dedicated to improving the conditions of women in the male-dominated Arab world.

In Iran, of course, though women have to wear *chador* but *chador* has not been a constraint for them as far as work is concerned. Iran has very active women's movement in whole of Islamic world. They are active in practically every field of work and are present in large numbers in Iranian parliament too. In Indonesia too women have entered in educational field in a big way. There are large number of women in Islamic universities also and there is strong movement developing for women's rights.

Thus one must realise that reality is multi-layered and complex. Muslim women too are undergoing through throes of change the world over. The orthodox 'ulama can hardly restrain this forward march. More and more Muslim women are either challenging medieval theological formulations or simply ignoring them. They are trying to carv out their own niche in this male-dominated world.

10

ON A MUSLIM WOMAN LEADING THE CONGREGATIONAL PRAYER

Amina Wadud, an Islamic scholar of repute from US, led the mixed congregational prayer on 18th March 2005 in New York and also delivered *khutba'* (sermon). It was a historic step as it was a unique development in the history of Islam. Not that it was the first time but it had happened after centuries. Amina Wadud invoked the principle of spiritual equality of men and women in Islam. She led some 130 women and men in prayer. Subsequently, another woman led Jum'ah prayer and delivered a sermon in Canada too. Ms. Asra Nomani, a former *Wall Street* journalist also led prayer in the University of Brandeis near Boston in USA. In fact, Asra was the main motivator behind the movement for a woman leading the mixed gender prayer.

It greatly disturbed conservative Muslims who denounced it as against Islam. Fatwas were also issued against it. Some extremist Muslims in USA even threatened to throw a bomb and hence the venue had to be changed. Libyan leader, Gaddafi in condemnation of a woman leading a mixed gender prayer went to the extent of saying that women-led prayer 'creates millions of Bin Ladens' according to *Daily News* (March 24, 2005). There was a time when Gaddafi was a fervent advocate of gender equality and used to say that gender inequality in the Muslim world was a western colonial conspiracy to immobilise half the Muslim population. That time Gaddafi was more of a rebel and now perhaps he is finding back his mainstream roots in Islamic world. He has also given up his militant image and has come closer to USA.

In Egypt, the Great Mufti (*Mufti-e-A'zam*), Ali Goma also denounced a woman leading the mixed congregational prayer. He said it was not permitted in Islam. He said no woman can lead a mixed congregational prayer, much less a *jum'ah* prayer and she cannot deliver *khutbah*. He said that majority of the imams and the muftis agree that a woman cannot lead a mixed congregational prayer. However, all 'ulama agree that she can lead only women in prayer.

It is important to examine this claim from the Qur'anic viewpoint. Is there any authoritative argument (*nass*) against a woman leading a mixed gender prayer in the Qur'an? Certainly not. All agree that there is no such denial in the Qur'an. Though the Qur'an does not refer to the issue directly, there are verses in the Qur'an, which can support a woman leading such mixed congregational prayers. We will throw more light on this a little later.

Prophet's *hadith* also allows a woman to lead a congregational prayer. The Holy Prophet had asked Umm Waraqah bint Abdallah to lead prayer in her *dar*, which included men. She was well versed in the Qur'an compared to others, including men, and hence the Prophet asked her to lead the congregational prayer. Now generally, *dar* (house) is interpreted as her family and according to this interpretation she was asked to lead her family members in prayer including her husband. But it is also stated in *hadith* that the Prophet appointed a *mu'addhin* (caller to the prayer) who was a man. This means it was not her family but most probably her locality. Here *dar* should not mean household or family but locality as *dar al-Islam* would not mean family of Islam but a locality, even a country of Islam.

This *hadith* relating to Umm Waraqah has been narrated by Abu Dawood, also by Ibn Khuzaimah, who rates it as 'sound' (i.e., authentic). Umm Waraqah was also one of the few who handed down the Quran before it was compiled in written form. It was because of this *hadith* that jurists like Al-Mozin, Abu Thawr, and Al-Tabari held the opinion that a woman can lead prayers of mixed congregation. Ibn Taymiyyah, another noted jurist, was of the opinion that a woman can lead Tarawih prayers of mixed congregation.

Though there is unanimity among ulama' and jurists that *hadith* relating to Umm Waraqah is authentic, but then there is debate whether permission by the Prophet was specific to Umm Waraqah or it implies permission for all women to lead mixed congregational prayers. However, there is nothing to indicate that it was specific to Umm Waraqah. Since she was an 'alimah who was well versed in the Qur'an and elements of *salah* (prayer) so she was asked to lead prayer in her locality. It was certainly her ability and sincerity, not her tribe or standing in the society, which earned her that distinction.

It is a well-known principle of jurisprudence that of the two, one who is the greater 'alim would lead prayer and of the two, one who is physically more sound would perform function of imamah and of the two, one who is from the same locality would lead the prayer. Extending this to sex, the 'ulama concluded that since a woman is physically weaker than a man so a man is superior and hence must lead the prayer. However, on this basis all 'ulama and jurists agreed that woman can lead other women in prayer.

But a woman can be a greater 'alimah than a man and it was on this principle that the Prophet allowed her to lead a mixed congregational prayer. This was 1400 years ago, and even now in the 21st century there is such opposition to a woman leading the prayer. It is really strange. Stranger reasons are being given to oppose a woman leading a mixed congregational prayer.

A leading Arab 'alim, Sheikh Yusuf al-Qardawi says in his fatwa that, "Throughout Muslim history it has never been heard of a woman leading the Friday Prayer or delivering the Friday sermon, even during the era when a woman, Shagarat Ad-Durr was ruling the Muslims in Egypt during the Mamluk period. It is established that leadership in prayer in Islam is to be for men."

With due respect to the Sheikh, I must say first of all Muslim men, particularly 'ulama, have decided that a woman cannot be ruler or head of the state. How then Qardawi is approvingly quoting that during a woman's rule in Egypt no woman led congregational prayer. Qardawi, like other traditional 'ulama, I am sure, considers a woman's rule as illegitimate. And if he does not, then he should not object to a woman leading a mixed congregational prayer.

Secondly, his argument that it is well established that "leadership in prayer in Islam is to be for men," the question is who has established that? The Quran? No. The holy Prophet's Sunnah? No. And every one agrees that Islamic Shariah is based on the Qur'an and Sunnah. It is not for anyone to establish Islamic rules. This assertion on the part of Yusuf al-Qardawi is not right and certainly not based on Islamic sources.

Sheikh Qardawi, in order to justify traditional practice that man alone can lead a congregational prayer comes out with very strange logic, even obsession with sex. He argues, "Prayer in Islam is an act that involves different movements of the body... Moreover, it requires concentration of the mind, humility, and complete submission of the heart to Almighty Allah. Hence, it does not befit a woman, whose structure of physique naturally arouses instincts in men, to lead men in prayer and stand in front of them, for this may divert the men's attention from concentrating during the prayer and disturb the spiritual atmosphere required."

I really wonder on the Sheikh's logic. On one hand he says, prayer is an act of concentration and submission to Allah and humility to Him and on the other he argues that a woman's sexuality will interfere with this concentration. Of what use is a Muslim's concentration if he gets sexually excited even in the sacred and spiritual act of prayer and submission to Allah. Better he does not pray. Allah says in the Qur'an that, "Surely prayer keeps (one) away from indecency and evil," (29:45) and our Ulama are arguing that a woman through her posture in prayer will excite a man's sexual desire. Whom should we listen to? To Ulama or to Allah who says prayer is an antidote for all indecency and evil?

Qardawi further argues, "Hence, it is to avoid the stirring instincts of men that the Shari'ah dictates that only men can call for Prayer and lead people in the Prayer and that women's rows in Prayer be behind the men." This may be the Sheikh's view; it is certainly not the Qur'an's and Sunnah's view. Qardawi thinks the Prophet did not know what he knows about men's sexuality and permitted Umm Waraqah to lead prayer. And he also thinks that only men's sexual feelings can be stirred, not women's when they pray behind men.

The problem is not with sexuality but with a man's ego that he does not want to pray behind a woman. Men have total control on all social and religious institutions and in no case want to give up this control. Islam came as a liberator for whole humanity, much more for women who were totally subjugated. The Prophet of Islam was personally a great supporter of women's cause. Apart from revelation, he did what he could for women and their liberation. He wanted women to be equal to men both in the material and spiritual sense. The Qur'anic verses as well as the Prophet's conduct are a clear proof of that. Not only did he want women to pray inside the mosque, but also wanted them to lead men in prayer. When some men obstructed women from entering into the mosque to pray, he said, "Do not prevent Allah's servants (amatullah) from praying inside Allah's house." Men do not allow women to enter into the mosque in several countries even today, particularly in the South Asian countries like India, Pakistan and Bangladesh.

Who do they follow? Their own version of Islam or Qur'anic and Prophetic Islam? The Qur'an stands for complete equality in human dignity, freedom, duties and rights as far as women are concerned. The Qur'an puts it in four words when it says, *wa lahunna mithlul ladhi 'alayhinna* (i.e., And women have rights similar to those against them in a just manner. 2:228).

These four words are of great significance. These words ushered in a revolution in gender relations in a period of darkness in the world. These words gave women what the world could give them in the early twentieth century. The Prophet naturally brought these words into practice in their true spirit. The world until then had believed animals and women have no soul. The Qur'an, on the other hand, not only preached men and women have been created from what it calls *nafsin wahidin* (from one soul) but also accorded them full human dignity.

The Qur'an made another revolutionary statement, *wa laqad karramna bani Adam* (And surely we have honoured children of Adam. 17:70). Children of Adam being collective noun, all are included, including men and women, black and white, Arab and non-Arab. Thus, to the Qur'an all human beings have equal dignity and no gender discrimination is allowed as no colour, racial or linguistic discrimination is permitted.

But when Islam spread to other parts of the world where all forms of discriminations, including gender discrimination, were practiced this revolutionary message of Islam was lost and all prejudices sexual, racial and linguistic began to be practiced. The Muslims who embraced Islam with their pre-Islamic prejudices, could not appreciate the Islamic spirit, and there was no person of the Prophet's spirit among them or of the status of immediate companions of the Prophet to infuse true spirit of Islam among them.

Women enjoyed a very low status in all cultures and races and this low status continued despite acceptance of Islam among those people who embraced Islam decades or even centuries after the death of the Prophet and his companions. The new generation of 'ulama from Persian, Roman and Turkish stock too engaged themselves in formalistic juristic issues, without fighting their deeply embedded cultural prejudices against women. And to serve these deeply embedded gender discriminatory opinions, new *ahadith* (sayings of the Prophet) came into existence and *qiyas* and *ijma'* (analogical reasoning and consensus) being purely human institutions, too were influenced by these cultural prejudices.

Thus, all sorts of discriminations began to be practiced against women. The early dynamism of women was severely restricted and she was confined to home. The Prophet had even allowed them to participate in the war. Umar, the second caliph had appointed a woman as inspector of markets and now she, wrapped in black cloth could not move out without a *mahrim* (i.e., with a man closely related to her whom she could not marry).

Now all this was thought to be strictly Islamic and the 'ulama and jurists issued fatwa after fatwa (legal opinion) making this low status of women as Islamic. She then became a mere appendage of her father or husband after marriage. Her salvation lay only in submission to authority and pleasure of her husband. She could not even step out without his specific consent. She lost her individual dignity. A *hadith* circulated, wherein the Prophet was made to say that if it were permissible to prostrate before anyone except Allah, I would have required a wife to prostrate before her husband.

Thus, one can see how later generations of Muslims immersed in their cultural values and completely alien to the Qur'anic spirit, degraded woman's status. No wonder she was not permitted to lead congregational prayers as she was thought to be inferior to men. Yusuf Qardawi's argument that no woman in history of Islam had led a congregational prayer is based on this kind of logic, not on the Qur'anic spirit.

During the Prophet's time, the women did not accept their degradation but fought for their Qur'anic rights. Once, when an argument ensued about their status, they went to the Prophet and inquired whether they were inferior to men. The Prophet waited for divine injunction and Allah responded, "Surely the men who submit and the women who submit, and the believing men and the believing women, and the obeying men and the obeying women, and the truthful men and the truthful women, and the patient men and the patient women, and the humble men and the humble women, and the charitable men and the charitable women, and the fasting men and the fasting women, and the men who guard their chastity and the women who guard their chastity, and the men who remember Allah and the women who remember – Allah has prepared for them forgiveness and the mighty reward." (33:35)

If one reads this divinely revealed verse, can he still argue that women are in any way inferior to men? If one still does, then all one can say is that he is either not appreciative of the Qur'anic teachings or that he is deeply immersed in his male-dominated values. To him the Qur'anic message is not as important as his own values in which he has been brought up. The real tragedy is that one is born in a Muslim family and formally accepts Islam as religion without being deeply affected by the Qur'anic spirit. Or the Islamic message reaches him through not only his cultural filter but also through the conservative 'ulama themselves quite alien to the real Qur'anic spirit.

After deeply studying the import of the verse 33:35, can one still seriously argue that women cannot lead mixed congregational prayers? That is why all those who are opposing women leading a mixed congregational prayer are simultaneously admitting that there is nothing in the Qur'anic and hadith against women leading a prayer. But since they are immersed in male values rather than Qur'anic values, they maintain women cannot lead a congregational prayer and invent strange arguments like sexual excitement by looking at the back of a woman. What is much more surprising is that such arguments are advanced by the 'alim of the status of Sheikh Yusuf al-Qardawi.

They do not realise that such arguments are external to the Qur'anic spirit. The Qur'an does not even remotely suggest that men are sexually more excitable than women and so women should be wrapped in cloth from head to toe to spare men the sin of rape or adultery. The Qur'an treats both man and woman equal even in this regard and proposes same punishment for both for such offences.

Even in case of polygamy men use such arguments. It is often argued that polygamy saves men from resorting to illegitimate relationships with other women. The Qur'an does not refer to any such argument. On the other hand, the Qur'an reluctantly permits polygamy to take care of orphans and widows (4:3) and warns that "if you fear you cannot do justice then (marry) one." Not only this, in yet another verse 4:129 it says, "And you cannot do justice between wives, even though you wish (it), but be not disinclined (from one) with total inclination, so that you leave her in suspense. And if you are reconciled and keep your duty, surely Allah is ever forgiving, merciful."

The message of this verse is very clear and if one reads both the verses i.e., 4:3 and 4:129 together it becomes quite clear that he can take more than one wife only in some exceptional cases but otherwise one should take one wife. Yet the 'ulama throughout history made it almost a privilege for men to marry up to four wives and justice never remained an issue. On the other hand, such arguments, totally external to the Qur'anic spirit that one needs to marry more than one wife to avoid a life of sin, were usually made.

Now women are much more educated and conscious of their rights and the time has come to put into practice the real Qur'anic spirit and understand the Qur'anic teachings in the right perspective, and small steps like Amina Wadud and others leading mixed congregational prayers should be taken. The Islamic world urgently needs certain reforms and for that an internal debate will be very helpful.

This step has stirred feelings and from the heated debate will come the much- needed light for healthy change. The vast gap between Islamic spirit and Muslim practices needs to be bridged through dialogue and discussion. There is constant attack from non-Muslims about gross injustices perpetrated by Islam against women. Non-Muslims are not aware of Qur'anic teachings and hence they blame Islam for these injustices. Those Muslims who understand the Qur'anic teachings must come forward and initiate discussions both with Muslims and non-Muslims.

Muslim women also need to be properly educated in the Qur'anic teachings and we urgently need women theologians to spread awareness among them. Thus, both Muslim men and women, committed to human dignity and gender justice, will have to seize initiative to bring about much-needed changes in the Muslim society. Thus, we should welcome the initiative taken by sisters like Amina Wadud and others and spread this message.

A believer (m'umin) must be totally committed to justice, benevolence, compassion and wisdom as these are oft repeated Qur'anic values and any injustice to women cannot be acceptable to a believer. Throughout the medieval ages, Muslims lost the true message of Qur'anic values and now in the age of human dignity and human rights, the Qur'anic message of gender justice needs to be revived.

If we do not bring the real Qur'anic spirit, even in today's circumstances we will miss the bus forever. Allah will never forgive us for this indifference to His Message. We have always sidelined reformers like Muhammad Abduh of Egypt who stood for gender justice and true Qur'anic spirit. We need not one but many Abduhs.

APPENDIX

THE LAW OF MARRIAGE AND DIVORCE AMONGST MUSLIMS, CHRISTIANS AND PARSIS IN INDIA

Law of Marriage and Divorce Amongst Muslims

A. General

To whom does it apply?

A Muslim is governed by his personal law of marriage and divorce, unless he has been married or his marriage has been registered under the Special Marriage Act 1972. This personal law, which forms part of the compendium known as 'Muhammadan law', is uncodified law derived from the Qur'an and various judicial decisions.

What is a Muslim marriage?

It is a civil contract—not a sacrament as amongst professing Hindus. It follows that it must be made between parties who are of sound mind.

Proposal and acceptance

As in all other contracts, a formal proposal has to be made by or on behalf of one of the parties to the marriage and such a proposal must be accepted by or on behalf of the other party in the presence and hearing of witnesses who must be Muslims and must consist of either two males or one male and two females. The proposal and the acceptance must occur at the same meeting.

Polygamous
A Muslim marriage can be polygamous—i.e. the man is entitled to have up to four wives. But a Muslim woman has to be monogamous.
Consequence of a Muslim marriage being a civil contract:
  1. The wife becomes entitled to payment of dower, which is usually agreed upon.
Dissolution by contract
  2. The agreement to marry may provide that if the husband marries again the marriage will be void.
  3. Again, the agreement may provide for the marriage coming to an end on the occurrence of some event.
  4. In what is known as a *muta'* marriage, it stands automatically dissolved on the expiry of the agreed upon period. Thus the agreement may itself provide for dissolution under certain circumstances.

B. Divorce or Dissolution of Marriage

Talaq
Under traditional Muslim law the right to divorce rests exclusively with the husband who can divorce his wife by simply repeating the word *talaq* thrice. In fact, the husband may delegate his power to pronounce *talaq* to another person. (The husband may even delegate this power to his wife.

Dissolution of the Muslim Marriages Act
Under this Act the Muslim wife has acquired the right to win a divorce on the following grounds:
  1. That the whereabouts of the husband have not been known for four years.
  2. That the husband has failed or neglected to maintain her for at least two years.
  3. That the husband has been sentenced to imprisonment for seven years or more for a criminal offence.
  4. That the husband was impotent at the time of marriage and continues to be so.
  5. That the husband has, without reasonable cause, failed to perform his marital obligations for a period of three years.

6. That the husband has been insane for three years.
7. That the husband suffers from leprosy or some other virulent venereal disease.
8. That she was given in marriage before she was fifteen, that the marriage was not consummated and that she repudiated the marriage before she reached the age of eighteen.
9. That the husband treats her with cruelty, viz.
   (1) He habitually assaults her or makes her life miserable by cruel conduct even if he does not physically maltreat her; or
   (2) He associates with women of bad reputation or leads an infamous life; or
   (3) He attempts to force her to lead an immoral life; or
   (4) He disposes of her property or prevents her from exercising her rights over it; or
   (5) He obstructs her in the practice of religious observances; or
   (6) He has more wives than one and does not treat her equitably (fairly) as enjoined by the Qur'an.
       (A false charge of adultery constitutes cruelty and is a good ground for a divorce.)
10. Any other ground for dissolution of the marriage.

The Court
The Court to which such application must be made is the High Court of the State.

Procedure
All those persons who would be the husband's heirs at the time when the petition is filed must be mentioned in the petition. Notice has to be given to all those persons and they have the right to be heard in the court proceedings.

C. Consequences of the Dissolution of Marriage

These are laid down by Muslim law.

Remarriage
1. If the marriage was not consummated the woman can remarry immediately on dissolution. If it was consummated she has to wait for the execution known as the *iddat*.

2. Naturally, marital intercourse between a divorced couple is unlawful and any children that may result are illegitimate.

3. The divorced couple can, however, remarry if they so desire. However, if the husband has pronounced *talaq* they cannot remarry unless the wife first marries someone else, that marriage is consummated, and has therefore ended owing to divorce or the death of that husband.

Where divorce is granted under the Act this rule will not apply.

Right to Dower

On dissolution the woman becomes entitled to immediate payment of dower (if it has not been paid already)—the full amount if the marriage was consummated before dissolution and half if it was not. If no amount of dower was agreed upon at the time of marriage she is only entitled to receive three articles of clothing. If an agreed upon dower is not paid, the divorced wife, and after her death, her heirs, may sue for it in a court.

Inheritance

As soon as a marriage is dissolved the wife loses her right of inheritance.

To this rule there is only one exception, namely, where the husband divorces her by *talaq* during an illness which leads to his death. In such a case, if the husband dies during the period of *iddah* the divorced wife is entitled to inherit but not if he dies after that period.

This is to prevent a man on the verge of death from finding an easy way to disinherit his wife in favour of his other heirs.

Law of Marriage and Divorce among Christians

A. General

Indian Christians are governed by two Acts in these matters. These are the Indian Christian Marriage Act of 1872 and the Indian Divorce Act of 1869.

To whom these Acts apply?

The Acts apply to any person professing the Christian religion regardless of whether he or she has been baptised. Every marriage in which either one or both persons is/are Christian is required to be solemnised under the provisions of the Marriage Act.

How is it solemnised?

A Christian marriage is solemnised in a church or other place of worship by a clergyman or in the presence of the marriage registrar under this Act, or by any person licensed to grant certificates of marriage between Indian Christians. The marriage will be certified under the Act if:

(i)   The man is not less than twenty-one and the woman is not less than eighteen.

(ii) Neither party has a wife or husband still living.

(iii) The parties make the prescribed declaration to each other indicating that they are taking each other to be their lawful spouses.

If either of the parties is less than eighteen, the consent of that party's father or guardian or mother must be given.

Furthermore, if the man is less than twenty-one and the girl is less than eighteen the procedure as to notice must be gone through.

Conditions for a valid marriage

1. The parties must be of age or if they are not they must have secured the requisite consent.
2. Neither party must be a lunatic or idiot.
3. The marriage must be monogamous—neither party must have a husband or wife alive.
4. They must not be related within the prohibited degrees.

However, a marriage within the prohibited degrees which has been especially permitted by the Church shall be valid.

B. Matrimonial Reliefs

The Indian Divorce Act

This Act governs questions of matrimonial relief among Christians in India. Passed in 1869 it has remained unchanged even though matrimonial law in the Christian countries of the West has changed a great deal, as for example in England and the United States.

The reliefs provided under this Act are:
(1) Divorce
(2) Nullity
(3) Judicial separation
(4) Restitution of conjugal rights
(5) Maintenance and alimony
(6) Custody of children

(1) Divorce

The only ground for divorce available to the husband under the Act is an act of adultery (wilful sexual intercourse with another man) by the wife.

Grounds available to the wife
The wife, however, cannot sue for divorce only on the ground of adultery by the husband. In her case, the husband's adultery must be coupled with:
(1) Incest (i.e. having sexual intercourse with a near relation, with a woman whom he could not legally marry).
(2) Bigamy (which here implies a previous marriage and sexual intercourse with the first wife.
(3) Marriage to another woman (here the other marriage is subsequent).
(4) Cruelty—mental and/or physical.
(5) Rape, sodomy, bestiality.
(6) Desertion for two years without reasonable excuse.

Note: None of these must accompany adultery to constitute a ground for a woman to get a divorce. Another ground available to a wife is that her husband has converted to another religion and gone through a form of marriage with another woman.

Factors the court will consider
As in the case of other matrimonial laws, connivance or condonation of the matrimonial offence, and collusion in the beginning of the proceedings will entitle the court to refuse to

grant a decree. Again, if the petitioner (party who applies to the court) is found to have committed adultery himself or herself, or is found to have treated the other party with cruelty or has deserted, or wilfully separated from, the other party, prior to the act of adultery complained of, or is found to have been guilty of wilful misconduct or neglect towards the other party that conduced (was partly the cause of) the adultery, or if the applicant has been guilty of unreasonable delay, then the Court may refuse to order a divorce.

Note: The concept of 'desertion' in matrimonial law in general has two facets, viz.:
(1) the intention to abandon the company of the spouse, and
(2) the fact of such abandonment.

If a person is compelled to abandon the company of the spouse for example, because of consistent ill-treatment by the spouse, it cannot be suggested that the abandonment is the result of a voluntary decision and therefore, it cannot be suggested that desertion has taken place. Again, consent to an abandonment will be sufficient to defeat any claim in redesertion.

(2) Nullity of Marriage

Grounds

The grounds on which the court is entitled to declare a marriage null and void are:
1. Impotence: that the husband or wife was impotent at the time of the marriage and remained so until the time when the suit was filed.
2. Prohibited degrees: that the parties to the marriage are within the prohibited degrees of the relationship.
3. Unsound mind: that the husband or wife was a lunatic or an idiot at the time of the marriage.
4. Bigamy: that the former husband or wife of either party was living at the time of the marriage, and the marriage with such husband or wife remained in force at that time.
5. Force or fraud: where consent of a spouse was obtained by force or fraud. Either spouse may present a petition to the court asking for a decree of nullity on any of the above grounds.

Children
As in the case of other matrimonial laws, there is a provision that the children of a marriage that has been declared void are deemed to be legitimate. This legitimacy carries with it the right of inheritance, i.e. the children can inherit their parents' property.

(3) Judicial Separation

Grounds
A decree for judicial separation can be granted on application of either party on grounds of:
  (i)   Adultery
  (ii) Cruelty
  (iii) Desertion, without reasonable excuse, for two years or more

Wife's property
All property acquired by the wife after the judicial separation shall be deemed to be completely under her control as if she were unmarried; also, from that date she shall be deemed to be an unmarried woman for the purpose of contract and suing.

This provision is necessary because (i) a judicial separation does not formally dissolve a marriage; and

(ii) among Christians, husband and wife are treated as one person, so that the husband has rights over the wife's property and is also liable for his wife's contracts and debts.

It is manifestly unfair that this should continue when they are no longer living together and, in fact, are living separately by sanction of the law.

(4) Restitution of Conjugal Rights

The provision is basically the same as in the other Acts already examined. However, if the other party wishes to resist or prevent the making of such a decree he/she must prove facts which would entitle him/her to a decree for judicial separation or for nullity.

(5) Maintenance and Alimony, and (6) Custody of Children

The provisions relating to these topics are broadly identical with those previously discussed and need not be separately considered here.

Other Miscellaneous Provisions

Protection orders

Under this Act, a deserted wife may ask for an order of the court to prevent her husband or his creditors from claiming any rights over property she acquires after she has been deserted.

This is because the marriage, being still in existence, the husband is deemed in law to have control over his wife's property.

Damages and costs

A husband who succeeds in establishing that his wife committed adultery can claim damages and costs from the person with whom she is alleged to have committed adultery.

However, a wife has no right to claim damages or costs from any one in respect of her husband's adultery.

This provision is archaic and stems from the medieval concept of the wife being property, or akin to a servant.

Settlements

1. Where the court decrees divorce or judicial separation on account of the adultery of the wife, then, if the wife has any property, the court may order the settlement of her property for the benefit of her husband and/or her children.

   There is, however, no such provision in respect of the husband's property if he is found guilty of adultery

2. Where a settlement of property was made on the spouses before or after the marriage, the court which decrees dissolution (divorce) or nullity may make orders to apply that property for the benefit of the parties and their children.

Court

The court for the purpose of this Act are the High Court or the District Court.

Law of Marriage and Divorce Applicable to Parsis

A. General

Parsis Marriage and Divorce Act

This Act governs the law relating to marriage and divorce among Parsis.

To whom does it apply?
The Act applies to members of the Parsi community professing the Zoroastrian religion only.

Conditions for a valid marriage
1. The parties must not be related to one another within the prohibited degrees.
   An exhaustive list of prohibited relationships for both man and woman is provided in the Act.
2. The marriage must be solemnised by a priest according to the Parsi ceremony of *Ashirvad* in the presence of two Parsi witnesses.
3. If either party is below the age of twenty-one, the consent of the father or guardian of such party must have been previously obtained.

Registration
Provision is made for the registration of Parsi marriages and such registration is compulsory. However, non-registration, while punishable, will not affect the legal validity of the marriage.

B. Matrimonial Reliefs

The matrimonial reliefs provided by the Act are:
(1) Nullity
(2) Dissolution—which is different from divorce
(3) Divorce
(4) Judicial separation
(5) Restitution of conjugal rights
(6) Maintenance and alimony
(7) Custody of children

(1) Nullity

Ground
The only ground on which a marriage may be declared null and void by the court is that consummation of the marriage is impossible because of natural causes.

(2) Dissolution

Ground

Dissolution can be decreed (ordered) if either spouse has been continually absent from the other for seven years or more and has not been heard of as having been alive by those who would naturally have heard had he or she been alive.

(3) Divorce

Grounds

The grounds on which a divorce can be granted at the instance of a spouse are:

(a) Non-consummation of the marriage within one year due to the wilful refusal of the other party to do so.

(b) That the other party was of unsound mind at the time of marriage and has been habitually so till the date of the suit. In such a case, the party applying has to show his/her ignorance of this fact at the time of the marriage and must approach the court within three years of marriage.

(c) That the other party at the time of the marriage was pregnant by someone else, that the party applying did not know this at the time, and that on discovering this the sexual relationship ceased. Here too the court must be approached within three years of the marriage.

(d) That the other party, since the marriage, has committed adultery or bigamy, indulged in illicit sex or committed an unnatural sexual offence. In this case, the court must be approached within two years of the discovery of the fact.

(e) That, since the marriage, the other party has:

  (i) caused grievous hurt to the applicant.

  or

  (ii) has infected the applicant with venereal disease.

  or

  (iii) has compelled the applicant wife to submit to prostitution.

  In these cases, suit must be filed within two years.

(f) That the other party has been sentenced to imprisonment for seven years or more for a criminal offence of which at least one year's imprisonment has already been undergone.

(g) That the other party has deserted the applicant for at least three years.
(h) That, following an order for judicial separation against the other party, the spouses have not resumed marital intercourse for at least three years.
(i) That the other party has failed to comply with a decree of restitution of conjugal rights for one year or more.
(j) That the other party has ceased to be a Parsi. In this case, the court must be approached within two years of the applicant coming to know of it.

(4) Judicial Separation

Judicial separation is granted:
(i) On any of the grounds on which the divorce is granted.
(ii) On the ground that the other party is guilty of such cruelty or has done personal violence to, or behaved in such a way with the party applying and/or any children of the marriage that the court feels that it would be improper to compel the parties to live together.

(5) Restitution of Conjugal Rights

The provision is more or less the same as in other matrimonial laws.

(6) Maintenance and Alimony, and (7) Custody of Children

The provisions are basically the same as in other matrimonial laws.

Considerations
Collusion, connivance, condonation and delay may disentitle a party to relief as under other matrimonial laws.

Courts
Special Parsi Matrimonial Courts are set up under the Act, which are the Chief Courts in Mumbai, Kolkata and Chennai and District Courts in other places.

Maintenance Under Section 125 of the Criminal Procedure Code

Under this section the magistrate is given the power to order a monthly allowance for the maintenance of a man's wife or child or father or mother. Such allowance does not exceed Rs. 500 per month

To claim this allowance a simple application is to be made by or on behalf of the wife, child, father or mother to the magistrate. It must be shown that the wife or child or father or mother for whom the application is made has no sufficient means of maintenance and the man has enough means to maintain the wife, or child, etc but that he refuses to do so.

The wife or child, etc can claim such maintenance even if they are not living with the man concerned. They must not, however, live apart from him without good reason.

Before the magistrate, the man may offer to maintain his wife on the condition that she lives with him. But if the wife shows good reasons for not accepting the offer, such as that she is treated cruelly or that the man has married a second time or that he has kept a mistress, the magistrate will grant her maintenance.

However, if the wife is living in adultery or without any reason she refuses to live separately or if both husband and wife live separately by mutual consent then the wife will not get maintenance under section 125.

Where can the proceedings for maintenance under section 125 be filed in the Court of the Magistrate?
(a) where the husband lives;
(b) where the wife resides; or
(c) where both husband and wife last resided together.

The magistrate is empowered to increase or reduce the allowance if the circumstances change.

If a woman receiving maintenance under this section marries again, the allowance will be cancelled.

INDEX